SOCKS
CIGARETTES
AND
SHIPWRECKS

Berryman Family, 1896

Back row: Ben, Ted, Dick, Jim
Middle row: Mater with Raymond, Dreda with Christopher (Topher), Charles with Ruth
Front row: Rosamond, Jinny, Peter, Paul

SOCKS CIGARETTES AND SHIPWRECKS

A FAMILY'S WAR LETTERS 1914–1918

EDITED BY
FÉLICITÉ NESHAM

ALAN SUTTON
1987

ALAN SUTTON PUBLISHING
BRUNSWICK ROAD · GLOUCESTER

First published 1987

British Library Cataloguing in Publication Data

Socks, cigarettes and shipwrecks.
1. World War, 1914–1918——Campaigns
2. World War, 1914–1918——Personal narratives, British
I. Nesham, Félicité
940.4′81′41 D640.A2

ISBN 0–86299–227–3

Typesetting and origination by
Alan Sutton Publishing Limited.
Printed in Great Britain
by The Guernsey Press Company Limited,
Guernsey, Channel Islands.

For the family,
past, present and future

PREFACE

The letters were in a black, square tin box along with a lot of other papers my grandmother had hoarded: school reports, receipted bills dating from the last century and newspaper cuttings of long-forgotton events, all jumbled together. However these were tied up with pink tape in neat bundles, labelled 'Ted, 1914', 'Dick, 1915', and so on – the correspondence from my grandmother's five surviving sons who served in the First World War and one of her daughters.

I knew that the letters were there and that one day I would have to go through them – when I had time. There was one which had been kept separately, describing the Christmas Truce of 1914, and I had sent this to the Imperial War Museum, mentioning that I did have others. From time to time the Museum gently reminded me that I had promised to let them have the rest, 'when I had gone through them'.

At last I started work and, as I sorted through the letters, I showed them to friends who expressed interest. One of them said to me, quite fiercely, 'You've got to edit these before you hand them over!' but the Imperial War Museum, asking once again for the originals, came to my rescue. They took them over, providing complete transcripts, and allowed me access at any time to the originals for checking. I was also given anything I wanted in the way of illustrations.

As I read through the letters, the writers and those to whom they wrote, who had been part of the grown-up world of my childhood, took on a younger life of their own. Caught up in the turmoil of a world war which had brought them together even more than it separated them, they provided an unconscious record of a loving family who, wherever they were, wrote home regularly to their mother, ending most of their letters, 'Best love to all'.

I have tried to cut the bulk of the correspondence to a reasonable length and I must say 'thank you' to the many who have helped me in this enjoyable but exacting task.

First, of course, Roderick Suddaby, Keeper of Documents at the Imperial War Museum, who nagged me and then did all that I have said in a previous paragraph and has since kept me up to the mark and to whom I have turned for help and advice time and again. Then the late Frank Waters, who helped so much with advice and encouragement in the early stages; his wife, Denise and their friend

John May, who took up the burden. Next, my friends and relations who have severally and collectively said 'Get on with it!'

I am also grateful to those who have helped me try to trace the owners of the copyright of those letters not from the family and of some of the illustrations. After this lapse of time it has proved very difficult but every reasonable effort has been made to do so.

FÉLICITÉ NESHAM

CONTENTS

PROLOGUE: THE VICARAGE FAMILY

They were a typical Victorian family: thirteen children, of whom ten grew to adulthood and we can meet them all, except one who died as a baby, in the photograph taken with their parents, Charles and Gertrude, outside the Vicarage at Camberley during the summer holidays of 1896.

Dick, the eldest, is sixteen and in his second year at Felsted, having failed for the Navy – perhaps he just did not work hard enough. He is already something of a dandy with his light-coloured trousers belted by what appears to be a tie, his buttonhole and a generally casual air. By contrast, Jim, just over a year younger, is still very much a schoolboy in his knickerbocker suit and cap, holding a bicycle. He will be going to Lancing next term with an Exhibition which he appears to have won as much by his personality as by academic achievement.

Ted, standing behind his mother, completes the trio of the three eldest boys. He has at least another year to go at Cordwalles (now St Piran's) prep school near Maidenhead. All the boys who attained school age went there, the headmaster at the time being one Charles Hunt, an Oxford friend of their father. Ben – Benedicta after her godmother – almost exactly a year younger than Ted, balances the picture with another bicycle. In her full-sleeved blouse, Tam-O'-Shanter and buttoned boots she looks as if she is posing for an illustration to an E. Nesbit story.

The next sister is Dreda, sitting down and firmly holding a younger brother in place. Her second name is Mary but her parents could not decide on the first until they were actually setting out to the church for her baptism. Then Charles exclaimed, 'I know what we can call baby: today is St Ethelreda's day!' Another variation her brothers were to use later was 'Dryden'. There is a three year gap between Dreda and Peter, the schoolboy in the leggings and stiff collar sitting beside her, as Angela, the sixth child, died at the age of two months. Paul, who comes next, is the only one wearing a sailor suit. He has probably already decided on his future career.

Now come two more girls. Jane, sometimes known as 'Jinny', is her mother's acknowledged favourite daughter – partly, it was said, because the curls that tumble over the lace collar of her velvet dress were a rich auburn in colour. That dress is the envy of Rosamond, who, with her short hair and white pinafore, looks a little as if she were a choirboy strayed from her father's church. The boy in front of Dreda is Christopher. His parents chose that name because they liked the shortened form, 'Chris', but his siblings promptly dubbed him 'Topher' and, as they outnumbered their parents at that time at the rate of nine to two, 'Topher' he became as far as the family was concerned.

Ruth, the youngest girl, is where she is happiest, ensconced on her father's knee, with his arm round her and her hands in his, while the baby of the family, Raymond, in his frilled frock and wide sash, seems to be waving to the camera from the security of his mother's lap.

Of that happy family group, Raymond was the first to go, dying on Palm Sunday the following year, aged fifteen months. Charles died in 1901, just before Easter. Dick attained his majority that September.

Gertrude was at least able to stay at the Vicarage. The next incumbent, Charles Kirwan, was a bachelor and did not want the large, rambling house, so from the Vicarage which had been their home for the last seven years the elder boys went out into the world, and here the younger children began to grow up. Like all large families they had their own words and expressions – almost a private language – which they used among themselves.

An 'F.F.' was a 'false friendship', the kind that can spring up suddenly between two people flung together by circumstances such as a sea voyage. By calling this relationship an 'F.F.' you were acknowledging its nature and the fact that it would probably not last, at least not at that intensity.

Gertrude was known as 'the Mater' (though Charles had always been 'Daddy') and if her anger were roused, there was said to be 'mud' about and they could expect a 'cop' – a severe ticking off. The Mater was tiny and indomitable. Probably the only way in which she could cope with eleven lively children ranging in age from twenty-one to six was to rule them with the proverbial rod of iron. They were terrified of her but they adored her. She was *not* the perfect mother. She had her favourites and made no secret of the fact. Dick, the first-born, could not put a foot wrong, but it was the third surviving daughter, Jane of the auburn curls, who had the velvet frocks. This probably did not matter much in a large family. In fact it could be quite useful to have an ambassador who was sure of a welcome ('*You* ask her, Dick'), but those frocks still rankled, at least with the younger girls, long after they had all grown up. Of course Gertrude did love them all and their devotion to her and to each other was, in every case, lifelong.

Another family expression was the word 'krewst' which can best be translated as 'activity' or 'action'. When things got too much for her at home Gertrude would leap on to her bicycle, pedal furiously to the village, buy a bun and ride out into the country. Here she would sit and eat her bun in silence and solitude, returning in due course with her peace restored to find all quiet and in order. The word would have gone round that 'the Mater's on a bun krewst'.

The most famous bun krewst of all was when a seventeen-year-old friend of the family, James Tucker, later to be her son-in-law and later still a High Court Judge and a Law Lord, came swinging across the lawn by means of a rope and pulley slung from one tree to another – the 'razzle-dazzle'. How was he to know that the maid – even clergy widows had servants in those days – had just come out of the house with a tray laden for that Victorian speciality, tea in the garden? She put it on a table in the middle of the lawn just as James launched himself from the tree, and the inevitable happened. His feet caught the edge of the table, scattering bread-and-butter, cakes, sandwiches, tea, sugar, milk and crockery from one flower-bed to another. The Mater came out and looked at the ruin in throbbing silence. Then: 'That's your tea,' she said coldly and marched off for her bicycle. As the subdued children picked blades of grass, clover leaves, daisy petals and other flora from the buttered slices before they ate them they could only be thankful that it was a guest and not one of themselves who was the culprit.

They had surprisingly few relations. There were some Palmer cousins of Gertrude's in Windsor and Ireland and a rather formidable Aunt Edward, widow of Uncle Edward Gibbs, but on Charles's side only his younger sister, Nellie, had survived. A wide circle of friends went some way towards compensating for this. The Lloyds of Hartley Witney and Bené Yeatman date from before Gertrude's marriage, while the Dudmans, the family at the Big House and the patrons of Charles's first living at Pitney in Somerset, were still taking a proprietary interest in his children after thirty years. James Tucker, who comes into the story again, and Bunchie Quentin were friends from Camberley days. All the boys were a little in love with Bunchie but she married a curate with TB and has to be written out of the script. Other friends are frequently mentioned in the letters: sometimes whole families like the Gabbs of Guilford, the Drews, the Davids and the Moodies; sometimes individuals – Willie, George, Specs, Eric, Chubbie, Charlie and others. No one now knows who they all were.

Dick was already a medical student at Barts when his father died, and a place had been found for Jim, failing the necessary scholarship to University, with a wine merchant in Portugal. Ted, who had paid for his secondary education with a useful Scholarship at King's School, Canterbury, was a cadet at the Royal Military College (now Academy) at Sandhurst. (Here the riding instructor, aware that he had the son of the Vicarage among his pupils, shouted sarcastically: 'If Jesus Christ had ridden his donkey into Jerusalem the way you're riding that horse he'd never have got there!')

Peter, an Exhibitioner at Kelly College, Devon, died there of meningitis following mumps at the age of sixteen, while Paul went on from Cordwalles, which specialized in preparing boys for the Navy, to HMS *Britannia*. Topher followed Ted to Canterbury and was sent out to the Argentine to farm sometime between 1912 and 1914.

No serious effort appears to have been made to educate the girls for a career although they all went to boarding school. Jane went on to Bedford Physical Training College, probably because she wanted to ('Conduct: noisy' say her reports succinctly), Rosamond to a school of church needlework, and Ruth embarked on a training as a sick children's nurse. Ben and Dreda seem to be the daughters at home, although Ben did begin to learn to play the harp; not so much because she was musical – she had beautiful arms which could be seen to advantage playing such an instrument.

When Charles Kirwan went to Holy Trinity, Guildford, Gertrude had at last to leave the Vicarage at Camberley. As she had by now become a friend of his and was used to his churchmanship she decided to move to Guildford where the family were established in a three-storey house with a basement and a small garden: Delaford in the London Road, which was to be 'home' to the Berrymans for another generation.

The three eldest boys were of course off her hands by now and in 1913 Dick and Ted were in India, Dick a doctor in Assam and Ted an officer in the 39th Garhwal Rifles, Indian Army. In November that year Ben went out for what was intended to be a year-long visit, staying in turn with both her brothers. She went first to Dick but by the summer of 1914 she had evidently been staying with Ted in Lansdowne, the tiny hill station that was the regimental depôt in the United Provinces, for some months. Here she had made friends with the wives and sisters of the other officers, particularly one Alix Mankelow, a pretty, vivacious twenty-three-year-old, who was staying with her brother, Archie. Ted was due for some leave and plans were afoot for him and Ben to meet Dick at Shillong for the races (where Dick would be riding his own horses) when war broke out in Europe and Gertrude began to keep their letters home.

LETTERS FROM THE RAJ 1914

Lansdowne
6 August 1914

Dear Mother,

Just a line. Exciting times are they not, and heaven knows what may have happened by the time you get this if you ever do. But you mustn't mind, mother; I know the state of mind you must be in. Don't be frightened. War is a horrible thing and this was *bound* to come, and the sooner the better . . . You need have no fear at home, you won't be troubled there.

And of course you are proud of having a son in the Navy who is a member of the finest service the world has ever seen, and whatever else you feel you *must* be glad that he's to have a chance of doing his duty and distinguishing himself. So don't be anxious; rather consider him lucky to get this chance; and I know Paul will play the game when it comes to the real thing.

I feel very out of it out here; you can quite understand my anxiety as a soldier to be where the show is, but I don't see much chance. . . . I fully realise somebody has got to stay behind, and look after England, India, Egypt and the rest of them, but it galls just the same. I would give *anything* to have a look in at the war.

I'm afraid we are all going through a trying time, but you must be brave, mother; I know you will be, and don't be frightened or let the girls get frightened; there's nothing to be afraid of; the Fleet will see to that. I only wish you had a son at home to help you through it all.

Best love to all and wish your service sons the best of luck.

yr loving son,
Ted

For Dick, a civilian, the war was principally a nuisance. He wrote from Lahoal, in Assam on the historic 4th August.

My dear Mother,

Very many thanks for your letter. Really this wretched war is frightfully upsetting, and we being so far away know so little. Yesterday we did hear

Gertrude Berryman

Germany were fighting Russia; goodness knows how long it will be before England is let in. P'raps we'll hear more news today. I wish I was at home. Everything of course will be upset. No tea is being shipped and it is all accumulating here. How is Ben going to get home? No one will have any money! But p'raps it will all be over quickly and settled up, anyhow I hope so.

Well best love to all
I had a touch of fever last week but am quite fit now
your loving son,
Richard

Ben's letters were longer. She had more time, of course, as Ted had the usual retinue of Indian servants to run the bungalow, and, as well as all she had to say about the war and conditions in Lansdowne, she was more interested in affairs at home than her brothers were. Where Dick would comment briefly, obviously in answer to his mother's letters, 'That wasn't Leonard Pullman after all then' or 'I thought you would remember the Passey boy', Ben would write in detail about the family and their friends. She wrote almost entirely without paragraphs or punctuation, covering both sides of large sheets of paper, usually ending with several sentences strung, sometimes word by word, round the small margins, switching breathlessly from comments on a new dress to plans for the future.

5 August 1914

Dear Mother,

Very many thanks for your long letter. The dress you have got for me sounds ripping thank you ever so much. I shall hear if you've sent the box to Calcutta or here but it doesn't matter much I can get King Hamilton to send it along if I should still be here as it seems I am for life the dreadful war has and will upset most things I expect, one can't make any sort of arrangements, and all leave from here is stopped unless within 48 hours recall, so at present Ted will not get his for Shillong, but I expect I shall go at the end of Sept. . . . and if I can't get home in November I shall go to the Nobles, they will always have me. We hear very little up here of course in way of what *is* going on but it seems pretty dreadful and at home you must all be in a fuss. I don't suppose any officer will go from here but there is a chance of course, and they are all of course dieing to be off and everlastingly grumble at being so poked away, it's all very cheery for us poor females but at most they will be ordered to stations down below to take places of other officers gone. Alix and I see ourselves stranded but I shall go to Assam. Thank you *ever* so much for the ninon coat I'm sure to love it. Jane and Eric don't seem to have been over successful at Broadwater, but they had fun I expect and ripping whizzing about in the little car; Jane *will* be one up on me in driving by the time I get back as I have forgotten all about it I'm sure. A good idea to go to Holmwood I'd love to see it again and the girls won't remember much at least of course Dreda ought, and I can hear Jane making wild shots and pretending she does!

Holmwood, near Hartley Witney, was Gertrude's old family home. Although it had been let since the death of her mother it still had a special place in their affections. Several of the children had been born there and it was not far from Laverstoke, where their father had been rector for ten years before going to Camberley. Dick was to comment in his letter of 11 August 'I wonder how Holmwood looked, have you arranged to leave the estate to the eldest son. Remember how we used to argue about it.' One feels that Gertrude was not meant to take the question seriously, although Ben also has a point to make:

I suppose you did alter that part of your will (nice subject!) didn't you, but you certainly ought to make some compensation for us girls and go on [with] Grandmother's scheme of the females being provided for! Glad Fay and Maurice have been down – You do seem to be doing a lot with jam and pickled walnuts and I hope you do the cherries. I rather like brandy cherries. I don't hear from Bunchie, she owes me two letters too. . . . I'm glad my room is to be papered, I should like it a plain white if I can, but it will have to be started or rather finished by the time you get this and it doesn't matter a bit really. I expect it's the same as Dreda's as there was some over wasn't there, I suppose you'd better leave the pictures for me, but I feel I shall *never* have a moment once I get back! And may I please have the gas taken away and electric light put, I feel sure I used more gas as I never turned it down hardly. Ted is very well but has lectures etc. today but I daresay he will write tomorrow. He's very distressed he can't be in this war and swears all day – well so does everyone at not being on the spot. What about Paul. Suppose he'll get in for some of it tho' I suppose the Home and Channel Fleets will get most of anything there happens to be. The rains here *never* cease, I didn't think it could be as bad as it is, really it's awfully depressing, it gets on your nerves after a bit and we've now had it for nearly 3 weeks, we just had two more or less fine days and that's all, and more rain during July alone than there is in England in a year. Nothing going on, I don't see anyone but Alix and even we can't get to each other some days tho' we are so near, it means changing both times as NO umbrella or coat keeps *this* rain out, and after a lesson or two one fights shy of chills. I have a fire going, you have to watch your things so carefully, all my shoes go mouldy in one day. . . . I am sending off the little book I got for. . . . your birthday and many happy returns of tomorrow, Aug 6th, your wedding day. I expect the girls won't forget some flowers, Dreda generally remembers, the excitement of Selsey *may* have put it out of their heads. I *do* hope you have a nice time. Everything has gone up in price I suppose, one doesn't in a way realise how dreadful a war can be. Wish we heard more, we only get summaries in the *Pioneer* and they are never satisfactory somehow. All leave has been stopped out of this country, I do pity the poor officers who were just sailing for home. . . . Two babies born here last week, oh, I told you that before. Mrs Stack is rather a friend of Ted's and she writes yesterday to say that she is going into the drawing [room] and is ready to receive visitors à la Mrs Archie Grey in a rapid recovery! I would love to be with you at Selsey I *can't* say life is very enjoyable up here at present I shan't be sorry for a change, and I shall be too disappointed if I *can't* get home this year as it will also mean I sort of stay about as both Ted and Dick will be houseless! Something of course will turn up and I've plenty of friends to go to but I'd set my heart on November but one can't tell how bad things will be as yet. Well I must end.

Heaps of love
your loving daughter
Ben

Go on addressing here for the present.

Dick's next letter, as well as his remarks on Holmwood, contains a mixture of walnuts and the war.

11 August 1914

Very many thanks for your letter. The song arrived safely and many thanks too. I forget if I told you I'd had fever. . . . I have been very lucky really not having had malaria yet, everyone seems to get it. . . . I suppose you are at Selsey now, unless the war has interfered with everyone's arrangements. We get a lot of good news, but we never hear any of the English or French losses. I hope it is soon over and if the Germans are getting beaten as they seem to be I should think they would soon give in. Fancy pickling 400 walnuts; you will use a fair amount of vinegar I should fancy . . . It's been raining here now for about 16 days to make up for the drought we had in July & June. Wish I had some gooseberries! I wonder how Paul is getting on in the Mediterranean, he surely must be in a scrap somewhere, he will be pleased I expect. I wish I was at home, it must be so exciting and we who are abroad will never realise what it was like. I haven't heard from Topher for a long time – he said he was going to write and tell me where to send some shirts to. No one I suppose talks anything else but war. The last we heard was that 19 German ships had been sunk or captured in the North Sea. Funny hearing all that firing, it must have been very awe-inspiring. I am afraid Ted may not get his leave now, but nous verrons. Well, I must stop,

best love to all,
Dick

As we know from Ben's letter Ted's leave had been cancelled, although she was confident that he would not be going overseas. Her next letter tells a very different story.

Very many thanks for your letter and much news. I expect you [will] hear ere you get this that the 39th Garhwalis are ordered to mobilize for active service, they are part of the 7th Division . . . and are going from this country and this time next week Lansdowne will be left destitute. Each regiment leaves an officer and a certain amount of men at the depôt and that's all. All three regiments go from here. At present only ordered as far as Kodwhara, the railway at the bottom of the hill 28 miles down and then to Bombay to embark the worst of it is they'll go under sealed orders so we shall never know where they go until they arrive. You'll know before us. Some rumours say Egypt to wait, some Harvre, and yet again England. Everyone dreadfully excited of course and they'll die of disappointment if they don't get into the thick of it. Ted is worked off his feet being adjutant. I can't tell you the things he has to see to, he leaves the house at 10 and I haven't seen him again for three days until 5.30 or 6.30 when he comes back for *lunch*. They are only allowed 60lb kit so for himself there is little to see to really, I've to make khaki pillow cases and small hold-alls and that's all. This war is absolutely dreadful, I've told you all about here first because you will want to know about Ted, but I can realise how dreadful it must be at home, you are safe I suppose but I am naturally *very* worried and we get so little news. It shows how sudden it all was because your mail mentions not a word and yet it was dated July 24th. Our mails will be more or less all right but they go round by sea which takes a week or so longer, so there'll be a gap at first, we don't get a mail on August 21st, it will be a week late I see, that's your mail dated August 6th, the *very* one we want badly to hear how you are (this will be your end too). Still send my letters *here* till I tell you, I hope and pray I shall get a mail soon as one clings to that so.

'*One clings to that so.*' They all did. Again and again during the next four years Ted's letters begin 'No mail yet', 'Mails delayed', with an occasional 'Mail just come: 37 letters!' The post between

England and France was to be quick and surprisingly reliable. It was the mail that had to run the gauntlet of enemy submarines and compete with essential supplies on the more distant fronts that was inevitably held up or lost. Before the war letters between India and England took three weeks and it was important to catch 'the mail' otherwise there would be a six-week gap in the correspondence. That the system is already breaking down is apparent from Ben's rather incoherent remarks on the subject. She goes on:

Don't worry about me as I am more or less all right as I've got Dick thank goodness out here though at present 4 days journey away. *Alix and I will stay together in this bungalow for about a month then I shall go to Assam again either meet Dick at Shillong as arranged before or go straight to him by middle Sept.* . . . I should go down to him now but it would be foolish in a way for I've got this house and I couldn't stand the heat and poor Alix is so stranded I feel I must see her through a bit at first. Heaven knows when I shall get home now, we *can't* tell yet. But if Dick has to give up his job and has no other I can always go to the Nobles *for as long as I like*. But I'm hoping I shall get back to you all before Christmas anyway. You must be worried about everything and I suppose the prices of everything are dreadful. Even out here they've gone up already. We hear of a great Naval Victory off the Dogger bank but NO details. If Paul had been in the Channel fleet I fail to know how I could have stood the suspense. Such heaps in fact everyone must be involved in one way or another – I suppose all the Aldershot division have gone. We know very little. I shall be feeling very miserable and sort of stranded till I get to Dick, but thank goodness I've got Alix. I shall manage to look after myself a bit but you know what it's like. I can't think what it will be like on Wednesday when the 39th Garhwalis go, apart from having Ted going which I refuse even to think of every officer one knows and some of them so awfully well somehow; I feel sorry for the poor wives and the station has so many brides. Two officers have gone today under sealed orders, to catch Sat. mail and they will go to the place where the regiments go eventually but that doesn't help us knowing. It makes it all the worse not knowing where they go as there can be no letters or anything. Ted is wild with excitement and so are they all. We poor females are *supposed* to feel the same but it's jolly hard and I find I can't *inwardly* get the right spirit. Parcels will get to me *in time* with a certain amount of safety, our mail won't really come to harm unless by an accident, see? so I shall get the things you sent all right I expect. As regards money don't you worry because I'm to draw on Ted's pay. He'll want very little and Dick will see to that part when I get to him. Ted says I shan't be left short in *any* way and Alix and I can certainly live on very little the time we are together. My getting to Dick will cost a lot but that will be all right. . . . Your day at Hartley Row must have been nice, you seemed to get a great deal into one day! The girls didn't tell me anything about the day and yet they were hard up for news! I wonder if you went to Selsey . . . I can imagine *your* feelings at being away from home at this time. The Territorials are getting a look in I suppose, I was wondering about Willie but I suppose they won't be sent out of England. There's no fear of an invasion, thank goodness, but you must all be in a dreadful state of worry, I *wish* I could know more, our mails will tell us most and we will have to wait another 2 weeks before you mention much. . . . Please tell Rosamond I may miss the mail with her letter this mail, and also tell her the bracelets arrived *perfectly* safe and *beautifully* packed. Thank her please. The other girls I'll write to next week. Nothing doing here. I don't go out much except to Alix and back and she here, because messages and things are going the entire day and I never know when Ted may want a meal. . . .

The sun is out once more, the first time for *weeks*, it makes all the difference in the world, let's hope it's fine when we are alone, that everlasting rain and mist I could *not* endure. I'm very fit these days which is a blessing. We appear to be going to be left minus any doctor but I do *hope* not, such a lot of people are always ill too. About 5 or 6 of our officers are on leave at home, they've been recalled but they won't be out in time. They pick up the others somewhere I suppose but no own kit whatever. Captain Lumb will only just get back in time, he's got twelve days *marching*. He was miles away on the snow line and had started before the war was thought of so the wire must have been rather a shock. I must end now do please take care of yourselves I *wish* I was home one feels so stranded somehow away from one's people – having Dick I'm only too thankful with any luck I shall be with him in about 6 weeks. . . . I don't suppose Ted will be able to write and if you ever can write to him you *must* remember to be *pleased* that he's going. They *can't* understand our feelings of fear *one* bit. You may hear where they are sooner than I especially *if* they go to England which is one of the rumours, but there are so many. Some still think they won't leave this country but transports are ready at Bombay.

Ted did write by that mail, on the following day, Gertrude receiving both letters on 4 September.

Just a line as I am frightfully busy and haven't got a minute to spare. The air is full of rumours, and I don't know where or when we are going. I expect Ben will have told you all the news. However I'll fix her up all right before I go, but I'm afraid you won't hear much of either of us owing to delayed mails and censorship.

Anyhow we'll both be all right so don't worry. I do hope you've not had too much to worry you but these are anxious times, but I think England is

Ben

as good a place to be in as anywhere though I expect you are a bit uncomfortable owing to rising prices. But there is nothing to be frightened of so don't let Dreda and Jane get into a panic!

He managed to write again on the 18th and after a couple of paragraphs on much the same lines as his previous letter he goes on:

As regards old Ben. I often wondered how I managed before she came to stay; how really dreary life must have been. She's a perfect little person, and her staying here has been too charming and delightful for words. She is a *great* favourite with everyone and has made one or two real friends I think. But to me she has been perfectly sweet, and I can never thank her too much for all she has done for me. It has all been perfect, absolutely, and I can never thank her enough. My only regret is that I could not give her a better time, but amusements here are limited and I'm a busy man. If she has derived one quarter of the pleasure from her visit that I have, well I am more than amply repaid.

Ben, for her part, was only too glad to have been with him at this time.

19 August, your birthday.

Thank you ever so much for your letter. I must try and get a letter off to you today, and will you please tell Dreda and Jane that I may not be able to catch the mail this week but they shall hear next, I've so little time for writing there are such heaps of things to do and see to. Here is all hussle and fuss as the regiments leave tomorrow and the 2/39th on Friday. They've been all ready for some days and are very anxious to get off. Alix and I have been awfully busy making and mending, but the little they are allowed to take is awful, I consider, only 60lb personal kit and the Lord knows when they'll get back. I've got all Ted's things packed up in his lined cases, I wanted to get it done before he left, I'd so hate doing it after. I simply won't realise he is going off to war, they all seem to think in time, and if it lasts they will see some fighting. I am so glad that one of the family is here to see him off. I rather expect our letters will be the first you'll hear of their going – or the officers on leave have of course all been recalled and are to join at the destination (no one knows where *that* is) so you may know through that. They are to be at Bombay early next week, in the 2 Divisions there will be about 50 regiments and that means about 30 transports. I suppose they'll use any old ship they can get. We've heard very little news and it seems it is scarce even in England, in the next few days we shall know more after this big battle, I hope and pray the worst will be *well* over by the time any of these people get there and then they'll have had the excitement of going and all and be more or less safe. I suppose such heaps of people we know and hear of are in the expeditionary force and have gone. I've just heard from Dick . . . I shall go straight to him as soon as ever it is cool enough, anyway I shall go in a month's time as I can stand a little of the heat and would sooner be with him, but we shall fix all that up and I haven't heard from him since my letter telling him for certain Ted was going. Dick seems very fit and cheery. Thanks very much for saying you've sent my parcel. It will arrive *some* time I suppose and I shall be sure to love all the things [though they] won't be of very much use if I am buried with Dick at Lahoal but I shall have them for when I *do* get home. I'm hoping it won't be very much later even than November as most people are going home then, I mean the wives and families left here. . . . Please when you get this, address me c/o King Hamilton & Co, Calcutta, letters and everything, as I shall have left here and I'll keep them up to my movements. I heard from Paul from Alexandria; it must have been a day or two before they dashed to Malta. I'm dreading a naval battle with the Austrian fleet.

When Ben wrote again, less than a week later, Ted had gone.

25 August 1914

I must get a letter off to you today if I can to be sure of catching the mail. It seems ages since Ted went off on Friday. I haven't had a moment, there have been such a lot of things to see to packing away everything of his. We are now left destitute, the station seems the oddest place and of course the regiments absolutely made the place; there are no civilians here at all you see. Ted went off in very good spirits on Friday, seeing the regiment off was rather a struggle as all that cheering and bandplaying is unhingeing enough at any time, when the 39th went off I didn't go to the parade beforehand but Alix and I went down the road and saw them all pass, Ted marches at the head of the regiment with the Col: all the officers fell out as they passed and we wished them luck. I did feel so dreadfully sorry for some of the poor wives especially the several brides but I must say they kept wonderfully brave. . . . The three regiments from here are no further than Kodwhara, the base of the hill here waiting to entrain for Karachi, it is sickening for them being kept down there because it's frightfully hot and unhealthy but we can send them things and hear from them. . . . At present the idea of Egypt is very much to the fore. I only hope and pray it is true and for the moment they will be more or less safe there. I may come home now earlier as I've a chance of a free passage, journey from here to the port as well, in the trooper they are chartering for families of officers going on service. . . . The thing is I shan't get to Assam or see Dick again out here, but originally I was not going to Assam at all after here, it was only when Ted could get leave and go too that it was to have been so ripping, so under the altered circumstances I think I may as well come home a month sooner and save about £30 or more. . . . Alix will come home too. We are all right up here tho' it seems very lonely and deserted without any of our menkind. Alix is engaged to Nobbie Clarke in the 39th, it is rather dreadful for her his going off but he is very lucky because he is only 22 and so will see some service early in his career. We've got 11 dogs with us (how *you'd* enjoy this!) 4 of mine, 4 of Alix's, 2 of Nobbie's, 1 of Molly's, so you can imagine the pack they are; we have to be fearfully careful after tea because the panthers swarm around here now the place is empty. This sounds alarming but they wouldn't hurt *us* really, but they take the dogs before you know where you are. Phyllis Morris' birthday today we are going to dine with her, she was to have given a dance but of course that's out of the question now. We are very lucky to have Mr Fox at the 39th depot. He is looking after the messing well as he never minds being worried over anything, on your own like this you have to have a head of sorts and you know how good I am over money matters at any time and when it's not English money I'm more of a fool than ever. You needn't worry about money for me because I can draw on Ted's pay, but with this trooper business I shan't want any hardly as Alix and I will stay on *here* till we sail, and living up here doesn't come to very much; anyway I'll get it all fixed up and Ted made every arrangement necessary. I wonder how you all are, the papers say England is very peaceful but the expeditionary force going off must have made things seem very close. . . .

There was a long postscript all round the margin in this letter.

There's no news from here. We do nothing these days, nothing to do and the rain still persists. I daren't think of the packing I shall have to do because I'm bringing home lots of Ted's books and things, and we have collected such a lot of odds and ends somehow. They give you such short notice with these troopers but this one will be different I expect and it is just for the families and no one else. They won't send us either till it's quite safe from these dreadful mines. I suppose you've no news of Paul. No mail to answer, we expect one on Sunday. I am longing to hear again, I do so hate the mail going wrong. I shall be able to tell you my passage in the next mail or two. I must try to write to the girls tomorrow.

Ted's short letter from the camp at Kodwhara did little more than confirm the news expanded in Ben's longer letters. His next letter, written on a piece of paper torn from a Field Service Pocket Book, was from Karachi.

3 September 1914

Of course you have seen that 2 divisions are coming from India to help in the show, and you must have guessed by now from what Ben and I have already told you that we are coming. Anyhow, we have got as far as this, and embark in a day or two and ought to land in Europe somewhere about the end of this month, where, I don't know. But it's all so secret we aren't allowed to tell you anything, except what you can get from the papers. I'll write whenever I can, of course, but I don't know how often that will be. . . . Keep all press cuttings you can get about Indian troops in the war and the *Gloucester* [Paul's ship]; I see she has already distinguished herself. . . . So wish me luck & don't worry about me please, mother. You'll be having Ben home soon I expect, she'll have told you all the news. Lovely sea breeze here, and I'm as fit as a fiddle.

Ted's letters were delayed, possibly by censorship. This took a month to reach Gertrude, whereas Ben's written on the same day from Lansdowne arrived on 25 September.

I got your letter last week, I was so thankful to get a mail as I'd had to wait more than a fortnight, and just at a time when one wants to hear so much. All your letters were of course full of the war, it was so funny reading your remarks about Ted being out of it. I expect that you gathered that the Indian troops were being taken by the papers & Lord Kitchener's speeches before you got our letters saying they were mobilising here. You will also know the 3rd & 7th Divisions are going straight to Europe; the Egypt affair is quite off, so by the time you get this Ted will be very near the front. I fancy they'll keep them a bit to get acclimatised. I'm afraid you'll be very worried but I'm praying hard that the worst may be over by the time they get there, you see it will be almost another 5 or 6 weeks. . . . Look here, this is how you will know what the 39th Garhwalis belong to, they belong to the *20th Brigade 7th Division, Indian Expeditionary Force A*. And you can use this as an address, put Name & Regiment very clear, we from our end send them to the Post Office at Bombay but you would either put c/o G.P.O. or War Office I should think, you must find out. . . . No more definite news re the trooper. We may go now in lots of about 100 with the reinforcements from the country . . . there have been 700 applicants from both divisions but they cut out any that are not genuine. I should think Alix and I are almost sure for one. . . . I haven't heard really from Dick since I told him I shouldn't go to him again but it would be a hopeless running away of money, the journey alone being close on £10 or £11, and it seems it would be till November and he will get home I expect, as ship's doctor or something. He says he will send me to Shillong to the hotel there and he won't go as it costs such a lot but I *don't* want to go

Fred Lumb, Alix, Ben and Ted, 1914

Tennis party, Lansdowne 1914

alone, after all it was going to be so ripping with him & Ted, beside I am longing to get back.

In fact, as the time drew nearer, Ben's thoughts turned more and more to the family and friends in England.

I imagine it must have been dreadful for you everyone going off. Willie and all too, but when you wrote the expeditionary force hadn't gone and with the first lot no territorials went did they? Splendid Paul having that go at those German cruisers, I don't quite know why they didn't finish them off more, it must have been gorgeous for Paul, now I hope there won't be much more, *he*'s had his little go, hasn't he. I suppose George wasn't with the Scots Greys, I do hope he's all right. It must be dreadful for you as I daresay you have casualty lists by now, I doubt if we get them at all. I shall so dread landing in a way, as one gets so little news on board, I shall be thankful to get home, one feels so useless out here and I suppose everyone is doing something at home. Alix has had six months hospital training which ought to come in useful, we feel fearfully useles with nothing to do in the useful line out here and besides being so far away now all our people have gone to Europe. It's gorgeous weather here and I hope the rains are over, we can have all our meals in the garden as it is not too hot, and we've a nice shady place. We can play tennis again but ladies fours seems so odd, especially out here where there were always more men than girls.

But she cannot keep off the subject of the war for long.

I feel dreadfully sorry for Flossie, but I suppose most of the naval show is over. It was gorgeous that we did so well, but a fearful *suspense*, all that time with no news only rumours. I was so thankful that Paul was not there and he hasn't been out of it either. . . . Fred Lumb got back in time, but only just, he'd gone over the border into Tibet so never got any of the wires recalling him, he did 35 miles over impossible country for 7 days. I just saw him and had tea with him in the mess the few hours he was here, he had to go straight on, too thin for words and fearfully tired but only too thankful not to have been left behind. It was touch and go if he'd catch 'em up.

In her next letter, written on 10 September, she still did not know what her movements would be.

I got your mail letters yesterday. I was waiting for them to answer also I *did* think I'd be able to tell you for certain about my passage on a trooper, there is a good chance of getting a passage in one leaving Karachi on the

18th. 10 of us from here are moving heaven and earth to get it. Otherwise they say we are sure of one in late Oct. I shall be tempted to use my P&O before then I feel sure, but otherwise I find I can save about £50. Staying on here of course means using Ted's money so I am wanting to get back, also I can't bear the idea of being up here, it's miserable, and Dick only within 4 or 5 *days* journey and that impossible to do alone, but he advises me to take this trooper as he has given his service to government in November. . . . Shillong is off, needless expense and I certainly don't feel like going anywhere for enjoyment these days; and without Ted or Dick I should hate it – it was all going to be so different before with them both. It seems so funny in your letters to hear you say how sick Ted must be to be out of it, when he'll be so very much in it. . . . I'm relieved to hear about Paul. If we get this trooper on the 18th we go under the same escort as the 7th Division but of course I don't suppose we shall see anything of our friends and relations. It will be quite a historic voyage anyway.

During the next four years Gertrude was to receive many requests for a great variety of things to be sent to her sons. In a way she was used to this. She had always sent them back to their various schools equipped with a stamped addressed postcard: 'Have arrived safe with luggage. Please send . . .' on the assumption that they were bound to have forgotten something. The first request came now from Ben, on Ted's behalf:

Will you get and send to Ted under the address I gave you last week with additions found out by you *3 refills* [batteries] *for an Ever Ready Baby electric torch and one new bulb*. He gave me one of these a ripping thing but I gave it back to him to take, and by the time the parcel reaches him he'll want refills; just risk sending them because there's a chance of them reaching him, but you'll know more your end about that.

Her thoughts turn more and more towards home.

I do so wonder where Willie is, he is in it by now I feel sure. The casualty list must be dreadful, we haven't had one at all yet – I shall hear so little news once I start that I shall dread landing. The troopers arrive at Southampton, I don't suppose anyone will be able to meet me, it's a long journey and you may not know exact date, but I shall be quite all right. . . . Anyway I'll wire directly I land but it would be a waste of money to meet me, since it's so different from what my original home coming was to have been. The girls tell me they do heaps of work in the house. I suppose most people are grabbed for nursing, I think I might help with the cooking as well. *Splendid* you being able to put your art to such good use, I feel as useless as they make 'em now, so stranded and Ted having gone, I'm no good to anyone and it all means spending money being up here alone. . . . Will you when you get this join some *Press Cutting Agency* and get them to send you *all* cuttings about the INDIAN EXPEDITIONARY FORCE and the *Gloucester*? Ted tells me to tell you this: you send them a sub and they send you the cuttings and this way you miss none. I've some to keep till I get back, Ted says this is *very important* so start at once, see? You may not hear from him much, he says. He wants me to get home as soon as I can, and *you* are not to worry about him, easier said than done isn't it. Anyway I got a lovely lot of praise from him in his letters which has made me glad to have been here, tho it was so *awful* the very fact of seeing him off and all, it ended such a *ripping* time with him here somehow that I *hate* being here without him and *longing to get away*. Please tell the girls they'll get no letters this mail I'm afraid but I love them. . . . You must read them out of this and give them my love.

As part of a long postscript she writes:

Dreda's birthday tomorrow. I'll remember it as I did Peter yesterday. Lovely for Ruth to get such a gorgeous chance of nursing she *must* be pleased. You will have got Ted's name on the Intercession list now.

Her next long letter, dated 5 September headed 'On the way to Karachi' was evidently written on the train.

I must send you a line now in case I don't get time before we sail. Alix & I are on our way to Karachi; we've got passages in the *Dilwara* (you will have had my cable which I am sending before I sail) and you will also have had my mail letters telling you I had a good chance of a passage. We had a dreadful rush only 12 hours notice and *every*thing to pack and see to, goodness I don't know how we did it. Mr Fox ran all the travelling part – you see it isn't quite like starting from Guildford, we were 30 miles from the station! and coolies carry your luggage down, we had 28! Alix & I are awfully lucky to get that passage and together too. . . . Now we go along with the 7th Division under the same escort, so we shall be more or less with the 39th till they get to France. . . . We travel with warrants marked 'War 1914' in red ink, everything free. . . . I can never describe the journey, it is *dreadful* frantic heat well over 100 in our carriage & we are crossing the Sind desert & the whole carriage is really inches in dust and we ourselves are absolutely black and pour with perspiration the entire day. . . . Well it's good training for the Red Sea we are only going 8 knots . . . all the voyage, it will take nearly 5 or 6 weeks so I am sending this by the mail this week which will overtake us but I shan't be far behind. I'll wire the day I land and come along – I've got tons of luggage, 3 packing cases. I've brought all the china Ted and I had, rather a nice dinner service & tea set & all his books. The discomfort of this journey is past description but I shall be glad to get home so I don't mind. Ted will be glad to know I'm safe & on my way back before he sails too. I don't think he quite likes leaving me stranded, you see four days journey which one can't do alone, from Dick makes one rather alone. I don't suppose I shall see Ted as they have embarked but he will know I'm there, but I hope I may get a glimpse if we stay a few days before sailing. . . . Really the war news is better isn't it; *how* thankful I am & I hope & pray the fighting won't be so fierce by the time our lot get there. . . . I do hope Willie and George are safe, I don't know for certain if Willie has gone. I'm afraid such heaps of our friends must have been killed its too dreadful. It would be nice if the *Gloucester* formed part of our escort, I hope we go to Malta. . . . I must thank you *most awfully* for the gorgeous box of things I got just before I came away. They are all *too* ripping and so *much* what I wanted, please tell the girls how much I loved their little contributions. . . . they'll be useful at home & NO waste . . . You have been ripping sending me all the things I've wanted out here, everyone has spoilt me, the family I mean, Ted & Dick I can never thank enough & they vow they can never thank me enough for coming, but that's rot. I've loved it. I'm so longing to see you all again and I'd hate to be so far away with Ted in the show. . . . I must try and collect a few presents at Port Said! I'm living on Ted's pay at present! Dick wired did I want money so I wired back no I've got heaps! So he wired back if *you* are so rich I'll be on the borrow. Rather sickening for Alix she was out here for another year but she wants to get back before Nobbie Clarke & her brother get to France. . . . I feel so sorry for her, she & Nobbie were only engaged a week before he went. . . .

She added another page in the same envelope.

Karachi
Wednesday evening, September 16, 1914

Well, we arrive this morning after *the* most impossible journey. . . . Archie Mankelow met us & we had breakfast on this ship, the *City of Lahore*. The *Dilwara* isn't in yet so we are messing here at present. Look here after all you will not have had a cable because its not much point. I can't tell you the date we leave or anything because cables are so heavily censored. . . . I shall be home in about a month or 5 weeks I suppose so any day after you get this you can expect a wire from me saying I've landed. . . . Ted came along for a few minutes at lunch time; his ship is also in the docks here, but they can't get off much. He is looking most *awfully* well and very cheery. Such heaps of troopers here, the dock is full and we have three or four cruisers to escort us. We are hoping one may be the *Gloucester* as then perhaps we should see Paul. It does seem funny going really with the

Expeditionary Force. . . . We embark tonight – I see the *Dilwara* has just come. Alix & I have a cabin together, that we do know, so we hope it's a 2-berth one. It does seem funny that I'm really starting home. . . . I don't know if I shall see Ted again after we once sail because I don't suppose we land in many ports en route but we *hope* to see something of them. Tell the girls I'm longing to see them again & you all. . . . Just had a wire from Dick, I must write to him tomorrow, he says 'What about being alone in India' but he'll be home soon I feel sure.

Ted and Ben managed to see quite a lot of each other in Karachi as he was able to have all his meals on board the *Dilwara* until they sailed. He wrote to his mother on 17 September:

It is ripping seeing [Ben] again, but so odd somehow, as I left Lansdowne a month ago, & here we are still in India, & Ben stayed on for a long time after we've gone, & comes home in the same convoy! . . . under the same escort of cruisers as us. . . . As Ben says, it only wants Paul on the *Gloucester* to meet us at Port Said to complete it! Imagine Paul's face when he saw us! Quite possible and very likely the *Gloucester* will be our escort after the Canal. . . . Just off to have lunch on the *Dilwara*, & after that we leave the docks & go out into the stream about 4 p.m. So I shan't get another chance of seeing her I don't expect. We might if we go ashore at Aden or anywhere.

Ben's last letter from India was uncharacteristically short but in the same breathless style and with the usual marginal postscripts. Ted's ship had gone out early that morning, 20 September, and she had just heard there was a chance to catch the mail before the *Dilwara* joined the convoy.

There will be about 40 of us all together in three clumps. . . . I'm sure there will be a good old muddle as these ships are so very un-used to sailing at close quarters. Very uncomfortable, full of babies who scream *all* day. . . . I've seen quite a lot of Ted & the others and we shall see the 39th Ghl ship all the way along because it is in the same block as ours.

And, in a postscript:

I shall be very much on the look out for the dear *Gloucester* all the way home.

Ted wrote at sea:

Here we are, well on our way to heaven knows where! All sorts of rumours where we are going to land, of course . . . but no one knows at all, it's being kept an absolute secret. My last letter was from Karachi, I think, when I told you I had met Ben. . . . We had awful fun there, she & I, as we were in dock for about 4 days before we sailed. I used to be fairly busy all day on ship, but always managed to get off in the evening & go up and have dinner on the *Dilwara* & sit & talk to Ben till far into the night. Well, one day we got orders to leave the wharf, & next day, the 21st Sept, we sailed so I haven't seen Ben since then. This is a huge convoy of transports, 40 in all, & we have cruisers and battleships escorting us. The old *Dilwara* used to be just alongside of us, but too far off to distinguish people. But half way across the Indian Ocean she went gadding off on her own, with a small cruiser as escort, most exciting for Ben, wasn't it. She went to land troops at Aden and pick up some fresh ones & this morning I can see the old *Dilwara* tearing along to catch us up. You see the *Konigsberg*, that small German cruiser, is still knocking about in these waters somewhere, hence the elaborate precaution of escorts . . . . There is just a chance that we may stay a day or two at Suez or Port Said. . . in which case I may be able to get over and pay the *Dilwara* a visit, I hope so. What fun it would be if Paul & the *Gloucester* were at Port Said too, & were part of our escort through the Mediterranean, & then we'd be quite a family party on the high seas. . . .

He refers to the weather:

Our men, who of course have never seen a ship or a sheet of water bigger than a bucket before were frightfully ill, poor devils, but are much better now.

and goes on with the second of many requests, 'Please send . . .'

By the way, I want you to do something for me, I want a camp lantern, to take candles, something after this style – [he sketches it] – you can get them at the stores [Army & Navy?] or Harrods or any stores like that, I should think. They are generally made of black tin, with talc sides which slide in & out, & weigh about 1lb. If possible I should like a *folding one*, but never mind if it doesn't fold up, an ordinary one will do. But it should be square shape, as above, & please send out one or two extra talc slides with it to replace them if they get broken. Anyhow the A & N stores camp furniture dept would know the thing exactly if you ask them, as I know they keep them, but I expect there's been a run on them lately. Anyhow, have a shot will you at getting one, p'raps some military stores in Aldershot wd have one.

Now came the problem of where to send it.

Well, having got it please pack it up ready to send to me when I can give you an address. Of course wherever we land we are bound to sit down for a week or two to get men & animals fit after the long voyage, as we shall be pretty soft, so we shan't go gadding off at once, & there will be lots of time to send it to me. P'raps the India Office will publish an address, but if they don't & we're not allowed to tell you where we are (quite possible this, as they keep things so secret) then you might ask the India Office what address to send things to. But they are sure to let you know some address.

He dismisses the problem with some reference to the improved weather and then goes on:

I can see the old *Dilwara* just off our starboard quarter, fearfully nautical these days, but it is too far off to distinguish people easily, even with glasses. Funny to think how hot we are now, & in about a week's time we shall be shivering with cold I expect. We've only got thin khaki drill kit, so lets hope they give us some warm clothes before we start. . . . We haven't heard much war news, just a few spasmodic wireless messages; but what we have heard seems favourable; I wonder what the situation will be when we get there. I shall stop this letter for a bit now, & finish off later, when we reach Suez or Port Said.

Suez
3 October 1914

Am sending this home by Ben. I believe we are going to Marseilles but don't know for certain. Awful hurry.

Tons of love,
from Ted

Ben also wrote at Suez:

. . . I hope I may see Ted at Port Said, after that I think we may leave this convoy and go on our own. . . . We are about 50 transports going along together, we have been quite near Ted's ship once or twice & at Suez yesterday we were in harbour together, but no one was allowed off. . . . We've heard very little news, but I see in one list of casualties that Laurence Russell is wounded. I did not find anyone else I knew but that was some time ago of course. I want to get back quickly now once we leave the convoy as they will be in France fairly soon. I don't suppose our people will go straight into it they are sure to let them climatise if possible at first. I shall hear from Ted at Port Said anyway even if I don't see him. The Irish Rifles [the troops on board the *Dilwara*] are an awfully nice lot and Alix & I are having a very good time. They have a band too on board which plays twice a day, and we dance in the evenings. The Irish Rifles are only going home to get warmer clothes & then straight to France so of course they are in good spirits. There was a Tommies' concert last night, there was quite a good deal of talent. . . .

The messing on board, however, leaves something to be desired. After some days of sea sickness and tummy upsets she writes:

[I] have been eating again now, tho' the food is *frightful* & not get-atable mostly as they have so few waiters, but we are all getting used to the discomfort & are more or less cheerful, under all the hopeless circumstances. I really wonder that we are because there is not one single person in the ship who has not a husband at the war, bar Alix & I and we've brothers and her fiancé. I love going through the Canal it's so peaceful, I hope we are able to land at Port Said. . . . I do hope you are all right. I'm longing to get back to you again. I hope you are doing that press clipping scheme for Ted. [And around the margin again] I live in hopes of seeing the *Gloucester* somewhere, there may be a chance perhaps. . . .

This letter is postmarked 'posted at Port Said', where the hoped-for, but not expected, reunion did take place.

Ted recorded in his diary:

Went straight through to Suez, through the Canal & coaled at Port Said – here I met Ben again, & we had a most cheery time, & bought half the place & finally had dinner at the great Eastern Hotel with Alix M., Nobbie Clarke & Archie M., great rag.

And he sent his mother an undated picture postcard of Port Said:

Ben & I having a great time here! Don't tell it's a strange place to meet. We go on tomorrow I expect. Ted. Quite a family meeting, Both fearfully fit. Just off to dinner. So long.

In the last letter of the voyage, written off Sardinia on 11 October he described the meeting in greater detail.

Ben and I had most awful fun at Port Said, & sent you some p.c.s from there which I expect you have got by now. I went and got her off the *Dilwara*, & we went ashore & made a whole lot of purchases & wandered about seeing sights generally. And it was a sight! Nothing but officers in uniform and *crowds* of them, also hundreds of French sailors, all waving little Union Jacks. Ben & I kept saying 'Vive l'entente' to them & they were fearfully pleased always. There were 2 French battleships in P. Said, & two or three British cruisers & torpedo boats, but the old *Gloucester* wasn't there; I wonder where she is. After we had walked all over the place, we foregathered with Alix & some pals & had a tremendous dinner at the hotel, where we met everyone we'd ever met in India, & I kept introducing Ben to officers who had just rejoined from leave, & I think she's met everyone in the regiment now. We had quite a good dinner, with a little French tricolour stuck in the flower pot on the table. I had to be back on ship by 10, so we wandered off & rowed back & then sent old Ben off to the *Dilwara*. It was a gorgeous day and I can't remember having enjoyed anything so much for years.

Somehow it seems almost surprising that the old *Gloucester* with their brother Paul was *not* there. The letter ends:

We get scraps of war news by wireless occasionally, & today we heard about the Zeppelin being burnt by our navy airmen & the seige of Antwerp.

There is, of course, much speculation as to where we are going. At *last* after many guesses, rumours & hopes & fears, we know we are going to Marseilles; from there we go to a concentration camp near Paris, and after that, heaven knows where they'll send us, wherever we are most wanted. It will be pretty cold on the continent this time of year, so could you send me along a khaki muffler sometime, a nice soft light but warm one if you can get one, also a pair of warm gloves, leather lined wool sounds all right, size 8. Ben has got my address, but I'll give it to you again unless of course you've had any other address given by the India or War Office. . . . You see I'm not allowed by regulations to tell you where I am, or mention any towns etc, just the barest items of news can be sent, otherwise one's letters are liable to censorship and much delay, & very often destruction. But of course you can send me what you like . . . and say what you like in your letters as they are not censored. . . . By the way can you send me 2 pairs of warm drawers, not too thick but thick-ish, short ones reaching to the knee, as I know it will be most infernally cold all the winter. But don't send too many things, as one's kit is limited in weight of course, and I've got as much warm kit as I can carry, almost. Doubtless a little baccy & cigarettes would not be out of place sometimes. But I leave it all to you. I expect everyone is making clothes etc for the troops, & so we *should* be plentifully supplied if only the things roll up.

Well, we live in stirring times, so don't expect to hear from me again till you *do* hear from me: the Indian troops should be a good deal in the limelight, so you will probably see references to their doings in the papers occasionally. So wish me luck and don't worry about me. Best love to all the family; I haven't had any letters for ages! Ben will tell you a lot of news first hand. I wouldn't have missed that day in Port Said for worlds. I wonder if she's got home yet.

Tons of love from your loving son Ted

This letter was posted in Marseilles on 12 October. The 2/39th Garhwal Rifles had landed in France.

INDIA IN FRANCE 1914

Ted wrote again on 14th October on some scrappy paper.

Just a line to say we've landed in France – not allowed to say where! and am absolutely all right. We disembarked two days ago, marched out 10 miles to camp (no joke after a month on board ship!) and got to camp about 12.30 at night, and to bed by 3 a.m., when it began to rain, and it's been raining ever since! . . . However we are all in high spirits & it could take a lot to damp them. Excuse a scrawl, but am writing in my tent on the floor. We have all our kit – such as it is – at present but we shall soon be on 35lbs only. . . . How splendid Jim enlisting, what a sportsman; I expect we shall meet some day, I hope so. I got lots of letters from you & Jane & Dryden, all the ones you posted to the India Office. Thanks awfully for them – very busy as I have to get acquainted with all the thousand and one orders of the force – so glad to hear you are all right at home.

It would not be surprising if, when Gertrude eventually died, 'Please send . . .' had been found written on her heart.

Please send me a khaki muffler, light weight but warm. Tell Ben the blue jersey is the warmest thing in Europe & the buzz of the force, really no rotting. Past 10 o'clock, so I must go to sleep. Still raining hard. I wonder if old Ben's arrived home yet. She'll tell you all my news. . . . I wouldn't mind some cigarettes and baccy occasionally – I am going to try to keep a diary through the war, but I expect it will be a pretty scrappy one when once we get to the mysterious 'front'! We get a few papers occasionally, & I see Antwerp has fallen; I wonder what their game is. By the way, send along a few picture papers occasionally, *Daily Sketches* etc, they will all help to amuse us.

He repeats his request for gloves and a folding lantern and goes on:

Old Ben will tell you all about our escapades at P. Said; I wouldn't have missed that day for worlds. All our letters are censored, *so* I can tell you *nothing*, not even where we are or where we are going; don't worry we'll be all right, but won't it be cold! Ugh! . . .

When he wrote again he was on the move.

23 October 1914

Just got another letter from you in answer to the one I wrote from Marseilles. At least I wrote it on board and posted it when we landed, by the pilot. Then orders came out that all letters posted in French post offices wd be destroyed, so we fondly imagined those wd never roll up. Anyway, I wrote again from camp, so I expect that's rolled up too now. I've had lots of letters from you all since landing including some forwarded from India, in which you say you expect I wish I was in the show! It seems funny reading them. . . . I suppose we must stick to orders, & refer mysteriously to 'this place' & 'that place', mention no names, silly as it seems. Anyhow we left the last place I wrote from – give you one guess! – on the 18th, & came by train here, by a most roundabout way, arriving on the 21st. The camp was in an awful state, feet deep in mud, & we had persistent rain for 6 days. We got orders on the morning of the 18th to entrain at 2 o'clock that night, or next morning rather. There was an awful muddle of transport, & owing to the mud, well, I never *saw* such a mess! To cap it all it poured in torrents from 2 till 4, & made things 50 times worse of course. . . . Eventually we got the transport off, & marched off at 8 p.m. arriving at the station at 12.30. We loaded up the train, & started off at 6 a.m. next morning. We had no sleep of course for 24 hours, & had been working hard all the time, so were of course rather tired. We had been soaked through & had got more or less dry again marching, but none of us had our clothes or boots off for more than 36 hours; this I know is nothing to what others have been doing up at the front, or to what we shall doubtless be going through in a day or two now, but it just shows how one can be quite decently uncomfortable miles away from the war really. . . . Such fun in the train; every station *crowds* of people, stare, stare, & shouting & waving. All the girls asking for souveniers, & almost tearing buttons & badges off one's uniform. However, I managed to hang on to all of mine, as I couldn't spare any, though I gave away one or two odd stars – interrupted here by ten million orders coming in. Sorry.

24 October 1914

Not had a chance to get on with this till tonight. We got here at 10.30 one morning & marched straight out to camp, almost as muddy as the other, but mud of quite a different kind, sort of sticks to your boots. . . . We went for a route march this morning, through most lovely lanes etc & gorgeous trees, poplars and vineyards, all the autumn tints were lovely. . . . Thanks awfully for all the things you are sending out, they sound gorgeous & I am daily expecting the parcel. . . . By the way, what's wrong with an air pillow, a small one, it seems to be the thing to have, so light and convenient, & I've had to bang a pillow out of my 35lb kit – tell Ben this! – so sleep on clothes or any old bundle, but have one of the khaki pillow cases Ben made me, which I stuff with grass etc when I can so manage to be fairly comfortable; anyhow I sleep all right. And there's stuff called CREX for tired feet which our Colonel says is v. good to put in water when washing; tabloids, I think, would you send some along, or any similar stuff. The great thing is *small* parcels, only *letter* post if poss, to ensure quicker & more certain delivery.

Well, my old horse had to go to hospital as I told you, but they are so short of gees that, though we want 8 for officers, they have only given us *one*, for our interpreter who has never ridden a horse in his life, so I shall be able to have his. Poor old Araby, I wish he had kept fit; Ben will be awfully sorry. I imagine Ben is arriving about today; how the house will buzz with talk; I wish I could be there to join in it all. I heard from Paul yesterday, just a scrawl, wishing me luck . . .

Ted's diary tells of all this in more detail.

How amusing the people were in the train coming up from Marseilles and from Orleans too. They crowded round the carriages at every halt, and gave us all cigarettes, nuts etc etc. In return they asked for souveniers in the shape of buttons and badges. One fair damsel I saw [was] wearing the badges of every regiment and corps in the division. She must have made herself very nice to everyone, but I did not make her acquaintance.

Well, the morning of the 29th we left Calonne and marched about 8 miles and halted, about 11 o'clock. At 6 we moved again, the weather being bitterly cold, and found we had orders to relieve the King's Own Yorkshire Light Infantry in the trenches that night. . . . We got to the trenches at midnight and, after having them explained and receiving a few final words of advice from the officer, we entered into the war proper. We had hardly settled down, in fact had not finished taking over the trenches, than the enemy began his favourite night attacks. Whether he came on in force or not I don't know, but we opened a heavy fire on him, which lasted about ½ hour, and then all was quiet again. I know I was just taking a company to man a little shallow trench when it began, so we lay down and opened fire. But there were very few – if any! – Germans in front of us, so I think it was really a false alarm, though they certainly fired back at us from their trenches with rifle and maxim gunfire.

Considering how anxious his mother must have been, he spares her surprisingly few details.

3 November 1914
[in pencil on a scrap of paper]

Thanks awfully for your letter which I got in the middle of last night! Well, at last we have reached the front! We left — on the 26th I think, did a 2 days journey, marched 10 miles a day, billeted in a village on the 28th, marched 8 miles on the 29th & relieved a regiment here in the trenches in the night. And we've been in the trenches ever since, night & day. The Germans have made a lot of attacks on us, & all along the line, but – tap wood – as far as we are concerned they have not been successful. We had a few casualties. Anyhow I am allright. Being Adjutant I have to be at Bn Hd quarters with the C.O., receive & write messages etc, & generally be in a central position so that all may know where we are & can communicate with us. All day long incessant artillery & rifle fire goes on between the two forces, & the first 3 nights we were here we were attacked each night, one night we had *5* separate attacks! at 6, 9, 1, 3, & 5, but only two of them were heavy & we managed to keep them off, Lord, what a noise goes on on these occasions. Banging & banging, bullets whistling about & shells bursting, you never *heard* such a noise. . . . Cold at all – I should think so, & we all dressed in thin khaki drill. Isn't it wicked, I shiver all night – you see, we came in here as I say, on the 29th (having left our kit & heavy baggage – if you can call 35lb heavy baggage! – behind as usual to come on later) in just what we stood up in and that's what we've been in ever since, & are likely to be for some time, as there seems no chance of getting our kit up. So we've all been eating, drilling, sleeping in our kit as we are, & I haven't taken a single thing off for 6 or 7 days and *dirty*, well, we are black! – our Head qrs are in a farm here, & the Colonel & I live in a little bunk-hole underground, out of the way of Maria & J. Johnson & Co. Today is a lovely day, & they are fairly quiet, so we are sitting put in the garden under a haystack out of sight, but the men are all in the trenches ready for anything. Your parcel came last night too, but I couldn't possibly open it here, so sent it back to my kit, it sounds lovely, & I am longing to open it . . . Tell Ben the blue jersey saved my life, I've had it on continuously – there goes Maria again! – for a week now – I got a letter from her postmarked 23rd. I must end now.

His next letter was to Ben, in pencil, on paper torn from a Field Service Pocket Book.

8 November 1914

Very many thanks for your long letter full of most interesting news. . . . it must as you say be truly funny seeing all your friends dressed up as Tommies and going about with them all, Wiggs is an awful swell being an officer of course: no I hadn't heard it before, the others hadn't told me about it. Yes the 'historic' voyage in the DilDil, however unpleasant and trying at times, will surely live in your memory as quite a good show on the whole, and as you say you probably made some good friends on board & saw some new life. I expect you can put them all in their places when it comes to soldiers, eh, even Jim & Wiggy! Mother says Jim expects to be out here very soon, but he seems to have had very little training, I'm not crabbing the show, only I should think they'd want some more yet. . . .

We are still in thin khaki drill; what a contrast to that day at Karachi! *You* remember, in the first cabin you had on the *Dilwara*, when we simply bathed in good honest sweat. I don't really think I've got enough on, but I can't get any more just at present. You see we came out to occupy the trenches on 29th Oct, & are still here; that makes 10 days. . . . Devilish long to be in cold damp trenches with only the kit you stand up in! I read a glowing account in the *Standard* a day or two ago of life in the trenches, but it was very misleading. First of all, it talked about 'spade-hewn, straw-spread' trenches; true in a way, but all our digging here has to be done at night, as it would be impossible to dig by day, as the enemy's trenches are 300 yards off, & his little advance trenches, in which snipers sit & pick you off if you show a finger, are only about 150 yards; so the digging isn't very grand – and there is some straw, but it's mostly trodden into the mud. Again he says we do 3 days in the front trench, 3 days in the support, & 4 days rest. Divil a bit, this is our 10th day in the front trench, & no hope of relief yet awhile. . . . These damn Germans seem to think the barn, where we have – or rather used to have – our Battalion Headqrs is a most important place, because they persistently shell it. Every day for the last 4 days we had a whole lot of Jack Johnsons all round us, & they've knocked the farm buildings to hell. Such a pity, as 'it's a nice little farm', & has a lovely orchard and looks lovely in the evening sometimes – but of course it's absolutely wrecked – I don't think one can imagine these things unless you see them . . . all the furniture, crockery, clothes everything lying all over the shop anyhow – I don't know what the poor people will do when they come back after the war.

Last night, in fact all yesterday, the Germans were very active. For some reason or other they seem very anxious to break through our line just here, where we and the Seaforths are. . . . They again made a special effort against our headquarters, & dropped shrapnel & howitzer all round, but we were quite safe in our trenches, though of course we had a few men hit – Poor Nain Sing [his orderly, whom Ben knew] was hit on the head by a piece of shell a few days ago & died shortly afterwards; I'm awfully sorry as he was such a good chap, & had done me most awfully well on this show.

I don't suppose you've seen any casualty lists, perhaps you have; I'm not supposed to mention them I believe, but I'm sure they must have been published by now. Poor Stack has been killed, I don't know *what* Mrs Stack will do, I'm most awfully sorry – Wright has been killed too, & Davidson & Hayes Sadler, & 2 more in the 8th [Gurkhas]; Maclean wounded (he's gone home) & Col Morris, in fact they had a rotten time, the 8th, though they didn't lose many men – awful, isn't it. . . .

I want a balaclava cap, so if anyone wants to do anything say that; it's bitter at night, sleeping in just one's kit & no blanket or anything – I cover myself over with sacks and straw & so keep fairly warm. You remember that warm coat I had made well, I've had that on all the time & it's ripping & warm; but I believe mother said she had put a sweater in that parcel, & that will be lovely. She sent me the most *gorgeous* silk muffler, much too good for these shows, but it's been an absolute blessing & I couldn't have got on without it, and as for the blue jersey, well, saved me life, & caused a great stir among the troops!

I have picked up several German helmets, rifles, uniform, shells, etc. but I can't send them home as I should like to, so it's no good. I must try & collect a few trophies of the campaign before we've done.

We are just hanging on here while bigger developments take place elsewhere, & never a day passes without a furious shelling and an attack or two, & bullets go whizzing all over the shop; most exciting. There are hundreds of aeroplanes about, &, as you know, I've never seen one before – Col D-B & I were standing in a trench the other day, quite still, as the orders are to do so when 'hostile aircraft' (that's good, and will make your soldier friends sit up!) are about, & a German Taube was careering about overhead; you see it's awful hard to spot people except by movement. Anyhow we suddenly heard a little shrill hissing sound and an explosion in the turnips in front; this happened 3 times; & the stinker had been dropping bombs! But they didn't do any damage. . . .

What I shd have done without 'torchers' in the trenches I *don't* know! He's been absolutely *invaluable*, and you shall have him back again after the war as a trophy.

He managed a letter to Jane on the same day, enlivened by one of his characteristic drawings: 'Me having dinner when Jack Johnson is about'

Dear Jinny – sporting effort –

Thanks awfully for sending along the cigarettes I'm sure they'll be much appreciated. . . . My word, it is cold at nights, last night we were expecting an attack, so had to keep awake, but I got fed up towards morning & went off to sleep, or tried to, but it was too darned cold. And the enemy never fired a shot, so I was had all round. The first night we got here I was taking about 40 men from one trench to another smaller one, which we had to enlarge (you have to do most of the digging by night, as they spot you & pip you if they see you by day, snipers all over the place) when suddenly a furious fire opened on our right. We fairly flung ourselves down in the teeny little trench & the fun was fast & furious for about forty minutes. Luckily we had no one hit, though they had maxims on us, which make a most horribly alarming noise. . . . You should see me, staring at aeroplanes; 'Mr Stare' had never seen one before & the first one I saw had just dropped a bomb on the station we detrained at, but missed luckily – we have been congratulated (the 20th Bde I mean) by General Hillocks on our resistance, as these damned Germans have attacked us several times, but we have managed to keep them off so far; also Sir John French has sent us his congrats & gratitude to the Indian troops as a whole. So lets hope we keep it up – I'm doing the real heavy soldier, sitting on an ammunition box, & writing on the lid!

Still using indelible pencil and leaves torn from a signal pad he wrote to his mother on a date that was to have more significance than he knew then – not only for the rest of the world but for himself: 11 November

Very many thanks for your last letter. We are still in the trenches and no sign of being relieved yet, and we are all very tired and weary as the continual strain takes it out of one a lot. Shell & rifle fire goes on all day, and one has to be very wary walking about the trenches by day, as the Germans have special picked shots posted in houses, trees etc who poop off at anything they see moving about. . . . But as we have now been 13 days and nights in the trenches we have of course burrowed about and made quite a rabbit warren of them. Still, if one does get careless & show oneself a bit too much, as sure as fate 'zip!' comes a bullet whizzing along from somewhere. We sent 50 men the other night under Major Taylor (Ben knows him) to round up some Germans in a trench close to us. We cleared them out of the trenches, & bagged six prisoners; they seemed quite cheery and not at all down-hearted at being captured. While this was going on, all the rest of the enemy let us have it very hot, & we had a very hot ½ hour, but were fairly safe in our trenches & didn't suffer much; I don't know what the German losses were but I fancy we did some damage. . . .

We are all very fit up to date, though tired & sleepy. But every day they try & attack us to break through, & every night too, in fact one is always on the alert, & one simply longs to get out of the trenches & go for somebody; but our orders are to sit tight here and hang on till all's blue while bigger things develop elsewhere. We are much too weak a force to advance, & only just able to keep off these attacks; our line is appallingly thin in parts, and we can only hang on with difficulty.

Old sportsman Bobs is out here, & has sent for 3 men from each regiment in the trenches to see & talk to them; jolly sporting of the old man isn't it.

I have had several papers from Rosamond I think & some cigarettes from Aunt Nellie, please thank her & I will write when I have time. Her gift was much appreciated by the men.

So glad old Ben arrived home safely, I had a long letter from her a day or 2 ago. Can you send me a weekly newspaper, say the weekly *Times*, as we never hear any news of the outer world here, & I don't know in the least what's going on. I wish they would relieve us; the regiment we relieved in the trenches were here 12 days & said they never wanted to see a trench again; its the awful waiting, doing nothing but sit still & get shelled daily as regular as clockwork that palls so; if we could only advance or get a move on of sorts it would be an improvement. The farm we are round about is full of apples, potatoes, cabbages etc, so we go round at night & loot the garden for our meals, as we get no fresh vegetables from the commissariat, only tinned meat, jam, bread & cheese, so one wants a little green food occasionally.

It's awfully cold here, especially in thin Indian khaki. But thank goodness we are going to get warm kit soon, at least we have been told to apply for it, but when we shall get it I don't know. . . . I have got a lovely Jaegar Balaclava cap, just like the man in the picture in the stores list! So tell Ben I shan't want one now. The gloves you sent are gorgeously warm; you see it's so raw nowadays, & very damp living underground such a lot. . . . 'Jack Johnson' just beginning his daily visits; yesterday they shelled us all the morning but without much result except noise. Very heavy firing going on up north, so I expect there's a big battle going on up there, we never hear any news.

Matches are always welcome, as there is an appalling slump in them just now.

Ted sent his mother a postcard dated 21 November, thanking her for letters and the parcel – 'ripping and *just* what I wanted'. He was too busy to write at length, but hoped to send a long letter in a day or so. He began to list things he wanted: a metal flask, a map case, a waistcoat and 'something else which I have forgotten, but I'll let you know in a letter'.

Gertrude must have read his next letter with mixed feelings of relief and apprehension.

22 November 1914

I can now snatch a few minutes to write to you a line and tell you all about it. First of all I really must tell you how much I appreciated that ripping parcel you sent. You remember I told you I got it in the trenches a long time ago, but couldn't open it there, so sent it right back to our kit with the transport miles away. That was nearly three weeks ago and I managed to retrieve the parcel on the night of the 17th when we came out of the trenches. It *was* a ripping parcel, & full of surprises. The shetland woolly is topping, & I wear it all day, & couldn't do without it – all the little food things are lovely too, and I have them all carefully tucked away in my haversack to use when the occasion demands, as doubtless it will all in good time. At present we are feeding like fighting cocks so there is no point in using up little things like you sent, which will come in much more useful in an emergency. I like the little writing case awfully too, & have sent you a p.c. out of it, which I hope you got. The lamp has arrived too, & is most useful, in fact I am using it now. Please thank the fairy who knitted the Balaclava cap; it's lovely, & one wants one badly this weather. Jane's chocolate was ripping too and the dubbin, and the new batteries for the torch were just in time to replace my last exhausted one. The warm pants I haven't got into yet, as I *still* have a pair I bagged from Bobby Reed, but I will be wearing them soon. The pillow I sleep on every night, lovely, & it's so awfully neat the way it folds up. So you see the parcel was *most* acceptable, & thanks most awfully for it.

Now comes one the longest lists of 'please send' she must have had from any of her sons.

Before I forget, I will note down one or 2 things I want you to get for me, I'm afraid I am asking now for some rather expensive things, but I will arrange with Cox to send you some money if you will let me know what they cost.

(1) A small flask, metal, curved shape, to carry in pocket to hold Rum etc . . . I have already asked for this in a p.c.

(2) a *light* chamois-leather waistcoat, if obtainable, to keep the wind out.

(3) a map case. These are made of leather, & have a talc slide inside through which you can read a map, & *a leather cover on the talc slide*, otherwise the sun glints onto the slide & the enemy shoots you! Obtainable at A & N stores.

Also some uniform. They are issuing us with thick khaki *some*time, but only Tommies coats, so please get the following:-

2 officers F.S. jackets, regulation khaki pattern, Captains badges of rank.

1 pair Bedford cord riding breeches, same colour as jacket.

As regards *Fit* – I suppose I'm about the same size as Jim, anyhow I should think you could fairly judge, say 38 chest and 34 waist, height 5–9, ordinary length of arm; I have put chest and waist measurements *on the big side* so as to allow

(1) making to fit if necessary

(2) wearing lots of warm clothes underneath.

Tell the man *to sew no buttons on the jackets,* but just to make holes to take moveable buttons, ones you fix with a split ring and remove for washing, same like we have on our Indian khaki, Ben will know. You see we wear black buttons, that's why, and I have the buttons here with me and can stick them on myself. . . . *Finally*, go to MOSS, Covent Garden, he makes coats in 48 hours, & may even have some in stock, & send along 1 coat as soon as ready and don't make the parcels too big.

That was not really 'finally': all round the margin he added:

Tagamy & Randall, 10, Simons St Sloane Square, has my measurements – but *do* allow for warm clothes to be worn underneath!!! Ask them for my measurements and give them to Moss. Don't forget to leave *lots* of room in the uniform for warm clothes; allow for a thick flannel shirt, a cardigan & a shetland! I shall wear all three!!

Page 2 of this letter was on proper writing paper – probably from the writing case in the parcel.

Now for such news as I can give you. We have come out of the trenches after 20 days – just three weeks – in them, and quite long enough too. Every day was much the same, perpetually shelling us, & rifle fire all day. . . . We had a good many men killed and wounded, and it's most awfully trying sitting in trenches and being shot at all day, & shooting back of course, but with no known results. . . .

One night we sent a party of about 300 men out to try & rush one of the enemy's trenches; it was a mixed party, some of our men and some of the 3rd Gurkhas – you see, all along our front the Germans had sapped up and had trenches only 50 yards off in some places! Imagine it, 50 yards away, & men sniping at you all day, so that you couldn't put a finger up above the trench without getting a bullet at it. Well, they tried to rush this trench, but the Germans spotted them, & I'm afraid we had very heavy casualties. They got a searchlight onto our position which lighted up the whole place like daylight, & it was impossible to move out into the open, the place simply hummed with bullets – some of the party managed to get into the trench and account for about 30 Germans, but the whole show was very unsatisfactory.

One day as usual, they started giving us our daily ration of Jack Johnson & shrapnel, & the shrapnel were bursting all round our headquarters where the Colonel & I were sitting in a little dug-out underground. All the shells burst quite close, & one knocked a huge branch off a tree, down right on top of our dug-out, busting the roof a bit, *and* setting fire to a haystack just outside, so we stood a good chance of being roasted alive; so we cleared out into a neighbouring trench, but the poor old farm where we were living was burnt down, and for the next two nights the whole place was lit up, & of course one couldn't move about much then, as it was just like daylight. So we had lots of adventures you see, & no day or even hour passed without an exciting moment. At last on the 17th we were relieved, and not too soon either. Work in the trenches is most frightfully trying & wearing; one gets little or no sleep, and the continual banging of shells & rifle fire all day gets on your nerves after a bit. On the night we were relieved, while the actual relief was being carried out, I mean while the regiment who was relieving us were just coming into our trenches, the Germans started an attack, *of* course! But we were up to all their little games, and nothing much happened, & it didn't last long, but the bullets were flying about pretty thick. We came out of the trenches weary & worn & oh, so dirty! And the poor men were very tired too, and had done awfully well, & we have been congratulated by 3 generals on our work. We had a particularly hard section of trenches to defend, as it was very weak, so the Germans paid particular attention to it. But 3 weeks is a lot to do on end; we went back out of the firing line for 2 days, & on the second day we were sent up here in reserve, & have to remain in a 'state of constant readiness' to support any part of the line in case of need, so don't really get any rest now. . . . Tomorrow we go back about 2 miles for a rest, which we badly need. I will write more fully from there – meantime send along those things, especially the uniform, and there's something else, but I *can't* remember it! I'm awfully well & don't worry about me.

Rather hard advice to follow after getting a letter like that. The next, begun on 1 December was not much better, although he had been sending field postcards regularly.

Very sorry I haven't written for so long, but really & truly I haven't had a minute. In fact I quite forget when I last wrote, I think it was about the 20th or so, when we were in reserve. Well, we came out of reserve for a week's rest, into some very comfortable billets here. We arrived one night, and next day got orders to go out into the trenches again to relieve another brigade which had a rotten time and had got rather badly mauled. So much for our week's rest!

There appears to have been some confusion, which is hardly surprising in the circumstances. The A.D.C., sent to recall the brigade, found the other three regiments but missed the 2/39th.

That's how we managed to get one night's rest anyhow & weren't hauled out till next day. Well the story goes – [He changes to indelible pencil]

Dec 3rd! Sudden interruption 2 days ago and I haven't been able to resume till today, out in the trenches again – how the story goes, or *what* I was going to say I haven't the faintest idea!

The trenches had been fought over, taken and re-taken several times until the Germans finally established themselves in them, with machine guns.

Our troops tried several times to retake them with no success, & then it was that our Brigade was called up, all except ourselves as I say, whom the A.D.C. couldn't find. So off they went, and our 1st Bn covered themselves with glory, recapturing the trench, & getting a lot of prisoners, & capturing 2 machine guns, and they made quite a name for the Garhwalis, which is a good thing as they certainly deserve it. After capturing the trench they stayed there one night, and then we came up and relieved them, as they had had a pretty hard time of it for 2 days. The trenches were in an awful state when we got into them, but that was after they had been cleaned up; what they must have been like when our 1st Batt. captured them after all that fighting I can't imagine; I heard some pretty ghastly descriptions. We went out ostensibly for 24 hours, but stayed there eventually 3 days and nights! Another instance of elastic time. The enemy's trenches were in parts only 20 yards off ours, & never more that 100, so you can imagine we had a lively time and so did they. . . . and my dear in one part of the line the Germans & ourselves were actually occupying the *same trench*, with a barricade & a bit of empty trench between us! We spent the days throwing bombs at each other, nights too: bombs made of a bit of gun cotton inside an old jam tin, which you throw, and they go off with a huge bang. . . . Well, we had 3 days & nights of this, & just before we left we got orders to exhume all the bodies from the trenches, & bury them behind, which we began to do, & got 40 odd out before we left, but there were lots more, all buried in the bottom of the trench, in the walls and parapet, in fact it's no exaggeration to say that in one part you couldn't put a spade into the ground without finding a body. Excuse the ghastly description, but I think it's as well to tell you some of the things that happen.

[Then] we were relieved, & went back into billets, that was a Saturday, & we stayed in billets till yesterday, Wednesday, so had a good rest, except for me as I was fearfully busy with office work & writing up records etc & never got a minute to send you a line.

I'm afraid I have several letters to yours to answer. One I have here, dated 26th Nov, in which you say you see the Indians have captured some trenches; yes, that's the show of our 1st Batt. I told you about it in the beginning of this letter, but I wish they'd give the name of the rgt. But you see it was really a bad show at first, till our 1st Batt. came up & sloshed them, so I expect they don't say much about it in the papers.

You seem to have large parties of soldiers in Guildford, but what a shame that big lot didn't turn up when all preparations had been made for them. Yes, I wonder what Dick is doing, & whether he is on his way home yet. [He was. See 'What the Others were up to']

½ a mo, just going to have breakfast, & will finish later. It's a wet miserable day, just our luck as we get into the trenches again! Now to fry some bacon for the Colonel & me –

We are in the same trenches now as we first came into on 29th October, so this is our third whack in trenches. But then there's nothing else doing, of course, it's all trench work nowadays. But I expect the great Russian success will make some difference this side, at least I hope so. . . .

I should like another tin of Bivouac Cocoa, which is top hole stuff, & very handy; also some Oxo cubes. That little extra Balaclava cap you sent out is most useful, & I always wear it as it's so light & handy. I've just been reading again your letter written 'behind the bar', what a sporting effort! Yes, isn't Bob's death sad, but what a gorgeous end; a wonderful man; if only the public had listened to him! And he was such a gentleman that when the crash came he never turned round and said 'I told you so!'

By the way, could you send out 2 more refills for 'Torchers' as Ben used to call him in Lansdowne; he's absolutely indispensible. . . .

I wonder if I ever wrote and thanked Aunt Nellie for some cigarettes she sent; will you thank her if you see or write to her, and explain things, they were most welcome. . . .

I really must try and get some more correspondence off now. I hope my letters are interesting, but it's rather hard to make 'em as most days are the same. Do you keep 'em, at all, as they might form a sort of diary of the show afterwards.

Catching up on his correspondence, he wrote a letter to Dreda and Jane:

Europe
3 December 1914

My dear girls, [your letter] is dated Nov 12th! *Would* you say a long time answering it. Awful sorry really, but these damn Germans keep one on the go pretty well, & I have little time for correspondence. Since Nov 12 we've been knocking around, helping another Brigade out of a mess it got into, had 3 days rest (so-called) and are now out in the trenches again. . . . And we haven't got our thick khaki yet, at least I believe it arrived yesterday, but we had to come into these trenches . . . so we shan't get it for at least a week, as they will probably keep us here. We spent 3 days and nights in some *awful* trenches, where there had been a lot of fighting for 2 days and you never saw such a mess. All the corpses had been buried – or ½ buried – in the trench itself, & the whole place was a mass of abandoned German kit, rifles, bayonets, haversacks, everything you could think of – you see, the Germans captured the trench from some of our troops, and we sent two or three regiments to try and retake them, but suffered very heavily, then they sent for the 20th Brigade to help . . . and our 1st Bn retook the trench, captured 2 maxims & a mortar for throwing bombs, & took 100 prisoners; jolly good wasn't it; tell Ben [that] Fred Lumb did most of it, & was in the thick of it all, & did very well I believe, & sloshed a German over the coconut with a rifle butt & laid him out as flat as a pancake, & shot several with his revolver – a great show, & we are all awfully bucked of course. We went out next day & relieved them in the trench they had captured, which as I say was in a beastly mess, but nothing to what it was when they captured it, which they tell me was 3 deep in dead & wounded. Jolly, isn't it! . . . Now we are back in our old trenches once more, for a week they say, but I expect it will be longer. Anyhow this time I've brought out a toothbrush & some soap, as last time they shot us into these trenches without any warning. They are much quieter in front of us now than they were when we were here before and, barring sniping which goes on incessantly all day we get no rifle fire at all. . . . Of course we haven't had the awful time those extraordinarily brave Britishers had at Ypres, but we've done a good whack; and I expect we'll see some more before we've done, – Well, so long, girls, nothing doing here,

Tons of love from Ted

To Ben, who of course knew the regiment, he wrote on the same day about the casualties they had suffered.

3 December 1914

Thanks most awfully for your letters, so nice & long & interesting. . . . Yes, it's very sad about Glag & Toc isn't it, we haven't heard yet what happened to them. It happened like this – One night Toc & 50 men made a most successful raid on a German trench 50 yards in front of our line, & rounded up 6 prisoners & lots of rifles etc. So successful was it that the Brigade determined to repeat the operation, only this time with more men – so 250 of the 2/3rd & 50 of us were told off for it. Well, they crawled out, but were evidently spotted, for the Germans opened a heavy fire & maxims, & the whole line changed. Well, on the *right* some of the 2/3rd with Uncle Smash, Alexander, & McSwiney got into the trench, but the fire was too hot on the left and they were beaten back. Toc was on the left, & in the dark none of the men seemed to know what happened to him, though one of our wounded men say that Toc was hit the same time as he was, but I don't know how much truth there is in this. In any case he has not been seen since. Meantime Alexander was wounded in the foot, & was lying on the parapet of the enemy's trench – Uncle Smash & McSwiney were actually in the trench, and some men too, so between them they managed to knock out 30 odd Germans. They then came to a sort of barricade in the trench, and McSwiney leapt onto this & was promptly bowled over, shot through the chest, & a big hole under his arm. (He is, you'll be glad to hear, all right, at Osbourne, & doing well & the bullet missed all vital parts). So there was old Smash with 2 wounded British officers & about 5 men, & Lord knows how many Germans! So he came back (meanwhile the Germans had opened a heavy fire from their rear trenches) to our trench to take more men up; but he never got back to the German trench as they had placed a searchlight all along our line & though he tried to get across every man with him was hit, an officer called Drummond (attached) was killed, & he had 2 bullets through his hat. So he had to come back again – meanwhile, when Smash started, for the 2nd time, we sent out another party, under Glasgow, to help Taylor on the left. He had 20 men with him, & only a few came back, & none can say what happened to him. There was a tremendously heavy fire going on all the time, & we had a lot of men hit – so the whole thing was chucked, as nothing could possibly live in that fire under that searchlight, & we had no supports, so couldn't attack the trench, not enough men to do it – meanwhile McSwiney & some wounded men shouted to Alexander that as no one seemed to be coming they'd better clear out. It appears that Mac sent some men to help Alec, & he wouldn't let 'em, or something like that, anyway Mac & some wounded men crawled back to our trench. Not finding Alec there, *Mac went back to the German trench*, but couldn't find him anywhere in the dark, (our guns were all the time playing on the trench as we were supposed to clear out at 12 midnight to let them do it, but they didn't know we had failed) so came back & fainted from his wound in our trenches.

Jolly plucky wasn't it. From our trenches now (we are back in them once more) we think we can see poor Alec's body lying there, but not a sign of Toc or Glag, so let's hope they are prisoners. This war is awful, especially here, sitting opposite each other like this, one can't go out & bury the dead or find out who they are or anything, as the Germans are so inhuman they won't respect the Red Cross. Maclean was wounded at the same time as all those fellows in the 8th Gurkhas were killed. Most of them were killed by shellfire I think. The poor 8th have had a rotten time; of all their officers who started from India or joined them from leave, *only Buckland remains*; he got a scratch from a bullet on his face & a bullet through the heel of his boot. Isn't it awful? Poor Maxwell is missing, but it is almost certain that he is killed, in an attack on some trenches which the Germans had taken, & our troops had to retake, & which were finally retaken by our 1st Bn, led by Fred Lumb, who did awfully well I believe. I have told Dryden all about that

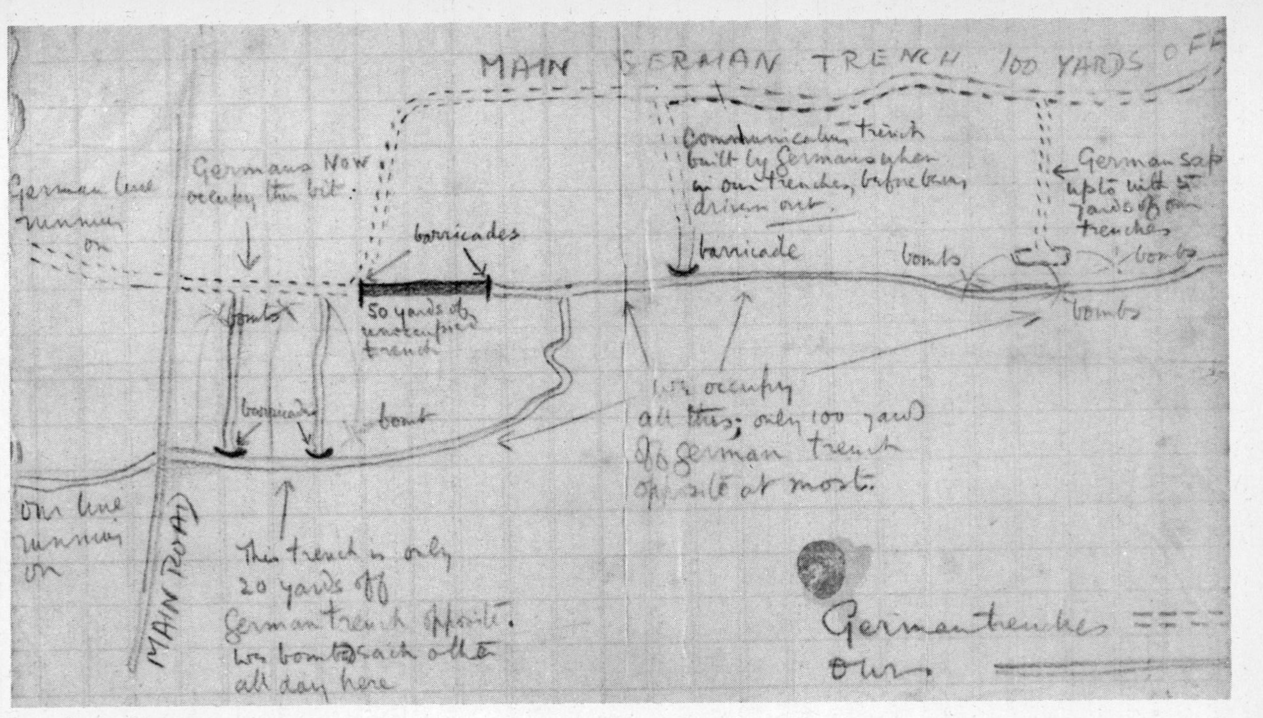
MAIN GERMAN TRENCH 100 YARDS OFF
German line running on
Germans NOW occupy this bit.
barricades
50 yards of unoccupied trench
Communication trench built by Germans when in our trenches, before being driven out.
barricade
German sap up to within 5 yards of our trenches
bombs
bombs
bombs
bombs
barricade
bomb
We occupy all this; only 100 yards of German trench opposite at most.
Our line running on
MAIN ROAD
This trench is only 20 yards off German trench opposite. We bomb each other all day here
German trenches
Ours

Dryden's Map

show in her letter. Old Wardell is missing, but there are many stories about him. He is known to have been wounded, & is supposed to have been treated in a Field Hospital, or may have lost his way & wandered into the German trenches & been captured (see Dryden's map). You see, the Germans bagged about 300 yards of our trenches, & they tried 3 times to turn them out by frontal attacks (in one of these the 8th lost so heavily, & one of the Baldwins was killed, H.L.C. his initials were, I think) but each one failed. Not surprising, considering the enemy had 5 machine guns against us, & our troops had to advance over 600 yards of flat open ground, madness to send them. However our 1st Batt came along, & sneaked into one end of the trench, and by throwing bombs ahead of them, cleared the trench, captured 100 prisoners & 3 machine guns & generally covered themselves with glory. Sam Orton was slightly wounded, but not very bad I believe. We went into this trench the next night, & I've told Dryden what a state it was in; and the open ground over which the attacks were made is not a pleasant sight either, but one can't get at the poor fellows (all dead of course) because the enemy are so close that it is impossible to move out of one's trench; we had 1 man killed & some wounded burying corpses. . . .

It's awful sweet of you to send those things out for the men, & we do appreciate it awfully, & they'll come in awful useful, as they often lose their scarves, gloves etc, & are absolutely done without them . . . . but I think a good thing to send would be common or garden coloured handkerchiefs, very cheap & any colour, as our men use them a lot for all sorts of purposes, 'Jharans' as you know well; do you remember giving them out every morning at Lansdowne from the linen cupboard! I often think of those ripping days we had up there and what fun it was. But, Ben, can you imagine Lansdowne after this. Think of the 8th, hardly one left, isn't it awful. Poor Mrs Stack, I have had 2 letters from her, one you forwarded, addressed Guildford, she said she was glad to see I was at home, & could I come & see her. What on earth made her think I was at home I wonder – since then she has sent me one or two things, baccy & an air pillow – Poor woman, I *am* sorry, & must write to her soon, but what am I to say? I *hate* it. You might just drop her a line of sympathy [he gives address]. I wonder what it all means, her letter was most extraordinary.

I got a parcel of cigarettes and matches from you today, from that baccy man; will you thank him awfully, and say the men *loved* them. They also like peppermints & chocolate. . . .

All our kit we left at Marseilles when we landed has been sent to Southampton. Mine is one of those little leather trunks you know, I'll tell Cox or someone to send it to home & you can open it up. I quite forget what's inside; I know some flannel bags are there, which we never wore on board, also a spare pair of boots, & some other kit. But you can open it up & spread it about. My dear, we are paying 1/9 a day for our food; isn't it a shame, when we are risking our lives etc etc for the paternal Government.

The food *has* been good, very good, but is getting worse and less now – never mind.

Well, I'm afraid I asked for a lot of things last time I wrote, but I'll try not to ask for any more, I'm fairly fixed up now I think.

So long, Ben, and keep smiling & don't worry about me; write when you can won't you, your letters are always interesting – & just note the *date* of last letter from me.

Ted now began to write almost daily, letter cards and post cards as well as sending regular official Field Service cards, always leaving in the same messages: 'I am quite well'; 'I have received your letter'; 'Letter follows at first opportunity'. He wrote to Ben again on the 5th.

I got your parcel last night of mitts & Balaclava caps for the men. Thanks most awfully for them, my dear, they are most acceptable and the fellows I gave 'em to are fearfully pleased. You see, Government issue them with a Balaclava cap each, but they lose them or tear them or something, so can always – or nearly always – find a use for one or two of them. And the men seem to like those little knitted wristlets too. . . .

We have got a lovely underground room, about as big as the Delaford dining room, only not so high of course. It is floored with doors from the ruined houses all round, & roofed in the same way, with earth and turf on the top. We have bagged chairs, tables & crockery from the houses too (this is not looting, but quite fair, as the houses are mostly flat on the ground and you may have to grovel among the ruins to find anything) . . . so we are awfully cosy, it is our mess, where the C.O. and I live, also the officers of the company in support. We have a little charcoal fire, & cook our bacon & potatoes over it. All the other officers of course live in the trenches, but change about, & get their turn here. . . . The C.O. and I make periodical tours of the trenches & have a general look round. . . .

I like this pencil I'm using, it's called the 'Eagle copying ink pencil, No 1522', it's a short one, with a tin cover thing; do you think you could manage to send me one a week, in an envelope, as they are infernally useful. This is rather a good card you have sent, there's such a lot of room on it. I see accounts in the papers of officers getting 96 hours leave in England, so don't be surprised if I turn up one day, only for *goodness sake* get some mufti ready for me, & a hot bath. Our guns are firing at the Maria battery now, & she's stopped thank goodness, as you never quite know where she's going to fall. Must end up now & get this censored.

And, all round the margin, as Ben herself was wont to do:

I think we are in for another whack of cold weather, as there's a bitter wind today, & rain, which will turn to snow soon I expect. Hurry up my new khaki as this drill stuff is awful. Am getting the weekly *Times* regular, please thank Mother, it's awfully interesting always. Good news, a man in the 1st Batt has got a V.C. The King gave it him yesterday. I think Fred Lumb will get something too.

The next day he sent a postcard to 'Dryden' (Dreda):

I've just thought of a good idea, could Delaford send me a cake every week, as they are so useful we seldom see cake & it's a darned handy thing for tea. Just mark the parcel 'cake' & it will roll up wherever I am. . . . 2 or 3 of our aeroplanes have been flying about above us all the morning, awfully pretty against the blue sky. It must be awfully cold up there I should think. O yes, another thing I want is a pair of khaki puttees, *Fox's patent special*, as worn with home service khaki, they are a sort of green khaki; I want *their* sort, not the great thick cloth ones; could you get me a pair & send them out d'you think. Thanks awfully I hope my new khaki turns up soon.

In a postcard to his mother on the 7th he writes, obviously in answer to a letter from her, that 'I've thought of a good thing the D.'s might give me, but I won't tell you here, or the censor mightn't like it!' The 'D.s' were the Dudmans, patrons of his father's first living, and in his next letter he says, 'Tell the Dudmans I should like a *waistcoat pocket Kodak* for Christmas, & please send some films.'

This letter was probably written on 9 December but he seems to have been too excited to put the date.

Isn't it simply splendid, and you must have seen it by now, a man in our 1st Bn has been given a V.C. *the first ever won by a native in the Indian Army*. What a gorgeous thing for the regiment, and it will make people know us now & no one can say 'Oh yes, the 39th, never heard of them who are they – We are all, as you may imagine, most fearfully pleased. The King pinned it on himself, not on himself I mean, but on himself, and said 'Let's see, this is the first one in the Indian Army, isn't it.' You see, the V.C. was only allowed to be won by natives after the Durbar, it was one of the Durbar concessions to India; and to be the first to win it is indeed an honour. . . .

It was at F—t that the man got his V.C. From what I hear, it was as follows: after 3 frontal attacks had been made on some trenches captured by the Germans (I told Ben all about this) the 1/39th came in from the flank and fought their way yard by yard down the trench – you must remember a trench is only a narrow little thing, 3 feet broad, so any fighting you do fighting down one you have got to do alone, or nearly so, as there's no room for anyone else. Well, trenches are made with things called traverses in them, that is pieces of the ground in which the trench is dug, are left there, & the trench runs round it. The idea of these traverses is that if a shell bursts in a trench, its effect is only local, & only hurts the men in that part of the trench. . . . Well, fighting down a trench, the enemy can of course hide behind these and it's exciting work running round them. That's what the chap got his V.C. for, for being in front all the time, and running round each traverse as he came to it & bayonetting the Germans in the next bit of trench; doesn't sound much, but it's jolly plucky, and 16 men were killed like this before the trench was taken. . . .

He also wrote to Ben about the V.C.:

Isn't it top hole a man of the 1st Batt getting a V.C. – simply splendid, and the 1st one too, ever won by the Indian Army; you'll be awful pleased I know, so I thought I must write & tell you, though I expect you have seen it in the papers by now. But I hope they say *Garhwalis* & not Gurkhas. . . . Some cavalry are coming to 'be broken into trench work' as their orders were, & we are doing some of the breaking, starting on a squadron of Billy's pack 9th Hodsons Horse. You see there's no use for cavalry in their true role, so they shove 'em in trenches to help the poor old footsloggers – so they send up squadrons to learn how it's done.

Sat up till all hours of last night talking to Nobby about marriage! How's the child? [Alix, Ben's friend and Nobby's fiancée] Nobby has got a rotten job, Qr Mr [Quartermaster] & has to fix up all rations etc, which have to be cooked right back behind & sent up into the trenches to the men. Nobby has to come up the road, quite a mile of which is always swept by bullets, & lots of people have been hit on it. So he has a pretty warm time, though few realise it, & I think people should know, as otherwise people might think he, not being in the trenches, was quite safe! Divil a bit.

Tons of love Ted

One can't help wondering whether this was the sort of thing that Ben and Alix really wanted to know.

There is a disappointment in his next letter to his mother, written on 10 December:

I see by some papers we got today that our 1st Bn man was *not* the first man to get a V.C. in the Indian army, but another man got one on the 31st October, apparently. Jolly sporting of the King to come out here, wasn't it; I see great stories of his going into the trenches, but I wonder if they are true or not, as it would be very risky with all these odd bullets flying about. . . .

Nothing is to be written on this except the date and signature of the sender.

Sentences not required may be erased.

If anything else is added the post card will be destroyed.

I am quite well.

I have been admitted to hospital.

Sick } and am going on well.

Wounded } and hope to be discharged soon.

I am being sent down to the base.

I have received your { letter. / telegram. / parcel.

Letter follows at first opportunity.

I have received no letter from you { lately. / for a long time.

Signature. Ted

Date 22/12/14

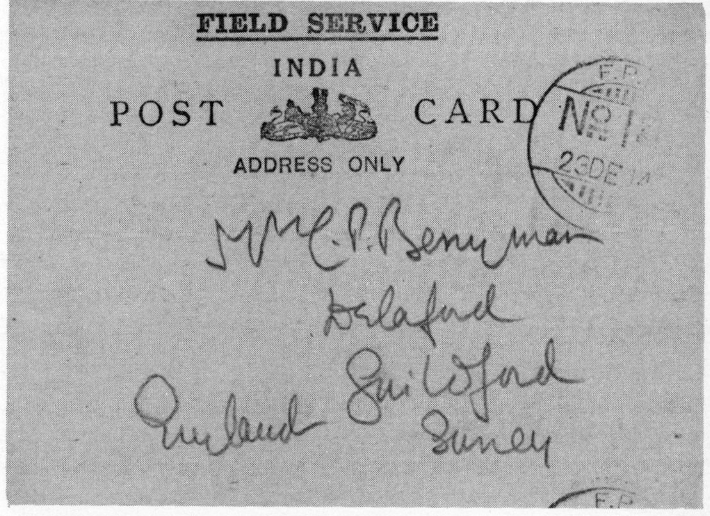

Ted's Christmas field service postcard

17 December 1914

Dear Mother,

Very many thanks for your letter of the 13th, arrived today. . . . Your letter was full of ripping news, *especially* the old war being over by the new year! The story of guessing the amount in the purse is truly convincing. Of course the stock exchange betting is on the war being over by Christmas, so we hear, and they generally know what's going on, quite apart from military point of view. I still say Easter, but of course it is useless speculating – Anyhow I hope they hurry up now and send out K.'s army and push things along a bit on the front; I'm fed up with sitting in the trenches. . . .

Thanks awfully for sending on the cakes, I hope they arrive all right. I have sent Dryden a secret code whereby I hope to ensure the safe arrival of cakes etc. I should like some cigarettes occasionally, Abdullahs will do, in tins, as cardboard boxes break so. . . . My uniform has rolled up I believe, but I can't get at it very well in the trenches. Wish I could as it would be warmer than this. . . . Tell people to write to me a whole lot, as I love getting letters, but the only drawback is I cannot guarantee to answer them, though I do my best. . . . Tell Ben poor Major Young has died of his wounds. She will be awfully sorry, I know, so are we all. What a beastly war this is. . . . No chance of leave just at present. I'm awful keen to know what Topher's doing. . . . What *awful* ROT the papers talk about the Indian troops 'stealthy forms' 'panther springs' & all that absolute tosh. It makes us all look such idiots. We're no better than anyone else after all, & not nearly as good as some. Why can't the papers be reasonable & treat Indians as ordinary human beings. Really the nonsense in the papers about the Indian troops is making us all awful angry; we've done no more than was asked of us, and all that appalling balderdash about Gurkhas & kukris, & 'grinning faces' – oh, law, it makes me SICK!

In his disgust he repeated himself all round the margins and forgot to sign the letter. He wrote again, more calmly, on the 18th.

I got a tiny parcel from you today containing some curiously strong peppermints & some Oxo & some bivouac cocoa, most acceptable and thanks awfully for them. I'm waiting for the Colonel to go to bed and then I'm going to eat one! . . . Our aeroplanes were very busy all the morning, buzzing about. Tell Ben I'm keener than ever to take up flying now, & tell Jane I'm not so much Mr Stare-stare as I used to be! Have you read about these small steel arrows they are all supposed to drop from aeroplanes? We have heard that both we and the Germans have them; they drop about 500 or so at a time, & they come whizzing down point first; jolly isn't it!

Yes, we've heard all about the old Kaiser being ill, & he's dead, & better,

& worse, & everything. I wonder which is true. I got a letter from Jim today, he seems very cheery; tell him I'll write when I have time. He tells me the *Gloucester* is the buzz of the fleet, which is a good thing. . . . One of our scouts got right up to the enemy trenches the other night, & heard them laughing & talking; then he peeped over the parapet & saw them all sitting round a fire, & they never saw him. And 2 nights ago one of the 1st Bn scouts got onto the enemy's parapet, but they suddenly got frightened & started firing; & he lay flat between 2 loopholes till they finished & then crawled back to his own lines unhurt. . . . What have you done with Topher? Is he going to the R.M.C. & going to take up soldiering as a career? It's worth considering I think. . . . I must write to the Dudmans, but I have no paper. A few things like this [a letter card] or some note paper & envelopes all in one would be very acceptable. . . . I'll send you a F. S. postcard tonight, just to see which gets back quickest. Glad you like my letters, but I'm afraid my last one or two have been very dull, but nothing much has happened. No news of being relieved from the trenches, this is our 15th day now – only a week to Christmas, it doesn't seem like it somehow. I haven't spent Christmas in Europe since 1903! When I was a spotty cadet!

He wrote two letters on the 20th. In the one to Ben he says:

Bobby Reed went in to officiate for poor Young – I told you he had died of his wounds, didn't I? – for a day or two at Brigade H. Q. and while there managed to get his parcel of uniform and now sides about in it! He says it is much nicer than this thin stuff, as being warm, you don't have to wear such tons of stuff underneath. Poor Young you know was just standing on the road by our 1st Bn Head Qrs, behind the trenches about a ¼ mile or so, & a bullet came along & hit him. It's the same road that Nobby has to come up every night with our rations, & it is very unsafe altogether, a lot of chance shots, which miss the trenches & come over, & some aimed shots too, as I am sure they can see the road in places. Wasn't it rotten luck, & we are all most awfully sorry, as I am sure you will be. . . .

My dear, Guy Mainwaring has got mumps! and has I hear gone home, but whether this latter part is true I don't know. Archie [Alix's brother] is doing adjutant now [of 1st Batt.]. . . . Tons of our aeroplanes have been very busy today; it was quite a clear morning, blue sky & all, & these mono planes looked gorgeous; the Germans fired one or two shrapnel at them too, which looks awfully pretty, little puffs of smoke against the blue sky. I'm fearfully keen on flying now. I hear Mac is going into the Flying Corps, lucky devil.

His letter to his mother has a familiar ring. After thanking her for a 'little parcel of peppermints and stuff' he goes on to ask:

By the way, can you get something of this sort, a little pocket mirror & comb, sort of thing one wd never *dream* of using in peace, but in this show, where one is days without one's kit, it would be most useful. If you could do this: get the above, & a tiny tooth brush (ordinary size with handle cut off will do) & a small size of toothpaste, & put the whole in a small tin box about the size of one of those bivouac cocoa tins if possible, nice & handy to 'slip into the pocket'.

When this letter arrived at Delaford, Rosamond, one of the sisters at home, went into the town to get these. Selecting a toothbrush at the chemist's she asked, 'Will this break?' 'Oh no, miss!' 'Then it's no good then, I want one that will.' History does not relate whether the chemist changed his mind.

In spite of the warning: 'if anything else is added the postcard will be destroyed' Ted, instead of crossing out unwanted sentences on the field service postcard he sent on the 22nd, wrote 'Merry Christmas' across them. It got through. He sent another on Christmas Day itself and then wrote again on 31 December:

Thanks most awfully for your last few letters. I'm afraid I've been very remiss in answering them, but I haven't had a moment really. We came out of those old trenches on the night of the 27th, after doing 25 days & nights there, pretty long time, wasn't it. We *were* glad to be relieved as you may imagine, the men were all absolutely doggo, as they had had to work day & night to keep the trenches from falling in, because the weather was so wet and beastly that the earth all got sodden & soaked and had to be simply propped up, & our trenches were simply lined with boards & old doors & anything we could get hold of. I am writing this in nice comfortable billets miles away from the firing line where the whole India Army Corps has come for a rest for 3 weeks or so. I haven't much news to tell you except an extraordinary thing which happened on Christmas Day. To begin with on Christmas Eve all the German trenches were lined with little lights, which we afterwards discovered were Christmas trees. Well next morning we heard them singing & shouting in their trenches, and about midday they began lifting up hats on sticks & showing them above the trench, then they showed their heads, & then bodies & finally they climbed out of their trenches into the open! Of course one couldn't shoot them in cold blood like that, tho' one or two shots were fired, and after a bit we also scrambled out of our trenches, & for an hour both sides walked about in the space betweeen the two lines of trenches, talking & laughing, swapping baccy & cigarettes, biscuits etc. They were quite friendly & genuine, & our Col who talks German had a long conversation with them, & asked them how they were & everything & you would never believe we had been fighting for weeks. After about an hour their officers shoo'd them back to their trenches, & we came back to ours, but for the rest of Christmas Day & night, & all next day, 26th, I don't suppose 2 shots were fired hardly by either side!

Wasn't it weird? By the way, leave is now open, & three of our fellows here have gone on leave. I am, I hope, arriving in London about 3 o'clock on the 8th if all goes well, as my turn is next; so you can expect me home, with a fair amount of certainty, on the evening of the 8th, probably by train leaving Waterloo about 5–6 o'clock. So if anyone likes to hang about Waterloo any time about then they are fairly sure to meet me. Isn't it GORGEOUS! Happy New Year to you all,

your loving son,

Ted

And on the 1 January he wrote to Jane, this time with illustrations:

Thanks most awfully for your 2 or 3 letters you have written lately. . . . We are out of the trenches now after 25 days on end, & the whole corps is now resting, & we all – as many as can – getting LEAVE. . . . Your concerts seem to be a great success; if you get up any while I'm at home I'll help you like a shot. I'll be home on the evening of the 8th, & leave again on the morning of the 14th, just 5 full days at home. I've got my new uniform now & have had a bath – in an old dustbin – but still it was a bath, & I feel so clean & smart, you wouldn't know me. . . .

We took 3 days to march here from the trenches, about 5 miles a day, as after standing in water & mud all that time you can't imagine the state your feet get into, soft & swollen & no good for walking on, but good enough to stand upon & no more.

I told mother about our palling up with the Germans on Christmas Day. It was most amusing, & so utterly out of keeping with the rest of the show that we can hardly realise it happened.

The above is exactly – liar – what happened; but I'll tell you all about it when I see you. I haven't seen anything in the papers yet.

And a final letter, before his leave, to Gertrude:

3 January 1915

Just got a ripping long letter from you dated 31st, written in the Parish Room, & I've just time to scrawl a reply. I have just been to church in the local theatre, as they said it was a special intercession day, but there were only 21 officers there. . . . Hope Dick is home the same time as I am. Why is Topher going into the R.N.R? I thought he wanted a mounted job. This is Sunday and with any luck I'll be home on Friday. I don't know what the trains are, but I ought to be able to catch one down to Guildford somewhere around 4 to 6 o'clock. Anyone going to hang around Waterloo on the off chance? I hope Ben's all right. See you soon & tell you everything,

lots of love to all,
Ted.

WHAT THE OTHERS WERE UP TO

With a reunion in prospect as Ted announces his longed-for leave, it might be an idea to see if we can find out what was happening to the rest of the family. Let us, to begin with, return to Dick, 'alone in India'.

Even before Ted and Ben sailed he seemed remote. He assumes, in a letter written on 18 August 1914, that:

. . . everyone you know is fussed, and of course you are too. Paul in the Mediterranean and now you will hear Ted is off under sealed orders. Ben of course will be all right as I shall get her down here about the middle of next month . . . I wish I was at home as we get such scrappy news here and nothing seems confirmed. On the other hand you are much nearer. How terrible all the slaughter must be, and how dreadful the North Sea being full of mines, goodness knows when it will be safe to go on board a ship again. . . . I wonder Holmwood looked tiny to you. Of course I knew it would to me. I am glad the place looked nice. I wonder Mrs Goodyear ever let go your hand . . . Things go on very much the same here. Extra recruits are joining the volunteer force, why I am not sure as the Germans can never get here. . . . Don't worry about us, I am sure this is the quietest spot on earth at the present time.

He sounds even more cut off and out of touch with the others in his next letter. Ben was already applying for her passage home when he wrote on 24 August:

Very many thanks for your letter. Even in yours (July 31) you did not say much about the war, and of course no one here really knows what people at home think and do nowadays. We don't know what regiments have gone on that Expeditionary force and of course there must be tons of people we know.

We get absolutely no news here nowadays, every bit of news is about German losses and we cannot imagine that they are always getting beaten. Ben will be coming down to me shortly. . . . Ted *does* seem glad to have had her with him, and so nice, he says, for someone of the family to see him off. I suppose he is fearfully pleased at going and Paul too at the idea of getting some fighting so, far from being sorry they are both inveigled, I am rather pleased. . . . Fancy pickling 425 walnuts. Whatever can you do with them all, I think you had better give them to Kitchener for the troops! . . . I suppose I shall have to go and meet Ben somewhere, but whether we shall go to Shillong as arranged I don't know . . . People here imagine there may be all sorts of excitements amongst the natives and so on but it is only the light-headed fools and I don't suppose there is a quieter place on the face of the earth at the present moment.

Of course mails from England were delayed but by his next letter he at least knew of Ben's change of plans.

No mail from you last week, no one got any letters from England, however we expect it today, a week late . . . So far we've really heard nothing about what England is like, whether there is very much excitement or what. I saw in yesterday's paper shots had been fired at a train at Crowhurst so I suppose there is a good deal of that sort of thing going on. Everyone must be very depressed as there must be so many killed and wounded amongst people one knows or knows of. Paul has been having some fun I see, his ship shot at a German battleship. Ted's gone I suppose by now, but apparently no one knows where. Ben I think is wise, she says she is coming back on a trooper with other dependants. . . . I shall be sorry not to see her, but she will save a lot of money and trouble.

Very little going on here, people are not much excited as there is really nothing to be excited over, we get very little news and can't believe half of it.

All I can say is I wish I was at home.

On 7 September, while Ted was still in Karachi, Dick wrote:

Ted must be getting somewhere near [the front] by this time. . . . Ben is quite safe anyhow where she is, but I am sorry I shall miss her. May possibly go to Shillong for a day or so but [it] will be a very tame affair now. Only two days racing. I hope my pony wins this time.

I am glad Paul is safe. You all seem hard at work nowadays dusting and cleaning. I wonder if you will do any cooking . . .

At least he knew they had sailed when he wrote again on 21 September. It was the usual mixture of the war and answers to her letters.

Very many thanks for your letter. The mails are taking a month now instead of three weeks, but we are getting them every week now as usual.

I am glad Paul is all right, but I suppose you are fussed about Ted now.

The tie arrived all right from Dreda I'm awfully pleased with it . . .

Ben hoped to sail on the 18th, I fancy she and Ted must have run up against each other in Karachi . . .

I have not heard when the doctor man [for whom he was 'locum'] is coming out, when he does arrive I don't quite know what I am going to do, I rather fancy joining a man in Calcutta for a few months but I doubt if I shall like it. I suppose something will turn up. . . .

I expect by this time you've heard Ted is going to Europe or somewhere, and I suppose you are having more fits, I can imagine how anxious everyone is about their relations & friends.

He still seems very far away when, in his letter of 6 October, he writes, 'So sorry I never wrote last mail but I was away in Shillong & missed the day. I had quite a nice time there only things are very quiet of course on account of the War . . . .' But in his next letter, on 11 October, his thoughts were turning towards home.

Very many thanks for your letter. Things don't seem to be improving much. We have just heard that Antwerp has fallen. I was surprised to hear Jim has come home to volunteer, I hope to hear in your next letter what he intends doing. I somehow feel I ought to come back & help, & when this man turns up if I don't get a decent job I shall come home I think. I suppose a doctor is sure to be wanted . . . I was away in Shillong & I think the change did me good. I got back here to find a fair amount of cholera about, but thank goodness it is better now, and not so many coolies are dying.

I had a long letter from Winnie Johnson. You remember she lives near Topher [in the Argentine]. She says his stammer is still bad. I always thought he had got rid of the habit.

I am going to sing one of the songs Jane sent at a concert next week for the war fund. Have you any money nowadays? I am afraid people are very hard up who depend upon dividends etc?

By his letter of 18 October he was getting restless.

Very many thanks for your letter. It seems so funny that you do not realise Ben is on her way home, but I daresay if I get a letter on Tuesday you will say something about it. We have heard during the last few days of the fall of Antwerp. I wonder what everyone thinks of that at home. We also hear of the awful cruelty to Nurses, cutting their hands off & poking their eyes out. Funny Jim meeting Cyril Manders [an old boy of their prep school, Cordwalles] I expect he will be quite happy in that Corps amongst decent men. . . . Your apples and pears sound lovely, we can get them from orchards in the hills out here but they are not up to much. I am getting quite interested in my kitchen garden here. . . . Of course the drawback is I do not reap the benefit of it as by the time the things are ready to eat I shall have gone. I can't say definitely what I am going to do. I may possibly join the army! On the other hand I may go to Calcutta & join a man in a practice there. I have not heard when this other man is coming out I hope he writes next mail. I have two ponies down here now and am trying to sell them, but no one seems inclined to buy a race horse nowadays!

His next letter, dated 26 October, is very disjointed. The one- or two-sentence paragraphs seem to be written almost entirely in answer to one of hers.

Many thanks for your letter. Poor George I am sorry I hope he's not badly wounded. And all those others, how dreadful their being killed and wounded. Is Charlie Anderson out there?

I wonder if Ben is home by now. I wish I'd told her to cable me. She ought to be with you by now. No, I suppose you haven't much to say about the war, but what I really wanted was to know about our friends out there & now you have told me, so I am quite satisfied.

Jim wrote to me & I have written to him. He seems very happy. Craigie [old school friend] has been down this way lately & we've had long talks over everything.

The Germans *are* cruel – it is awful.

Jim's address certainly is a bit long.

Fancy having all those men like the Drews have. Do they allow you any money for keeping them?

Jim must be pleased with his meat pies. Rather, I know yours & hope to be able to eat 'em again some day.

I dunno what I am going to do yet when this man comes out. So far I don't even know when he arrives. I *shall* be sorry to leave here, yet I feel I ought to come & help, no one dependent on me or anything. Most suitable.

I sang one of Jane's songs at a war fund concert the other night. Quite good the song is. Old Craigie was singing too.

He wrote a week later in similar vein.

3 November 1914

Very many thanks for your letter. Please thank Jane for hers. I am wondering Ben has arrived; today the mail comes in but I don't think you will have had time to write. Yes everyone seems quite pleased with the Indian troops. I suppose Ted is there by now. Yesterday we heard Turkey were at war, everyone will join in sooner or later I suppose, it's dreadful.

I am glad to hear George was not badly wounded. The Pringles' son is dead I see, he's an only son. . . .

I was staying with Craigie Manders last weekend. He is off home shortly & hopes to go to the front, but will return to tea when it's all over.

I hope this Turkey business does not upset shipping, or mails will take a long time to go round by the Cape.

Don't know yet what I am going to do, will let you know as soon as I decide.

By the time he wrote again, on 9 December, things had sorted themselves out for him.

I don't think I got a letter from you last week. I heard from Jane and one from Ben from Malta, which was opened under martial law! I wrote to the girls last night & told them I expected to be coming home. But this morning I got a telegram from Simla saying 'your services may be required military duty abroad very shortly please wire definitely if you will be ready to proceed'. I have wired them I'll be free at the end of this week as my old man is on his way up. Goodness knows what abroad may mean, Egypt or Africa I expect, so there is no need for you to panic. The worst of it all is I shall probably not be allowed to tell you. I fancy I am lucky as crowds of men are frightfully keen on joining the service in one capacity or another & no one had heard anything yesterday. It's lucky it's come now as I am just free, but I am sorry not to be coming home.

I wonder if Ben is home by now. She should be & I expect she is glad if she is. Craigie Manders sails on the *Kaiser-i-Hind* on the 28th, I would have come with him I think if I hadn't been called elsewhere.

I will cable you tomorrow not to write any more here, it's better if I can cable you a definite address later.

Awful nuisance trying to sell ponies & everything all of a sudden. I'm afraid they will have to go at a loss. You see there will be no racing this season so no one is keen to buy a race 'oss.

I see Dr Baker is commanding the Indian Ambulance Corps. How fat he looks in the photographs, of course if I had been home, he'd have given me a job in that.

The casualty lists are dreadful nowadays, I was telling Ben she must know quite a lot of people, having been mixed up in things.

I hope by tomorrow morning's mail I shall hear if she is home or not. Paul must be more or less in it now, only no one seems to understand what Turkey is doing. I fancy I would rather have been a sailor than a soldier.

I am sorry for you, a poor anxious mother, but I suppose there are crowds of others & you ought to be very proud if you get 4 sons all more or less fighting for their country.

At last he was on the move.

En route Calcutta
17 November 1914

Many thanks for your letter. . . . I hope you did not have 50 fits when you got the cable I sent yesterday. . . . I told you last week about the wire I had, well another came yesterday saying 'Please proceed forthwith Quetta and report Asst Director Medical Services for duty, pay etc now under reference to Secretary of State'. Result I am now on my way to Quetta. Far at all? I suppose about 10 days' journey! . . . I wonder how you are getting on with the two officers, I hope they are nice and clean. Many thanks for 'A Long Way to Tipperary', I think it's farther to Quetta! . . . I have not sold 'Summer' or 'Tu tu' but they are being looked after for me . . and should be all right. You see 'Summer' being a race 'oss & there being no races, no one wants her much, she's worth £100 but I am afraid I shall not get that. . . . I heard from Paul the other day, he says when he saw the *Breslau* last she had all her funnels! Aren't you glad the *Emden* is caught, every one here is of course.

Quetta Club
2 December 1914

Just a line to catch the mail today. Such a nuisance not knowing when we were going as I've been able to have no mail forwarded so all my letters are to come home. I'm going to try to catch some in Bombay next week, I may with luck.

I told you I was attached to a hospital (No 8a Indian General Hospital) and I believe at present we are to go to England! If so I'll try & get leave after we arrive & come and see you! But all the same I am not at all certain if we do go home.

Ted although in the thick of it I see is still safe.

I wonder what Jim is doing. I've got a 'British warm' tell him, I will give him when I get home, it's too big for me.

By the time he was on his way home he had lost track of time.

Dec 23rd I think.

I see a notice up mail bags closing at five. I dunno where it is or what to do but if I can find out I'll put this in. I'm a bit bored with this voyage & I don't see much chance of being home for another 3 weeks.

We're stuck at present here & are not moving on till tomorrow morning & we hope to stay in — for a few hours, as I'd like to go ashore. There are lots in this convoy, & I want to see a man called — who is in the —, — knows him, he will probably go ashore at —. Very cold for this part, but it was uncomfortably hot in the — Sea. Wish we could get some news. Hope Ted & Paul are safe so far. Fancy the Germans bombarding Hartlepool.

By 10 January he had arrived home.

Gertrude must have had mixed feelings about the war. Although Ted and Paul were both very much on active service it had brought her other sons home to England and they were, for the time being at least, reasonably safe. Topher, for whom an opening had been found farming in the Argentine, arrived in some trepidation. He knew his mother had gone to some trouble and expense to obtain the place for him and he was anxious about her reaction to his throwing it up to come home to enlist.

This anxiety did nothing for his stammer. 'Is there any m-m-m-mud at home?' he asked when his sisters met him at Guildford station and was overwhelmed to discover that, on the contrary, a hero's welcome awaited him. He enlisted straight away in the Public Schools' battalion and we lose sight of him for a while.

Jim, back from Portugal, had enlisted in the same battalion and some time that Autumn he wrote to his mother from Kempton Park.

Wednesday

Thanks for your letter. I also received the sausages which will no doubt be much appreciated by A.27

We are moving over to the grandstand today & just as we had got everything ready packed up & all it started to pour with rain & I'm sitting in the tent on a bundle of blankets writing this. . . .

The C.O. told us last night we should be going out to France in December. The Battalion drank the canteen nearly dry on the strength of it! – We are going to hurry on with the drill next week.

I shan't be sorry to get out of this old tent it is a fearful squash & things get so dirty – I hope the grandstand will be more comfortable. I'll be down on Saturday I expect.

In the event they did not go to France in December and he was able to join the family party on the occasion of Ted's leave. In fact, the only brother who missed it was Paul, as the following letter, from an old friend of the family, shows.

H. M. S. *Iron Duke*
C/o G. P. O.
19 January 1915

My dear Mrs Berryman,

Just half an hour ago I saw over the side a very smart and good looking naval officer. He had come on board about some job & then looked me up & had a long talk over yours & dear old times. The officer was Paul! He is very fit & keeping cheery & bright although life here is rather monotonous & decidedly damp & cold. How delightful it was hearing all the news of your family – it all seems so strange to hear of them grown up & how *very* proud you must feel that every son of yours is giving his time & work to the country – it's grand simply! Paul was telling me that he was the only one missing from a family gathering which has recently occurred. You must have loved that as it is ages since they all got together like that. . . . I shall look forward to seeing you all as soon as this terrible strife is over. I promise myself that if I am spared I will go on a motor tour for a holiday, willy nilly so will try & reach Guildford. I am so very glad to hear you are so well & as young as ever dear Mrs Berryman & the memories conjured up by my talk with Paul has made me sit down at once & write to you a few lines of remembrance & with best love to *all*

Ever yours affectionately,
Digby

Judging by his description of the weather Paul is no longer in the Mediterranean although of course he cannot say where he is. They seem to be settling down to the War in earnest as he is sending back a bag of some of his clothes:

I don't think there is much in there that's of any use to anybody. Would Capon [Gertrude's faithful gardener and handyman who had come with her to Guildford from Camberley] like the grey suit. I rather love it though and would like to wear it again – which I hope I shall before I finally discard it. Oh – and sometime or other a huge sea chest ought to arrive with various things I landed at Malta – pictures – greatcoats etc – but I should think that would be some time yet. . . . Willie Perkins seems to have got into the thick of it fairly soon doesn't he. . . . If anyone is thinking of making a cake, will they make me one at the same time and send it along. Goodnight, with ever so much love to you all.

As the new year wore on Paul was still very much on active service. On the first of February he wrote to say that her last letter was written on 'our day of action'.

I expect you have heard all about it & I can tell you no more – we were round & about there – but did not actually do any scrapping. . . . I've had two letters from Ted – just lately – he seems rather sick at having to go back to the trenches so soon – he wrote congratulating the Navy on our effort the other Sunday.

As a son of the church he dates another letter simply 'Next Sunday before Lent' and, knowing his mother will be pleased, he reports the presence of clergy: 'We seem to have been inundated with Parsons today. Two services this morning & one this evening & the R.C. parson is still holding his service on board.' In an earlier letter he reports 'We've got a parson now amongst the 3 of us small ships. Such a nice man . . . anyhow he impressed us yesterday when he took the service on board for the first time.'

Gertrude must have been pleased but she would probably have liked to have been told who they were as she might have known them.

The family still keep in touch with each other. Paul reports 'a long letter from Ted today – very interesting – he doesn't seem to have much trench work now' and 'Dick sent me a hamper of edibles yesterday – awfully nice of him. Food is fairly difficult to get but we feed *very* well really. Various fellows in the mess have cakes and things sent to them.'

Did Gertrude take the hint and, donning her blue overall, concoct another of her mouthwatering mixtures of fruit, sugar, flour and dripping known in the family as 'Delaford cake'? If she did it is to be hoped he got it before sailing out of reach. On 4 March he wrote from Hotel Reina Christina, Algeciras, Spain:

We are off on a warmer commission again and here we are at present – I'm just over here lunching with the Captain. You may not hear again for some time – because I don't know where I am going.

Very much love to you all
from ever yr loving son
Paul

The family in England were still managing to see a good deal of one another. Dick's hospital was established at Bournemouth and he wrote to his mother on 27 January:

Another man & myself are getting a house here. Do you think it will do. We are to pay £2.5.0 a week, a bedroom, a bathroom, & 2 sitting rooms. A fortnight's notice on either side and I fancy, Gas. I'm trying to work it out.

Rent	£2 5*s* 0*d*	
Servant Wge	10*s*	
Charwoman if necessary	3*s* 6*d*	per week.
Coal	7*s* 6*d*	
Garage for car	5*s*	

Then there's food to be bought & I've no idea what that is likely to cost, anyhow I don't fancy it can cost more than 3 guineas a week. Do you think so?

Write and say what you think as you must have had some experience.

One can't help thinking that Dick, by the age of 35, must have had a little experience of house-keeping himself. Anyway, having got a house, he invited his brothers and sisters to stay, to attend dances and concerts which they all obviously enjoyed. Ruth, the youngest, was still committed to her nursing while Rosamond was obviously looking for something more active than her church needlework, which she appeared to be doing at an Anglican convent in London. It was not long before she found what she wanted – a job on a farm in Kent where she spent the rest of the war, and where she met her future husband.

The three eldest girls were still at home and fully occupied with war work of one sort or another. In due course Dreda got a job in a bank, releasing a man for active service, but Jane and a girl-friend eventually established themselves in a tobacco shop in the West End. Ted was not sure he entirely approved but as it rapidly became a rendezvous for officers on leave she could be said to be providing comforts for the troops. She also organized and sang in concerts with unflagging energy and they all did their stint of voluntary work in the hospital, washing up and so on.

Ben, of course, had arrived home safely after her historic voyage and was soon as involved as the rest of them. There is one more letter of hers to her mother, which must have been written shortly after Christmas 1914. She is evidently staying with friends at St Leonards on Sea, and writes, as she always does, hopping from one subject to another and filling every available space.

Tuesday

I got your letter last night thank you so much. You seem certainly to have had rather a strenuous day on Sunday. Isn't it sickening the weather has been so alarming. I can't describe the rain and wind yesterday and really last night it didn't seem possible for the house to stand much longer but today so far is ripping so Wiggs & I are going over to Rye to lunch and down to Cumber if the little trains still go in the winter. I heard from Dreda this morning about Willie being ill, I do hope he'll be all right for the dance if we manage tickets, anyway I suppose Marjorie and I can go with Topher & Wiggie but we shall be disappointed if so many of us can't go, sickening for Jane but I really don't suppose Eric will have gone!

For once there is a slight gap on the page as if Ben had paused and drawn a deep breath before going on.

I don't know whether you'll be pleased No I don't suppose for a moment you will be I can't quite expect it but Wiggs & I have decided that it's best to be engaged. The unsatisfactory way in which we were going on was *NO* good, it isn't all done on the spur of the moment, much thinking has been done & I'm sure it's best. There are to be no great shoutings about it but anyone who wants to know can, you will I fancy think we are doing right, the other situation was rotten for me but I didn't want to sort of rush Wiggs into anything so things *had* to wait. If the dance is off I am going to stay here till Thursday so will you send me a line either here or Dollie's as that is where I shall be on Wednesday night for the dance, see? Will you give the enclosed to Dreda, I wonder if either of your billets *will* come back, on Wednesday or is the scare still on. Have a rest when you can I expect you were awfully tired after Christmas & all it was rather a rush.

Love to all,
your loving Ben

You'll iron my frock won't you, the ninon at the top too.

Dear Ben, what a puzzle this letter is! Why does she expect her mother not to be pleased in one sentence and to think they are doing right in another? And who was Wiggs? There is only one earlier reference to him, in her long letter from Lansdowne, on 10 September:

Wiggs tells me he was enlisting in Kitchener's 2nd army, well it's obviously the right thing to do however much against soldiering one is. I *do* consider the civilians are *fine* all the same, as it is *not* their job – after all one expects a soldier or sailor to *live* for a chance of active service their whole training leads up to it, but with a civilian he has all the *roughest* part and *none* of the nice.

Perhaps this is the clue. If Wiggs was against soldiering, Gertrude with a son in the regular army, probably didn't approve of him, while Ben's vigorous defence of 'civilians' with its sudden sprinkling of underlining is significant. Perhaps she was already in love with Wiggs when she went to India, which would explain how she came heart-whole through those eleven months of staying with her bachelor brothers and getting to know their friends, some of them, as she said herself, 'so awfully well somehow'.

There was certainly no 'shouting' about the engagement. No one else mentions it and it casts no shadow over Ted's leave, which was a wonderful family affair, to which he refers again and again in his letters after his return to France.

15 January 1915

Just a line to tell you I arrived safely after a very comfortable journey & a good crossing during which I was NOT ill! . . . Everything seems much the same as it was when I left, & the weather certainly is the same. They had wet days all the time, so I was fearfully lucky to get such a nice dry spell for the few days I was home. I must just say now how fearfully I enjoyed my leave & how ripping you all were to me, it was topping to see everyone again & I can never thank you all enough for giving me such a good time; I only wish I could have stayed at home longer, but of course I count myself fearfully lucky to be able to get home at all.

I hope the others got home safely after seeing me off. I'm afraid I dragged them out fearfully early & I appreciated it muchly. Rather a rush on the platform as I expect they told you, crowds of people & introductions & a final dash for the train as it was just starting. By the way, I find I never took my nail brush home, so it should not be on that list of things I left behind. But I *did* leave my purse somewhere behind so please send that out. Very cloudy & cold here, & we are off to the trenches again next week, but won't be in such a long time. I hear they are *entirely* under water! Jolly isn't it. . . .

Tons of love & thanks to all again for such a gorgeous time.

Sunday 17 January 1915

Very many thanks for your letter . . . I was wondering if you ever got that wire as I gave it to a promiscuous boy on deck who said he would send it off, & I'm glad he kept his promise. I posted some letters to you all on Friday night, which I expect you will get tomorrow. . . . Many thanks for Ruth's wire, which I had got before I left, it was very sweet of her to send it. Yes, I wish I could have seen her, but I will make a point of it next time I come home. I must write to her but don't know her address, so please let me know what it is. . . .

We've all just had a present of a tin of toffee from the Grocers' Association inscribed 'to our brave lads at the Front'! Hooray! People are really awfully good to us, & we are doing nothing. I do hope old Topher is getting on all right, but I expect he'll soon settle down after his experience in S.A. This time last Sunday I was talking to dear old Mr & Mrs Drew, hauled out of church etc, etc, & generally living in a sort of dream! Yes rather I'll store up some of the enjoyment, there was certainly enough to spare, & use it when things are dull. Are the girls washing up at the hospital now. I think it's splendid of them to take on a job like that & I'm very proud of you all.

To Jane he broke into verse:

Dear Jinny, I've just got your letter
And parcel containing my purse;
Yes, thank you, my cold is *much* better,
At least it's not any worse.
You remark how delightful it was, Jane,
Your brother from France to see;
Don't say any more, please, because, Jane,
It was far more delightful for me.

It was ripping to meet you again, dear,
After nearly four years in the East,
Far away from the mud and the rain, dear –
(The water, I mean, not the beast)
Far away from alarms & excursions,
From bathless existence of grime.
Thanks to all of your noble exertions
I just had the hell of a time!

I've of course often had leave before, dear,
For a month, or a week, or a night;
And it's sometimes been rather a bore, dear,
And others been fairly all right.

But THIS was a good 'n and sweet 'un,
And for solid enjoyment I claim,
Those five days can never be beaten,
The crème – so to speak – de la crème!

There's Jim – now I haven't seen Jim for
Twelve years – or is it thirteen?
And I wouldn't have missed seeing him for
A sum that would ransom a Queen!

Started this when I got back but never finished it! and haven't got time now. Freezing tonight, write soon,

lots of love from Ted

SPRING CAMPAIGN 1915

15 January 1915

Dear Jinny,

. . . Hope you all got back safely after your sporting effort in seeing me off. I suppose now you are busy in the hospital making yourselves generally useful. No news here, except that it is a rotten place & there's no place to *compare* with England . . . Thanks awfully for all you did for me at home, Jinny, I had a fizzing time & hope to be home again soon to rag you. Write me a nice long letter soon & tell us all about it. So long, keep smiling.

Dear Jinny,

. . . You do indeed seem busy at the hospital, however you are doing your little bit which is tophole. How you *stand* washing up dirty plates I can't imagine, as if there's one thing that puts me slick off it's a plate all over butter & jam; hence you have my sincerest admiration & sympathy. . . .

We are out of the trenches for a day or 2, but go back very soon. Same old story, they said they would keep us out 3 weeks, but they are going to keep us in barely one! Never mind, it'll all come out in the wash. We had a comparatively easy time this time, very little shooting or excitement. All that heavy fighting you must have read about at La Bassée was next door so to speak & we could hear it all going on, but they contented themselves with opening a very heavy fire on us while that was going on, but didn't actually attack. Mr Funk had to walk about a road behind the firing line, seeing everyone was ready, but very few bullets were coming our way fortunately, & those were only stray ones. Still these damn stray bullets can do all the harm sometimes.

After writing about aeroplanes – both German and British, and expressing a wish to get into the Flying Corps some day he goes on:

Well, Jinny, I must end up. Teatime & Genl Joffre & French are coming to tea, I met them on the road this morning & they said they might look in – they asked after you, & said they were glad to hear you were washing your country's plates.

Send a cake along, the last one was much appreciated.

3 February 1915

Dear Mother,

Can you please see about some cigarettes for me. Jim said he had fixed up a regular weekly or monthly supply, but since I came back from leave I haven't had any at all! except what other fellows didn't want. *Please* don't think I'm complaining, only I can't help thinking there must be some mistake, as surely *some* ought to have rolled up by now – if Jim hasn't arranged anything, could you please arrange with De Reske to send *200 a month* as if you buy them by the 200 at a time you get them a bob a 100 cheaper or something. But you might find out first what's happened to Jim's show, as I certainly understood he had fixed up something.

We go back to the trenches tomorrow after 6 days in reserve here. . . . As the trenches are full of water, of course we can't actually occupy them, but have a system of breast works & piquets out in front. I fancy most of the stories about standing in water are yarns, though of course there has been a tremendous lot of fighting in knee & waist deep trenches, & no doubt a lot of troops *here* had to stand for hours, & sometimes days, in water. But as a rule men manage to keep fairly dry, though mud is always ankle deep. The air is – here I was interrupted, and I'm sure I don't know *what* the air is! or what I was going to say! . . . Could you send along a *Bystander* or *Graphic* or *Illustrated London News* occasionally? A picture paper is always welcome, *Tatlers* or *Sketches*, as they go round & we hand 'em on to Tommies when we've done so a lot of people get enjoyment out of them.

4 February 1915

Dear Mother,

Just got your parcel at least the bulls' eyes & socks. Thanks awfully for them, the latter seem to be just the thing. We have just moved up into some new billets today just behind the trenches in a deserted and much shelled little village. . . . The church is full of holes, but not so bad as the last place we were at, which hardly had a stone left standing on another . . . By the way I met one of the Townsends a day or two ago, in the Sappers, & recognised him! . . . He asked how we all were, & said he rememberd Dick very well . . . Also one Stephenson, the Divisional Field Cashier, from whom we draw our pay, is a cousin of Morton & Esmé's. I met him the other day & when I signed my name for my pay I noticed he was Mr Stare-stare; & afterwards I hear he asked another chap if I was one of a large family & his cousins knew me if I was!

Must finish up now. How's Paul, I haven't heard from him for a long time.

7 February 1915

Dear Jinny,

My, they do know how to work you hard at the hospital, you certainly *are* doing your little bit. I have got an absolute first class cold and cough, a touch of 'flu I think . . . However by tomorrow I expect I'll be right as rain, though I should like to go to bed more than anything else. We go into the trenches tomorrow & I expect that'll cure me all right. *Could you send me a bottle of Somebody's 'Lightning Cough Cure'*, Veno I think it's called, someone said it was very good; or any old cough mixture.

I have been to church today 'in the school opposite the 44th Heavy Battery' as the notice was published in orders. And by Jove it *was* opposite the 44th Heavy Battery with a vengeance! They were only 50 yards off, and had found a suitable target just as church began – the noise was awful; and the whole thing was a curious mixture, church going on & quite close by the big guns killing & maiming the wretched enemy; so contrary somehow to the Church's instruction regarding one's enemies. The hymns we had were 'Lead Kindly Light'. 'Sun of my Soul' & 'Abide with Me'. No organ or piano, just about ½ doz officers and 30 Tommies, so the singing was a trifle awkward at times, & broke down completely in 'Lead Kindly Light', despite a valiant effort by Major Mac sitting next to me to switch 'em onto the right note again! I could only utter a hoarse croak! The guns were particularly noisy during this hymn and the result was something as follows, a quaint mixture of humour and pathos that made one want to laugh and cry at the same time:

Lead kindly – Bang! – amid the encircling gloom
   Bang! – thou me on;
The night is dark and I am – Bang! – from home
   Lead thou me on.
Bang! Bang! the garish day, & spite of fears
Pride ruled my Bang! remember not Bang! Bang! Bang! Bang!

the last four being from a French Battery of ·75s close by here, which, like all French batteries, always fire salvoes of 4 guns in rapid succession. I assure you, my dear Jane, the above is *no* exaggeration of the scene, and it was really very impressive in a way, and likely to stick in one's memory far longer than many an exciting moment in the trenches. . . .

Righto about the scarf, better give it ot Jim as I have one all right. Chubbie sent me a pair of mittens & a letter; . . . Cake *most* welcome, & stodged by my brother officers in no time. So long & give us a line sometime.

8 February 1915

Dear Mother,

Very many thanks for your letter this morning, & the handkerchief, which was most acceptable as I have a beastly cold & cough, & use a hanky pretty frequently. We go into the trenches tonight for 3 days. We are having a terrier colonel to stay with us, to learn all about trenches, it will be rather fun shewing him around everywhere.

Righto about the cigarettes, sorry to worry you, but I thought it best to find out about it & see if anything had gone wrong. As a matter of fact Abdulla sent us each a little tin of 25 as a present today, very sporting of them wasn't it. The one you sent hasn't rolled up yet, but will tomorrow I expect. *Sketch* & *Bystander* also not come but will doubtless come tomorrow & will be most welcome in the trenches. . . . I had a letter from Paul 2 or 3 days ago saying he was hovering round that last fight. . . . I hear Jim & Topher are going for commissions quite the best thing to do I should think as they seem to be using the corps as an officers training corps & nothing else. Why doesn't Jim shove in for a job as a motor cycle dispatch rider, they have heaps of them, flying about all the roads every day & all day. Suggest it to him, I don't suppose it's hard to get.

10 February 1915

Dear Mother,

It started today by being a nice blue sky day, but it's all cloudy again now. One of our airmen was out this morning, he *was* plucky, as the Germans kept plugging at him & went all round him, fearfully close, but he kept circling round, going sort of ½ way home and coming back again only to be greeted with another halo of shrapnel. He wound up by calmly flying through a huge puff of black smoke made by a high explosive German shell which burst just in front of him! . . . I *was* glad when he finally cleared off unharmed, & it was very exciting to watch.

13 February 1915

Dear Mother,

Very many thanks for your letter today. So glad you are getting a bit of a change and a rest, I am sure it will do you all the good in the world. My cold is much better now, and a few days in the trenches seemed to have a most beneficial effect, though I am still a bit snivvely, but I'm feeling perfectly well, which I certainly wasn't for a day or two.

And thanks awfully for the gloves, they arrived yesterday & are most welcome as my other pair were getting a bit shaky & the warm wooly part inside was getting rather thin & worn. The cake hasn't arrived yet, but I got the refill safe and sound, but I haven't used the original one up yet, so I have 2 refills in hand now. . . .

I hope Topher is all right again now, bad luck his getting 'flu, but there's a lot about . . . I fancy I must have had a touch of it, being somewhat prone to it, as you well know.

Have Topher & Jim had any luck with their commissions I wonder; under the circumstances it would certainly appear to be the best thing to do.

Must end up now; I got the *Sketches* & *Bystander* all safe thanks v. much, most acceptable.

The envelope of the next letter has 'Saxon story' in Gertrude's handwriting written across the flap.

16 February 1915
Shrove Tuesday, ha ha how did I know that!

Dear Jinny,

. . . An enormous parcel of anti-cough & cold mixtures rolled up, a lovely lot of things. The only objection being of course that my cold has now completely gone . . . and I am now sitting in draughts & discarding underclothes with a view to catching a cold so as to make use of all the lovely things you sent. No rotting, the parcel is *most* acceptable & will be sure to come in useful if not for me then certainly for some other snuffler. Cigarettes most welcome as none have turned up yet from Jim's patent man, but don't worry as I have enough now. C (Ben knows who C is; a man, how dull!) sent me 100 this morning . . . F.F.'s with the Davids indeed. Well, give my love to them all, especially Babs who was a great friend of mine. I enclose £1 for Ben for those watches she got me. . . .

Had a bath yesterday in a beer vat & am feeling awful clean today. Such a dull letter this isn't it, but we aren't doing much. Some of the aeroplanes were fired at today, awful pretty, but those high explosive shells make the most appalling noise in the air, & bits of 'em come careering about all over the place. They say the aviators themselves can't hear the bang because the propeller makes such a noise; they certainly behave as if nothing was happening, & take not the slightest notice of shells or anything else. Here's a true yarn: a Saxon regiment a day or two ago just opposite some regiment or other, I don't know which, kept shouting & yelling & finally climbed out of their trenches & began baleing water out. Our chaps didn't fire, much too cold blooded a job, but told 'em to clear off or they would fire. However the Saxons said no, they wanted to be friendly etc etc & loathed war etc etc. Finally the general commanding the Brigade came down, went over to the Saxons & said 'Look here, I'll give you 6 hours to dig yourselves some more trenches, as your present ones are flooded & after that I'll have to open fire on anyone outside.' So the jolly old Saxons started digging like blazes & got some sort of cover in the six hours & disappeared behind it; & as the 6 hours was up they hoisted a huge notice board up in the trenches with this written on it 'Don't shoot us & we won't shoot you; keep your bullets for the blankety blank Prussians who relieve us tonight.' That's an absolutely true yarn, I had heard rumours of it before & last night I got it from a feller who was there & saw it all. Isn't it weird, of course those were the Saxons who F.F.'d with us on Christmas Day, & they were really quite good chaps, & it's the pure Prussian who is such a blighter.

Dinner time. Keep smiling,

lots of love from Ted

20 February 1915

Dear Mother,

. . . Awful luck yesterday, Major Mac & I were talking along a road up by the trenches when suddenly a shell came from nowhere apparently & burst just behind us, about 10–15 yards off. However it fell in soft mud & went off with an awful bang & threw mud all over the place but didn't touch us! . . . We got a mail today, so the German blockade has not yet stopped the mails.

Have Jim & Topher managed to get their commissions yet? I trust so. I got a *Bystander* from Rosamond today, but haven't had any letters lately. I got some cigarettes from Dryden, but the regular supply hasn't started yet . . . Excuse a dull letter.

Love to all
your loving son
Ted

Oh by the way, I am sending home one khaki jacket & 1 pair breeches, as we have to cut our kit down & this is the only way I can do it. Please keep 'em & I'll write for 'em when I want 'em.

23 February 1915

Dear Mother,

Very many thanks for the cake which arrived today and is much appreciated by the mess. We are out of the trenches again now . . . and today & Major Mac & I were caught right out in the open, on our way up to the front trenches! It was fearfully muddy & heavy going so we couldn't go very fast. They weren't shooting at us actually, as I don't think they could see us; but at our front trenches, & all the bullets missing them of course came on to us! However nothing happened, but it wasn't exactly pleasant. . . . Isn't it splendid Lumb getting the Military Cross? Ben will be awfully bucked about Fred Lumb. He's home in England sick now, with a knee; tell Ben to write to the Willows, Marsham, Norfolk. . . . Many thanks for the *Tatler*; send another.

27 February 1915

Dear Jinny,

. . . I hope your concert is a success; it's coming off today isn't it? Have you got 'When We Wind Up the Watch on the Rhine' yet? I'm sure that will appeal to Tommy audiences; send me a copy when it comes out. Guy Mainwaring and I have just been bawling it out in the 1st Bn Mess (an old ruined pub!) I should think the Germans must have heard us! . . .
It's colder than ever today a very cold wind in addition – we are going back for a bit of a rest tomorrow, about time too as we have been in the trenches or in reserve continually since Jan 20th & one must have a few days off occasionally . . . I hear the Guards are relieving us, so I suppose all the Lords & Dukes will be paying us a call soon.

You seem to have good times on your birthday. Glad Babs liked my messages, give 'em to her again will you, & I hope she's all right again. So the Saxon story is the buzz is it. I'm afraid I haven't got any more to tell you. The Saxons are still opposite us here I think, & occasionally yell out Good morning & things like that. . . . I'm sorry this is such a dull letter but there is absolutely no news to tell you. Things are fairly quiet here, bar the shelling which is very unpleasant while it lasts, they've stopped now, but will begin again I expect about teatime, they generally do.

27 February 1915

Dear Mother,

. . . Yes, rather I got the cake all right, with a tin of sweets & 2 little packets of chocolate . . . I can't help thinking the cake before must have been stolen, as I think one is missing. So glad Jim is getting his commission soon, I think it's better on the whole; what about Topher? Has he managed anything yet?

About those waders, thanks awfully for suggesting them, & I should love a pair, but I'm afraid it is a bit late in the day now, and conditions in most of the trenches have much improved, though they are by no means dry. But I fancy now, between you & me, we shan't be doing *much* more trench work, so I don't think it would be worth while sending them. Still, thanks awfully for suggesting them.

9 March 1915

Dear Mother,

I got a cake from you a day or two ago which was much appreciated and thanks awfully for it. . . . I had a long letter from Paul yesterday; he didn't seem to think much of the *Gloucester* as a sea boat in really dirty weather. Otherwise he seemed very cheery. Ben also wrote me a long letter, you all seem to have had great times at that concert.

Any news of Jim's or Topher's commissions yet? I always scan the Gazettes eagerly to see if they have been appointed. I thought it took no time to get a commission nowadays.

Not much news from our part of the world, things are fairly quiet here I think, at present at any rate; though they seem to have had some lively times at Ypres.

France
7 March 1915

Dear Jinny,

Thanks most awfully for your topping long letter today . . . and the 'Watch on the Rhine'. Heaven knows if I'll ever get a chance to sing it, but you never know & it would be awful fun to sing it at a Tommy's concert . . . it's the sort of song that would 'go down' like anything. . . .

Ripping Dick having a little car, I suppose you all make yourselves awfully nice to him now. . . .

Why should you rag me about my letters – what's wrong with 'em anyhow? I know they're *damn* dull but there's nothing much going on – I will tell you some lies if you like, just to fill up. Yesterday a German aeroplane flew down the road where we were standing, whisked off my hat & flew up again. Then it looped the loop & came down & out stepped General French disguised as the Kaiser! He gave me back my hat & said he was sorry, but he was just having a day off and rolling round just for fun in an aeroplane he had found lying by the roadside. He asked after you all & said the war would be over on the 7th Sunday after Trinity & then flew away again. There, isn't that interesting.

No rotting, yours really *was* a nice long interesting letter, 6 pages . . . well written, & well expressed & well thought out & well – well, damned good all round. 'Well, very well, thank you.' Isn't that a joke or something? The latest thing to say (I saw it in the *London O.*) when you don't quite catch what anybody says is 'snow again, sonny, I didn't catch yer drift'. So I shall be always saying this now; awful, won't it be.

So you're going to sing at the White City are you; that's good, I shall look out in the papers for an account of the concert. Your concerts are always a great success my dear; I wish I could be home to help you pull up the curtain or sell programmes or something.

By the way, talking of Cicely, what about never meeting her when I was at home, under the clock in High Street at 3 o'clock on Tuesday 12 Jan 1915? Did you apologise and explain? Please give her my best love when you see her; I do wish I could have seen her as I hear she's awfully sweet & now Dick is cutting me out.

Had a long letter from Rosamond . . . I hear she is awfully pretty nowadays, but then I always thought she was. . . . I have been watching our 6 inch guns shelling the German trenches today . . . There is also a 9 inch gun too somewhere, called 'mother' & that makes still more fuss. What on earth a 15 inch gun does I can't imagine. I can quite understand the Dardenelles forts being blown to pieces by them.

16 March 1915

Dear Mother,

I have just a few moments to spare, even though it is nearly midnight, to write & tell you something about our doings of the last few days. You have of course seen in the papers about the successful 'British advance' & the Indian Corps doings, but I fancy the accounts lack detail & are very general. The part we played was small of course, but may be interesting, as I saw it.

To begin with – we left our comfy billets at the farm suddenly at 6.45 p.m. on the 8th, got a wire saying move at once; so off we went & reached a little village soon afterwards where we stayed the night. At 6 next morning I had to go up to the trenches to find out various things, not very exciting, & we stayed in this little village all the 9th, not doing very much. At 6 o'clock on the 9th we got orders to move at 1 o'clock that night, (it was freezing hard & very cold all this time) so off we went up to the trenches and awaited the dawn. Our orders were to attack the German trenches in the morning, after they had been heavily bombarded by artillery. Our regiment was only taking up a small front of course & was but a tiny unit in the whole show, which took place over a very long bit of the line, the whole of the Army being engaged; but you will understand how we only saw a small, but important bit of the whole thing. Divisions on our right and left were attacking as well.

As soon as it was light, the guns began, & my goodness, there never was such a row! Every conceivable gun in the Corps concentrated its fire on the front to be attacked by the Brigade, our Brigade that is, the Garhwal Bde (rather an honour to be chosen out of the whole Indian Army Corps to do the attack) and for half an hour they bombarded the German trenches. Lyddite, shrapnel, small guns, big guns, howitzers, field, horse & siege guns, all banging away as hard as they could. We were only about 150 yards from the German trenches, so we got the double benefit of hearing the sound of the discharge & the explosion too. Enormous shells burst in their trenches, poor devils, throwing up huge columns of yellow smoke, & heaving up trenches, dugout, trees, hedges, everything that came in their way. Precisely at a time previously settled the guns 'lengthened their fuse' as the saying is; that is they fired at the trenches and houses *beyond* the front trenches, so as to prevent supports etc coming up. And at the same moment our men jumped out of our trenches & charged across the open. It was splendid, & the men were into the first line of trenches before you could wink. They went on and rounded up the next trench behind that, but met with some resistance here, but overcame it & captured the trench. In all there were 4 lines of trenches, & they finally reached & captured the 4th line. In doing so they had captured 180 prisoners & 3 machine guns, & we had about 100 men killed & wounded. Alas! I was not in the charge, being Adjutant I had to keep with the Colonel, who went up with the last line. However it was all very exciting, & a splendid sight to watch. Well, having captured the 4th line of trenches, there, straight in front, was Neuve Chapelle; & nothing would stop the men, the officers there say they had the greatest difficulty in stopping them, & the whole Brigade rushed into & through Neuve Chapelle & out the other side, where they took up a line of entrenchments in front of the village. We all hurried on, there were bullets & shells flying about, but we managed to dig ourselves in, & found a whole lot of German sandbags & entrenching tools which were very useful. Perhaps this map will help a bit.

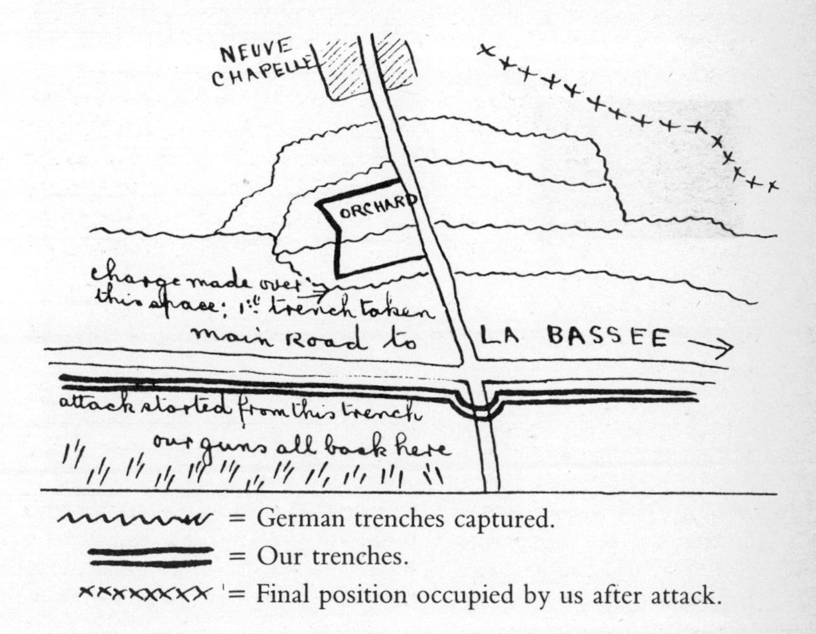

Well, we stayed there digging all day, & they fired maxims etc at us, & caused several casualties; they also shelled us a good deal, but by evening

Garhwalis attacking German trenches, Neuve Chapelle, March 1915. (Sketch by Fred Roe)

The Battle of Neuve Chapelle. (Painting by J.P.B. Beadle)

We had quite good cover. Late that night we got orders to go down & help the right flank, but owing to darkness & perfect maze of trenches (you must remember we were in the German lines now, at least in the lines captured from the Germans that morning, so we didn't know our way about much) and the guide who lost his way, we were ordered back. We spent the whole night trekking about, & then at 5 o'clock in the morning got orders to be attached to another Bde to help them in an attack at 7 a.m. So off we went again, trekking off into the unknown, & finally reached our position just at dawn, with an awful prospect before us, an attack over quite 800 yards of absolutely open country. We lay out there in readiness to move when the attack began, being fired at the whole time, & getting several men hit, but for some reason or other thank goodness the attack was postponed, & we got into some very bad trenches there with the Leicester Regt. Had we done that attack we should have been badly mauled, as the ground was absolutely open, & the Germans were well entrenched against us. Well, all that day we lay there, tired & no food (no one knew where we had got to, in the muddle); but we got some fun watching our guns shell a wood in front of us, and by Jove they did knock it about. We saw the Germans simply scuttling for cover when our high explosive shells got on to them. Late that night, 12 midnight, we were told to go back to billets, so we marched back, very tired & hungry, & reached them about 4 a.m. At 5 we got orders to move to more billets further back at 7 a.m. So we moved off & had of course no sleep that night. Well we marched at 7, reaching billets at 12, & settled down we thought for a day or two's rest. But at 4.30 that evening we got orders to go back at once, to stay in reserve up near the firing line. So off we trekked again, the men utterly fagged, for we had no sleep for 3 nights, but we managed to get there, & found rotten billets, & could get no food. However I got some tea off a tommy & went to bed (?) about 1 a.m. absolutely cooked. Nothing happened & we stayed there next day till 5 p.m. & then marched back to here, arriving at 11 p.m.; that was on the 13th and we are still here. The Brigade did *splendidly*, and got no end of praise from everyone, & the regiment has received heaps of congratulations on the good work done in capturing Neuve Chapelle, or helping to do so, for really the 2/ Gurkhas & Berkshires had a hand in it too.

Our poor 1st Btn got a very bad time; they got off the track a bit in their attack & lost very heavily. Seven officers were killed that day & 2 wounded: only 3 of the Btn were killed, Kenny, Welchman & Sparrow; and the Col was wounded; the other four killed were fellows attached. In the 2nd Btn we were very lucky, as we had no officers touched, though we had 150 men hit in the three days. I'm most awfully sorry, we all are, about those 3 fellows on the 1st Btn whom one knew so well, it's hard to believe they are dead; & the other 4 whom I only knew really by sight, as they were only attached to fill up vacancies caused by Lumb & Lane being on the sick list. Terrible, isn't it; but they were soldiers, & it was a soldier's death anyhow. But our 1st Btn did wonders next day: after having all those officers killed, they were heavily attacked & shelled all day, but they never broke, though they suffered terrible losses, they fought like fiends & earned absolutely undying fame, really they did; everyone says so, & our divisional General told us this morning that the name of Garhwal was famous for all time. Our men are really splendid, & 1st class fighters and soldiers, & I am fearfully proud of belonging to such a magnificent regiment.

And poor dear Major Mac [MacTier]! He's gone too, the very nicest man that ever stepped; one of nature's gentlemen, & a perfect example of courtliness. He went to command the 1st Btn on the 10th after their Colonel [Col. Swiney] was wounded, & was killed on the 12th by a chance bullet. I *was* so fond of him, & he was always a perfect dear to me. I don't know what the regiment will do without him, he always seemed essential to its welfare, & it is hard to imagine the 39th with no Major Mac; it has taken away a lot from the joy of victory. I would give anything to get him back. We buried him & Kenny in a little churchyard close here; I was so glad they buried him there & that I was able to go to his funeral; I was at least able to pay my last respects to a very dear friend. All gone now, 7 good men in the 1st Btn and 1 in the 2nd Btn, all given their lives for their country. Everyone has been loud in their praises of the conduct of the two battalions in the fighting, but I would rather they said nothing if only we could get those good fellows back again.

Well, it can't be helped. I have tried to describe to you the small part we took. It was all very exciting, & after it was all over we were all absolutely done, tired wasn't the word. We had been constantly on the move for three days and nights, food had been erratic, & sleep out of the question. But for all that, the men were cheery & hopeful, & you couldn't want better soldiers. I am frightfully busy now fixing up all the muddle inevitable after a show like this, & am very sleepy and tired, as I haven't had much time to rest yet. I'm afraid the casualty lists will be heavy when published. We all had narrow shaves, I had a fearfully narrow one, but must tell you about it some other time, as I'm too tired to go on writing now. Goodnight mother & I'm right as rain and awfully fit.

Love to all
yr loving son
Ted

22 March 1915

Dear Mother,

Very many thanks for your short note and the café au lait, much appreciated in the mess; also the chocolate which Mr Fox & I finished off today. . . .

Did you ever get a jacket & pair of breeches I sent home about a month ago I wonder, because you never said anything about them. . . . No news here, we are still resting but I believe move off further north in a day or two. Any news of Paul? They seem to be having lively times in the Dardenelles don't they. . . . Send along a cake when you have time. Excuse a scrawl.

24 March 1915

Dear Jinny,

Very many thanks for your ripping long letter. So glad you liked my letters & I'm glad I wrote 'em when I did because I'm blowed if I remember now what happened then, it's all a sort of dream. We are still in these secure billets but are now called Divisional Reserve . . . I don't suppose we shall be wanted unless they have a 'Bismark's birthday Biff' on April 1st, which is the rumour at present. . . .

I've been into Bethune today & had a damn good lunch. . . . I sent you some picture postcards, awful things, but I didn't put any stamps on, as I was told if I put FM (Franchise Militaire) on them they would go free; I wonder if they ever got home; do let me know if they did, & I hope you didn't have to pay on 'em. I feel much better for the change to Bethune, even though it was only for a few hours. I drove one of our interpreters in in our mess cart; you know what a good driver I am, & the road was full of traffic, but I managed very well really; anyhow no accidents occurred & we got safely back which is the main thing – I also had several short drinks which helped the world go round faster & the horse fairly raced home!

Lovely weather here too . . . hedges all budding & birds singing etc. No more cameras allowed now & we all had to finish off our films & send the camera home. I flew round taking anything I could find, & wound up by taking 3 ducks on a pond so you can imagine how I was put to it to finish 'em off! . . .

Fit as a fiddle I am nowadays; write again some old time & send us a *Graphic* or a *Tatler*; *Tatler* always welcome, I like reading 'Eve'.

25 March 1915

Dear Jinny,

All cameras are disallowed now so I am sending mine to you to look after for me; also two packs of films, unused, which you can take pictures with. . . . Hope (it) rolls up safely & you take some good snaps with it. I carried it all through the Neuve Chapelle show but didn't have a minute to spare; besides there wasn't much to take really. Send along a cake some old time, the Delaford cakes are always welcome in the mess & much liked – always thinking of our stomachs aren't we; pigs, I call us.

1 April 1915
[a postcard to Gertrude]

Just a line to say I'm all right. Sorry I haven't written lately, but I have been very busy these last 3 days; will write a letter & try & cope with some much delayed correspondence tomorrow. Lovely weather, nice bright sunny days & warm – Tell Ben Fred Fox may look her up, as he has gone on leave today.

3 April 1915

Dear Mother,

Thanks most awfully for the lovely parcel of things you sent . . . the contents have nearly all gone now! . . . Also an Easter card, which came today. Talking of Easter, the Bishop of London was round here yesterday & held a service in a huge field. He stood up in an old wagon & before he began he said he had a message for us all from the English people, who sent their love and wished us the best of luck. Then he said he had another message which was the thanks of the English people for winning the Battle of Neuve Chapelle; rather sweet of him wasn't it. A good many officers were introduced to him, I among them. He told us all to let him know at once if he knew any of our people, otherwise when he got back he would be taken severely to task by various mothers & sisters & wives for not meeting their sons & brothers & husbands! I couldn't remember if you knew him or not, so didn't risk it. . . . I thought you might be interested to hear all this; the padres out here are all working at top pressure now, especially round about Easter.

. . . I hope to get a little leave about the 8th or 9th – just a day or two but please don't count on it . . .

They have now done what we have all been fearing they would do, they have amalgamated the 2 Battalions of the 39th into one Battalion; so for the last four days . . . I have been as busy as possible & am still frightfully so – you see the 1st Batt had so many officers knocked out in that last show it was practically a new regiment as regards officers; & we both had a good many casualties among the men . . . I have been made Adjutant, merely by seniority, as I happen to be senior to Guy Mainwaring who was adjutant of the 1st Batt & who also is wounded; so it is a case of circumstances,

'Greatness (if it is such!)
thrust upon me!'

. . . I wonder when Jim will get his commission; I can't think why they won't give him one. I think I must pay a personal visit to the War Office if I come home & try & ginger things up a bit. I thought they were only too keen to get fellers to take commissions.

I see a huge panorama of Neuve Chapelle in one of the papers, really quite good, only it looks as if it was going on in the middle of the night, they've made it so dark. . . .

He did get his leave and wrote again on the 12th:

Just a line to thank you all for giving me such a topping time at home – I can't tell you how much I enjoyed my leave and what a lot of good I'm sure it's done me – I simply *hated* coming away, especially back to this awful business, but I suppose it couldn't be helped. Anyhow you were splendid and made it as easy as possible on the surface. It was ripping seeing all the family like that, and I only wish old Paul could have been there. I thought of him often while I was enjoying the family life, which never seems to change or alter in the least. These flying visits are really very good for one I think, the change of scene & thought and the extraordinary pleasure of seeing you all again all count tremendously though the actual physical rest is perhaps nil.

Well, it's over now, so I must just pick up the threads where I dropped 'em out here, & hope my turn for a few days leave will soon come again.

I didn't have time to write at Folkstone. We had an awfully nice trip up in the car, everyone was in great form; Jim turned up at Victoria, so I had a good crowd to see me off. I loved having them all there and they were all full of fun. We had a lovely crossing 'absolute ponders' it would be called at Delaford I fancy! . . . I found letters from you all waiting for me, thanks very much for them all, I will try & answer them all sometime, though I have done so verbally with a vengeance. . . .

What awful fun Dick's car was; I enjoyed my rides in that most awfully, & must get one when I come home on leave next.

I wish my leave could have been a little longer; it was a crowded hour, but I shall never forget how frightfully nice everyone was to me. . . . 2 cakes awaiting me here & 1 with me, so I am well supplied!

Best love to all & again ten million thanks,

ever your loving son
Ted

14 April 1915

Dear Mother,

. . . You say you didn't do enough for me. My dear mother, you *couldn't* have done more, you were all *much* too good to me and all helped to make my leave, as far as I was concerned, a complete success. I'm afraid I was away a good deal, but you know how hard it is to stay at home. Since coming back I have already heard from 2 people asking me why I didn't go & see them! But I stayed amongst the family as much as I could I think.

Anyhow it was lovely seeing you all again & I can never thank you enough for being so frightfully good to me. I *did* love it all so.

His next letter was written on a sheet of paper headed 'Indian Soldiers' Fund' and illustrated with a picture of Lord Roberts.

17 April 1915

They have sent a lot of this paper up with the Rations today so I thought I'd use a bit just for fun . . . So glad you have been away for a rest and change, I'm sure it's done you heaps of good, especially after all the strenuous days of last week, with never less than 12 sitting down to meals! The memory of my 4 pleasant days at home will last me a long time. I have heard from all the others and they all wrote such nice letters to me. I wish they would remember it was *I* who did all the enjoying & *they* who made my leave so absolutely splendid! . . .

I had a lovely long letter from Ben this morning; I'm glad to say she got all the letters I wrote her; I was rather afraid one I wrote just before I came home on leave might not have been posted. So Jane is going to Dick soon is she. I heard from him, he doesn't seem to get any orders, though I hear out here that his destination is probably Marseilles. The 'No stamp' dodge worked all right, but if there is no definite regulation it seems a shame to chizzle the Govt out of 1d everytime you write; besides it *might* not always work. . . .

21 April 1915

Dear Jinny,

I wonder if you would do something for me. I have taken the liberty of sending your address to a friend of mine, Mrs Stack (her husband was a pal of mine in Lansdowne in the 8th Gurkhas, and was killed out here last October, Ben knows her & knew him) because she wrote to me today & asked if my doctor brother would sing some songs for some soldiers in outlying camps etc just to amuse them. So I have written to say I thought perhaps you would help her if you could, only she is not to rely on you in any way as you may have lots else to do. As regards Dick, if he could possible manage to sing a song or two for her it would be ripping but I told her also to put no reliance on his help as he is a very busy man, etc, etc, I mean I haven't tied either of you down to help her & you can easily say no; but do go if you can.

No news; send along *London Opinion* & a *Mail* occasionally.

Tons of love
from Ted.

P.S. In case you are put to any expense over this show I enclose £1; if you don't go spend it on what you like.

29 April 1915

Dear Mother,

So sorry I haven't written to you for so long but we've been on the rush rather lately, & owing to unforeseen complications here have had to come back into the trenches after going back for a longish rest, which in reality only lasted one day. For no sooner had we got to our destination than we got orders to come back! . . . You have of course read all about the heavy fighting round Ypres lately, in fact you mention it in your letters; but we weren't sent up there, though I believe some Indian troops were employed – we are in the trenches, the same old game again, only the weather is of course much better now . . . the trenches are quite respectable . . . dry & clean, & dust has in every way taken the place of mud everywhere . . . I don't know which is the worst, I think it is just whichever you happen to be suffering from at the time. . . .

I got a cake from you last night; thanks awfully for it . . . .

I'm so glad your stay at Folkstone did you good . . . . These are anxious times & I know you feel far more than anyone would imagine from your splendid behaviour & you look all your troubles & anxieties in the face like the brave and splendid mother you are – It's useless talking about it, but we all think you are wonderful – but it's some satisfaction, isn't it, that, whatever happens, you know you & your sons & daughters are doing what they can for their country in this hour of trial; and even though it must be a terrible time for you we know you would not in your heart of hearts have it otherwise.

I'm afraid I have very little news. Things are fairly quiet here nowadays; all the excitement is up North, or round the Dardenelles. Any news of Paul lately? I wonder where he can of got to. . . .

Is the family still split up, or have any returned to the fold yet? I'm so glad to hear Jim has got his commission, & I know it will buck him up as he was so heartily sick of being a Tommy, wasn't he?

1 May 1915
Garland Day

Just a line to say all's well . . . The cake arrived safely, very many thanks for it. . . .

We have not been in all this heavy fighting round Ypres, though some Indian troops were employed I believe. Many thanks for the Neuve Chapelle story, the map on the back is really excellent. My dear, you must have been simply overwhelmed with cuttings lately, for Neuve Chapelle was the star turn till Hill 60 & Ypres knocked it out.

Not much going on here. Jack Lodwick has got a D.S.O. for good work with machine guns, did I tell you he was married? He got married when he was on leave last month.

Sorry about a dull note, but I must try to drop a line to someone at home each day.

A postcard to Gertrude:

3 May 1915

Just a line to say I'm all right. Not much going on here nowadays. Weather lovely except for a little rain yesterday. Very fit & smiling. Love to all.

4 May 1915

Dear Mother,

Just a scrawl. No news; all serene & quiet here. We have been in the trenches just a week now and I hear are being relieved tomorrow night.

The cake has nearly all been eaten now & was voted a complete success in our dugout; it wasn't a bit heavy but just right. . . .

Good North Sea news I see by the papers; any news of Paul by the way.

Just had a whole lot of mouth organs sent us! Imagine our men playing, they don't know one note from another.

A packet of Pink 'Uns etc has just come by post, looks like Jane's writing; many thanks.

5 May 1915

Just a line to say I'm very fit & well. We have been in these trenches 8 days now and are being relieved tonight thank goodness. . . . Send me out one of these new absorbent cottonwool face masks, but I expect you have already done so. I've got a rotten wire one, but I think the other kind are better & easier to carry.

I got a whole bunch of papers this morning, including *The Boy's Realm* which has been read with much gusto in the trenches.

Nothing much going on here nowadays; all the fun is going on up near Ypres apparently. We have got to bivouac tonight out into the open, so I hope it stops raining by then. I wonder why they can't find billets for us.

Another postcard:

6 May 1915

Very many thanks for your letter & the cake, most welcome. Fancy old Ben getting measles! I had a long letter from her today. Very muggy weather & thundery. All well here & I'm very fit & well.

and a letter the same day:

Who do you think came to see us today – the Prince of Wales. Absolutely informal, he just strolled in, *exactly* like his pictures, in that

Order of St. John of Jerusalem.

INDIAN
SOLDIERS'
FUND.

By permission of Copperfield, Limited, 12-15, Grafton St. Bond St. W.
Lord Roberts - by C. W. Furse, A.R.A.

HOSPITAL

6 May 15 191

Dear Mother

I wrote you a p.c. today & have been looking for it everywhere as I find I have time now to write a letter & I thought I'd tear up the p.c. but it doesn't matter. Who d'you think came to see us today, the Prince of Wales. Absolutely informal, he just strolled in, exactly like his pictures, in that mackintosh with the collar turned up & rather a rakish hat. He was very ordinary & talked to us all & asked after the men and all. Rather

Letter on Indian Soldiers' Fund writing paper

mackintosh with the collar turned up & rather a rakish hat. He was very ordinary & talked to us all & asked after the men & all. Rather funny, we were all in the mess & someone came in & tapped someone on the shoulder & said 'the Prince of Wales is outside'; and he really was, of course, but the chap thinking he was rotting, turned round & said 'Well, tell him to stay there!' However I don't think the Prince heard. He's an awful handful as he will want to go wandering about in the firing trenches & dangerous places like that.

So hot & muggy today & very thundery too. Just met some fellows back from Ypres; they say these 77 inch shells of the Germans sound just like a motor bus coming through the air and make a hole 15 feet deep & 35 feet wide! One chap was standing by a gun and a huge shell burst right between his feet & sent him sky high but didn't wound him! but he collapsed from shock shortly afterwards, but will get all right they say.

I hear the Canadians did awfully well up there as all the papers say; they were full of beans the whole time & went again & again into action singing & shouting. Splendid they must have been.

8 May 1915

The weather has now indeed changed . . . last week . . . it was really . . almost like India at times! . . . Today it is much cooler again with a lovely breeze. All the country round here is a mass of orchards so you can imagine how perfectly gorgeous they are all looking now, a mass of blossoms. And the meadows are full of dandelions and cowslips . . . I feel I should just like to wander about in a place like this always . . . one can almost forget the war and its attendant horrors . . . only there are a whole lot of guns round about here & they are constantly reminding us. . . . How lovely it must be at home now with all the trees & hedges coming out. . . .

I had a long letter from Jane yesterday, she seems to be enjoying herself with Dick all right. I'm so glad Jim is going to get a commission, I'm sure it's the best thing to do.

A postcard on May 9th

Just a line to say I have been *very slightly* wounded, by a shell, the calf & wrist, absolutely *nothing*, shall be out of hospital in 2 days. This is just so that if you see my name in the paper you needn't be alarmed. Fit as a fiddle. Ted.

NELL

Post Office Telegraphs.
Parliament Street OHMS handed in: 6.30p.m. Received here at 7.13 p.m.
Guildford 11 MY 15

To Mrs Berryman Delaford Guildford

Regret to inform you that your son Captain E.R.P. Berryman 39 Garhwal Rifles officially reported admitted No 3 London General Hospital Wandsworth Common 10 May suffering from gunshot wound left leg. No previous report of wounding received. Military Secretary. India Office.

Post Office Telegraphs 12 MY 15

Reference my previous telegram it is now officially reported that Captain E.R.P. Berryman 49 [sic] Garhwal Rifles was wounded in action 9th May Military Secretary India Office.

However Ted cannot have been in hospital long as it seems he arrived home before Gertrude even knew he had been wounded, according to the affectionate letter from M.A. Dudman of Pitney [Charles Berryman's first living].

My dear Gertrude,
We have thought so much of you during these last few days & are so sorry to hear that Ted is wounded, But glad only slight and how glad you must be to have him at home and safe for a time. It will be nice if you can all be together for a day even, it was nice Ted arrived before the news of his being wounded reached you and you had no real anxiety and I do trust his wound will not be very painful and that he will be able to rest well, he must need it after the terribly trying time he has had. What an awful war it is, really one feels as if one could not read all the accounts in the papers they are too sad and dreadful. We have Agatha Vansittart with us and she has made out a list of 29 relations all within the firing line or just going out to France or somewhere, 3 airmen among them, one relation, a Vansittart, has just been killed . . . I wish you could come and see us and we should like to see Ted, could he spare us a few days before he returns? We should be so pleased if he could. How nice Paul has leave now also. We are glad Jim has a commission, I hear Guy Crossman won't have one. Mrs Jocelyne's eldest son has one in the 9th Somersets, but her youngest son is a private and out in India with the West Kent Regiment. . . . I quite agree

Ted, 1915

with you about the *Lusitania*, people are foolish to travel unless absolutely obliged at present. Awdrey Sydney has just reached home safely from India but it was an exciting voyage. We have 200 soldiers now camped on the high ground between the Golf Links and High Ham. They are I believe rifle practising at the Paradise Butts and we hear 1,000 are to come altogether! and our yeomen are coming home in turn to see their families before going abroad.

Nearly every letter Gertrude received was on much the same lines: sorry that Ted was wounded, but she must be glad to have him safe, and with news of families and friends involved in the war. A girlhood friend, now Benedicta Yeatman and Ben's godmother wrote:

I hear you have Ted home wounded but not seriously and will have all the family party together for the first time in years. I am so glad – tho' Ted is wounded that you should have them all together. . . . I went to Salisbury this weekend to get a glimpse of Julian who is at Tidworth. Harry was to have been in the fight on 9th May and then the orders were countermanded. Julian is supposed to be going somewhere in 5 weeks but I expect it will be longer. He is only 18 in July. I do hope not the Dardenelles.

We at least know that Julian, although wounded later, came through safely to collaborate with W.C. Sellars in writing that classic of English history – *1066 And All That*.

102 Church Street,
Kensington
20 May 1915

I see in today's paper that Ted has been wounded, I do hope . . . that it is not serious . . . in that case it is almost a relief to feel they are out of the firing line. I know my aunt felt that – she has got her boy at home now for two months' leave after his second wound . . .

Molly O'Brien

33 Tregunter Road
South Kensington
20 May 1915

I was very sorry to see poor old Ted's name among the wounded this morning. . . . Poor you, you must be in continual anxiety with so many sons serving – and I do hope you get good news of the others – I should appreciate a postcard from one of you to let me know how Ted is getting on.

We have Reggie at home now, also wounded – it is such a blessing to feel they are safely in England and receiving the best attention. The dear old boy is very cheerful but in a good deal of pain as his sciatic nerve has been injured in some way.

I am thankful to say that my husband has not been in it very much lately and is quite well but I expect their turn will come soon. . . .

It is a most horrible time to live through and the only thing is to keep as well and as cheerful as one can, by being busy. . . .

Kathleen Broadbest

The letter from one of Charles's old parishioners at Camberley was much less encouraging.

Indoe House
Camberley
20 May 1915

I *am* sorry to hear about Ted, except that as it is slight he won't be able to fight again yet awhile and that is a mercy. But *mustn't* it be depressing to have all your friends killed? I think I should feel like exchanging into something else, you wouldn't feel so lonely. Gen. Bond's youngest son has died from his wounds. They heard a few days ago. He was wounded in the abdomen and they were told 'slightly', but that was a mistake for he died almost at once. He enlisted when the war began and came from Canada, I think, on purpose. Amy hasn't heard any more from Reg: when he wrote last he thought he would leave on March 12th but when you think he is walking from Central Africa and the nearest Rly Station! it doesn't sound a quick job. Elly Ward is on her way home . . . Poor Mrs B feels very anxious, I only trust she and the child will arrive all right, personally I should prefer keeping off the sea. You *will* all be at home this weekend, shan't you? How awfully nice for you. I thought it was so friendly and kind of Jim to come and see me. He looked so well in his uniform and his likeness to Mr Berryman struck me very much. It was the way he looks at you I think . . .

Mrs S. comes to lunch after decorating, it's always rather a trial although she doesn't sit amongst the tombs as much as she used.

S.S. Scott

As well as letters from several other friends Gertrude also heard from her Palmer relations.

26 Park Street
Windsor
Whit Sunday

I fear very much it is your dear boy who is reported as wounded. I am

Berryman brothers and family, 1915

grieved to think of your anxiety, but I trust his injury is slight and that he will soon recover from it, and perhaps you will have him home soon. . . . I have many friends and relations out, and I hear 4 of your boys are fighting for us – how much you have to think of. We have let this house to Capt Ascombe who is [in] command of the anti aircraft to defend the Castle. He has a very unrestful time during the visit of the King and is called up day and night with warnings . . .

Believe me, your affectionate aunt
Frances Palmer

Suirvale
Cahir
Co. Tipperary
13 May 1915

My dear Gertrude,

I saw amongst the list of wounded the other day the name of Captain E.R.P. Berryman of the Garhwal Rifles. I fear this must be your son Ted. I hope you can find time to send me a few lines to tell me about it and how he is – is he able to come home? Also please tell me about the others, Paul and Christopher and the girls. Has Richard come home from India? I fear I have been a very bad correspondent but believe me I do not forget you all. I hope this terrible war will not last much longer but I fear there is little sign of daylight as yet. Hoping to hear good accounts from you.

yr affecte Cousin
George Palmer

George's conscience might well strike him – he was Topher's godfather.

A letter from one S.M. Campbell of Eardsley Rectory, Hereford, sums up the theme of them all:

I was very sorry to see your son Ted's name in the casualty list yesterday but very thankful it wasn't in the first part of the list. The only time lately when there has been freedom from acute anxiety has been when our nearest relatives have come home wounded. One, alas, returned wounded for a blissful month with his young wife and was then killed in the landing of troops in the Dardenelles.

While the writer of a brief, undated postcard with no address was more prophetic than he knew:

Awfully sorry to see Ted's name in the list of wounded. I do hope it is only slight & thus a blessing in disguise and that he will get a good long leave. Let me know. JF.

Ted was granted extended sick leave until 16 August when he was ordered to report for light duties at home until fit for active service. He wrote to Gertrude from Perham Down.

I got to Salisbury all right today and reported myself as orderd. They gave me orders to report to the H.Q. of the South Midland Division at Churn in Berkshire . . . so I am off there tomorrow. Meanwhile I have come on to see Jim & Topher, and am staying the night here with Jim. I haven't seen Topher yet but I believe he is coming along soon. . . . Fancy Government paying 10*s* to get me to Salisbury, & about £1 to Churn perhaps, & a few more odd expenses, when a penny stamp would have told Southern Command that I was available for duty & another would have told me to go to Churn . . . absurd isn't it! . . .

I'll write again tomorrow & let you know my final destination.

Prince of Wales Hotel
Didcot
17 August 1915

Really, I've never known anything *like* this show! I left Salisbury today at 2.20 arrived Churn about 5, walked into the H. Q. office there to find Jos Lane of my regiment sitting there! He came home from France some time ago, sick, & is doing light duty at home . . . staff officer to . . . the South Midland Divn. We had a long talk, & he said he was very sorry he couldn't keep me, but he had orders to send me to join the 3rd Bn of the 5th Gloucesters, at Gloucester! . . . I came on as far as this tonight, & am going on to Gloucester tomorrow. I believe the Regt is out in camp, so I have got to chase them still further. I believe they are . . . terriers, who know absolutely *nothing*, and my services have been placed at their disposal. Heaven knows what I'm going to teach them! A letter addressed to me attd 3/5 Gloucesters, The Drill Hall, Gloucester will find me pro tem, but I'll send another address later. Touring the Southern Counties at all! My light duty seems to consist in careering about England.

This would certainly seem to be true from subsequent letters. He wrote from Malvern Wells on 30 August:

I arrived here yesterday to help in an exam for N.C.O.'s for promotion. . . . I am doing the musketry part of the exam with Lord Deerhurst, whoever he may be; never heard of him before. Anyhow he is a cheery old Colonel, with a nice round red face; he stands me drinks when we are not

Nell, 1915

on parade. . . . I am writing this in the Y.M.C.A. tent while the men are having a written exam. Lord D.'s chauffeur is cleaning my bike now; I hope the old boy doesn't find out as I collared him on the sly to do it.

Ted used this motor bike to visit friends in Bristol and Cheltenham because, as he said: 'I'm afraid it's much too far to think of weekends from here; but I can always manage to find something to do, I expect.'

He soon found something to do at weekends and indeed every spare moment. John Fielding, a director of a large Gloucester engineering firm, lived in a big house on the hill above the camp and, like everyone else in England, offered hospitality to the officers in the neighbourhood. The Fieldings were not a large family by Berryman standards – five girls and a boy – and only four of them were at home just then. Jack, due to go up to Cambridge to read engineering, was training instead with the Royal Artillery, and Marjorie, one of the three eldest girls, was on tour, having embarked on the theatrical career she was shortly to abandon for the duration of the war to work as personnel officer in a munitions factory in Woolwich. Gladys and Louie were involved with Red Cross work and Nell, the fourth daughter, was about to begin a shorthand and typing course with the idea of going into 'the Works' – the family firm. Isabel (Bellows), the youngest, was still at school.

It was these four who were invited to tea in the camp by an officer returning hospitality who asked Ted to come along to help him entertain them. They were still in mourning for their grandfather and were a little exercised as to what to wear. Nell compromised with a white blouse and a black skirt (she had only just left school) and tied her dark hair back with a black ribbon. She was not yet eighteen.

The party was a great success and led to further meetings, as Gladys, the eldest, wrote to Jack:

Broadsground
Upton St Leonards
12 September 1915

We have been wishing you were here this week. We had a real old pre-war madcap night of it on Friday – and longed for you and Marjorie. Captain Davis is now at the camp at Sneedham's Green and he asked us to a tea party on Tuesday and we had a jolly time of it and played 'up Jenkins' on his bath for a table! Two other officers – a Captain Berryman and Mr Culverwell were of the party, both very jolly and both home from

Officers at Sneedham's Green, 1915. Ted in the centre

the front – they belonged to the Indian Army and were wounded and are now temporarily attached here. Well – during tea someone said what a pity we couldn't have a fancy dress ball or some such jollification in the old Y.M.C.A. tent! So we suggested our house as a trifle more feasible and so we fixed it up then and there for the Friday evening! The only other guests were Auntie, Bertha [a cousin] and the Rector and Mrs Williams who are staying at Belmont and Helen Fox. We all dressed up and at 8 our guests arrived and were rigged up variously as Greek, pirate and Turk! Captain Berryman is a great sport, you'd like him awfully, he simply kept us in fits, Father was nearly ill and Auntie kept on gasping: 'I can't laugh any more!' I hope he'll still be here when you get your next leave . . .

A fortnight later Ted was writing to his mother:

Gloucester
18 September 1915

Very many thanks for your letter & the puttees & nail scissors which I got today. So glad to hear Jim is all right again, I expect he'll pick up fairly quickly now. Really today is too awful for words, persistent rain & *bitterly* cold, miserable. I'm just going to Gloster now to dine at the club & be comfortable for a few hours anyhow. I have been up to the Fieldings a lot, every day in fact, so I thought I'd give today a miss & of course it's just the sort of day one would love to go up. I play billiards with the old man a lot, of course he's *always* asking me up – I bought that Berlin puzzle for 'em & of course they do nothing else all day. Tell Ben Nell is as nice as ever; she & I are going out to tea tomorrow to an old gipsy woman to have our fortunes told! (I can hear Dreda and Jane saying 'what nonsense!')

It would be fascinating to know what the fortune-teller told them. It was probably Mrs Ridler, the gardener's wife, who had told Nell that she would meet her second, and true, love at a party and who made other true predictions. It was only a month later, on 29 October, that the Fieldings and some of their friends went for a walk in the beech woods along the ridge of the hill above the house. It was a glorious Autumn day and the anniversary of Ted's first going into the trenches just a year before. He could not but have been aware of the contrast and perhaps it was this that inspired him to 'speak'. That evening he and Nell visited her aunt, who lived a little lower down the hill, and under the spreading chestnut trees in her drive, on their way back to Broadsground, they became engaged.

The Fieldings seemed to be slightly taken aback, although the domestic staff were well aware: at that first evening party word had gone out to the kitchen that it was all right; he had taken 'the right one' in to dinner. Of course, they had three older daughters still un-married and, not only was Nell still only seventeen, but she had been engaged briefly at the beginning of the year to a young Sandhurst cadet who was about to go out to France. His mother had forbidden it on the grounds that they were both too young and the romance seemed to be fading when he was killed in action. Nell was always to feel a little guilty that she appeared to find consolidation so quickly with someone else and for years she wore the gold half-hunter watch that he had given her on their engagement.

The Fieldings, however, were loving parents and they compromised. The engagement was not forbidden but it would not be recognised until Nell was older, and Nell wrote cheerfully to Jack:

My dear old Jonathan,

I am so glad you are pleased to get one of your sisters engaged at last. The worst of it is that Father won't let it be made public for six months. As you can imagine it is jolly hard to keep it a secret as lots of people seemed to know about it before it ever came off. Ted wants me to go down to Guildford with him this weekend and spend Saturday in town and do a theatre. But if we aren't publicly engaged Father might not let me go. I do hope he will as it would be such fun.

Do you realise I am working? I'm learning shorthand and type writing & am getting really quite brainy. I have done all my work and Mrs Tyler isn't here to tell me what else to do so I am improving the shining hour by writing to you. I spent the weekend in Cheltenham with Ted and Jane in their rooms. It was a rag.

They had a concert on Friday and as the programme was too short, Ted sang some George Robey songs in costume and conducted the rag orchestra and it was a great success and there was a precious account of it in the Echo. We want to get him to come over here and do something at the hospital. . . .

I am so glad you know Ted. It is rotten that Marjorie doesn't. How funny it must be not to know your sister's fiasco. Ted is going to give me a white West Highland puppy for my birthday. I don't know when it will come as it was only born this week and I think it is going to be trained first.

Yours to a cinder,
Nell.

Ted also wrote.

30 Lansdowne Crescent,
Cheltenhan
9 November 1915

Dear Jack,

Just a line about the news which of course you have heard. You said in your letter home this morning that I was lucky, so I am, cocky, damn lucky, & Nell is an awful Dear; I thought something disastrous would occur the very first time I saw her! Of course your father wants us to wait six months before it's 'official', but that doesn't really matter, & most people seem to know already. I'm fearfully bucked at the prospect of becoming a relation-in-law of you all as I have always been awfully fond of the family who have been the soul of goodness to me.

They don't seem to want me back yet so I suppose I shall hang on for a bit longer. I hear the Indian Corps has been withdrawn from France, probably to Egypt. How's the course going, *and* the bike! I've returned mine to store & feel rather lost without it.

So long, cocky, & keep smiling,
yours,
Ted

Her parents' concern is evident in the letter that her mother had also written to Jack:

I wonder if you will be very surprised to hear that Ted Berryman is in love with Nell, he spoke to Father yesterday, it is arranged that if they are in the same mind at the end of the six months they may be formally engaged then, & in the meantime nothing is to be said to anyone about it, but I do not see how it is to be kept secret for so long. What do you think about it, I like Ted very much but Nell is *very* young for him, however I feel sure he will be *very* good to her.

The six months edict lasted exactly a week, during which Ted collected Nell every day from her typing school and gave her lunch at the Gloucester Club of which he was a temporary member. John Fielding, who also lunched at the club, realised that everyone else must see how things were and bowed to the inevitable, as much to his own relief as that of the young couple. The Berryman family were delighted. Paul, on hearing the age of his sister-in-law to be, wrote to Ted that he was 'now dubbed "cradle-snatcher"' but they were all very happy about it in spite of the war and the uncertainty of the future. At the end of 1915 who could tell what would be happening to them all in six months' time?

On Sunday, 28 November, Ted wrote to his mother:

Just a line to tell you that I have had orders to report to the India Office in writing, which I have done today, so suppose I shall be getting orders of some sort in a day or two. Will let you know what they are,
Love to all,

yr loving son,
Ted.

The orders were to sail to India, to rejoin his regiment, in the *SS Persia*

To E.P.F.

Once more to tread with you the path
Along the beech-strewn avenue,
Red gold with summer's aftermath
Against the sky's October blue:

To taste a Beacon wind again,
And watch it playing with your hair:
To feel the sting of driving rain,
And fill my lungs with Cotswold air:

To watch the straight blue smoke ascend
When all the Autumn air is still
And see where sky & landscape blend
In haze, the line of Malvern hill.

These are my dreams: no surer way
To bring the soul of you to me:
Dreams of a sacred yesterday,
Of a tomorrow yet to be –

And when I see you standing there,
Dream-daughter of my slumbering brain,
I wake to kiss – the empty air!
Then sigh, and turn, and sleep again.

S.S. *PERSIA*

These were anxious times for anyone with relations on troopships and Ted sent his mother a reassuring postcard from Malta, dated 28 December: 'Arrived safely all well here, nice and warm! Love to all Ted.' Two days later the *Persia* was torpedoed in the Eastern Mediterranean at 1 p.m. Casualties were heavy and Ted's name was not on the first list of survivors published. Nell's reaction was to go up to her room and write him a long letter. 'I know he's all right,' she said firmly when she came down. Perhaps the fortune teller's prediction that 'your man won't ever get killed or drownded' gave her confidence, but her sisters could not stand the strain as time went by with no news and they went to consult this same fortune teller, the gardener's wife. Mrs Ridler put out the cards, shaking her head. 'It's all black, all black – ' and then suddenly, as she turned up a red card – 'No! it's all right – the Captain's saved!'
Nell wrote to Jack:

Broadsground
Upton St Leonards
2 January 1916

My dear Jack,
By the time you get this I hope you will have got our wire to say that Ted is safe. We had a wire from him at Alexandria & one from Guildford this morning to say he was alright. I was at the hospital washing up when Gladys & Marjorie came & told me that the *Persia* had been torpedoed in the Mediterranean & in the evening we had a telephone message to say four boats had got to Alexandria. The nurse came to see us yesterday at tea & she told our fortunes in our cups & she said we were to have some good news from over the sea, of a ship from an 'E'. Marjorie & Louie went down to Mrs Ridler in the evening & cut the cards & she said it would all come right as the cards were so good round Ted & me, & there were some very anxious thoughts coming just before.

Broadsground
Upton St Leonards
20 January 1916

My dear Jack,
Many happy returns of the day. I am afraid I have not got anything for

you yet. Have you any ideas on the subject? We thought perhaps you might like a small gramophone to take with you, you can get such little dears with room inside for 12 records.

You will love Sandy, he is such a little dear & he grows! He is about twice the size he was when I had him & I haven't had him a month yet.

I had a long account of the *Persia* disaster from Ted the other day & he has sent back his watch & the miniature which he saved, but they are both ruined, and he sent three tiny scraps of hard biscuits which he was saving for his supper the night they were picked up. My dear, wasn't it thrilling & brave, he towed a woman for ages until they were picked up.

Several hand-written and typed copies of the account were made and circulated among the family and friends.

I will try and give you some account of the sinking of the poor old *Persia* while it is still fresh in my memory, though I don't think I am likely to forget it in a hurry, much as I should like to. It was just after 1 o'clock on Thursday Dec. 30th, and the gong had just sounded for lunch; consequently the majority of passengers were assembled in the saloon and a good many had actually begun lunch (as this is a personal account, you must excuse the continual occurrence of the personal pronoun 'I', but I am afraid it is unavoidable) I was a trifle late and strolled in about 5 past 1 o'clock, and was just sitting down in my place when there was a muffled 'bang', though it sounded loud and clear enough and one felt the concussion quite distinctly. Everyone of course knew at once what had happened and we all rose from our seats and began to file out of the saloon. There was no panic, no rush; as someone described it later, 'just like going out of church'. I heard only one remark, someone saying, 'not much doubt about that', otherwise everyone was quite calm and collected, outwardly at any rate. We all went to our cabins and got our lifebelts and went on deck, and proceeded at once to our boats. My boat was No 7 on the starboard side and when I got there the crew were already endeavouring to lower it. This must have been a minute after she was struck and the *Persia* was already beginning to list to port a bit. Our boat seemed to stick in the davits and refuse to be lowered, despite the efforts of the crew and ourselves. The list to port was now becoming very marked, and it soon became 45 degrees, and one had to hang on to the rail to prevent oneself sliding across to the port side, and anyone who was in the least bit late in coming on deck had perforce to go to the port side. It was soon obvious that our boat was never to be launched in time, as the old *Persia* was now almost on her side. Someone said 'time to go now', so in company with several others I scrambled over the rail and walked down the side of the ship, which was now of course nearly level, as she had heeled right over to port. No 7 boat was still fast in the davits, though a little lower than before, and I thought the best thing to do was to hang onto her as she might still get loose. However just then the *Persia* gave a final lurch and her keel appeared above water, and a huge rush of water caught me fair and square just as I was hanging onto the lifelines of No 7 boat and I was carried right away from the ship. I then saw it all, the last few seconds of the old barge, she half righted herself and then sank with appalling rapidity, the last thing I saw being her bows standing right out of the water, about 30 ft of them, and then these slid out of sight silently and suddenly. The sinking ship caused very little suction, but the water all round was of course very much disturbed. The whole tragedy had taken just 5 minutes, from the time the torpedo struck till the *Persia* disappeared. The scene that followed was too terrible to describe in any detail, even if I could do so. The sea (which had quite a nasty swell on, though not exactly rough) was full of human beings and floating wreckage. Chairs, tables, broken spars and beams were everywhere. The air was full of groans and cries, and everywhere one looked it seemed one saw human beings struggling in the water. It was awful. Our lifebelts kept us afloat easily, but we all hung on to wreckage. Each bit I got on to seemed to be chosen by several other people, so one had to change several times, as there were too many on several pieces to support the weight. I looked round, a bit dazed of course, and could see four boats some way off, and one upturned one. Obviously the thing to do was to swim for the boats, so, shouting out this to the others, I started off. It was difficult work, as the sea was so full of wreckage that one got knocked about a lot and it is hard work swimming in a lifebelt too.

The boats seemed miles off and I seemed to get no nearer. By now the swell and the current had scattered everyone over a very large area, and the boats were picking up as many people as they could. While swimming along I heard groaning and crying close to me and saw a lady lying on her back, apparently utterly exhausted, and just drifting helplessly away, supported by her lifebelt. She was delirious I should think, and kept saying she was dead and dying; so I took her in tow, though there seemed little chance of our reaching the boats, as I seemed to get no nearer. Fortunately she lay quite still, and though my legs kept on getting mixed up in her skirts and she was rather a dead weight, I managed to swim on and at last succeeded in hailing a boat. They fortunately saw me and waved back, (I had already got near one boat but they had no oars out and I was carried away from it by the sea. How hopeless it all seemed then) and after more struggles I at last reached the boat and after three ineffectual grabs at a rescuing hand I seized it and we were hauled on board. I *was* thankful to get in. I must have been in the water half an hour and felt quite done up. I'm afraid anyone who was afloat when she went down and could not swim must have been lost, as the boats soon drifted away from the scene, the swell and current being very strong and I'm afraid, too, may people got injured by floating wreckage.

The boat I was in contained about forty people. We got oars out but it was hard to make any headway in that sea and with amateur oarsmen. We looked round for more survivors but could see none, and, except for a few pieces of isolated wreckage, which were here and there visible, the rest having been scattered, it was hard to realise a ship had gone down. There were four boats afloat, all full, and one upturned one in the far distance with a few people clinging on. Some people swear to having seen a fifth boat full of people but nothing has been heard of this since. The chief officer of the *Persia* (to whom we owe our lives as he cut away three boats from the davits with a hatchet, there being no time to launch them; the fourth boat had been launched somehow or other) was in one of these and he shouted out orders to all keep together, so we laboured at the oars and at last got all tied together in a line. The chief officer then transferred some from his boat (which was only the small 'accident boat' for use in case of man overboard) which was carrying about 10–12 more people than it could hold, to ours and others, we had now just over forty, including 6 women, 2 children, and one ship's officer, 4 male passengers and the rest stewards and native lascar crew of the *Persia*. All our watches stopped at 1.15 or 1.20, but it must have been about 2 o'clock by now. We tried to keep our course SSE towards Port Said, so as to fall in with other ships if possible, but it was a difficult job in that sea. About 4 o'clock, I suppose, we sighted the masts, funnels and smoke of a ship on the horizon which cheered us all up, and her hull soon appeared (I must tell you here that there had been no time to send off an S.O.S. signal by Marconi, so no one knew what had happened.) Suddenly a huge column of water was seen to shoot up by her, followed by 5 shots from a gun. It seemed that she too had been torpedoed, or shelled by the submarine, or perhaps was firing at the submarine. In any case she got no nearer to us, and though she did not sink at once, she gradually faded away in the gathering darkness.

We now tried to make ourselves as comfortable as possible for the night. We were all wet through of course, and it soon got very cold. The poor women were very thinly clad, but we gave them coats and sail covers and there happened to be a very thin blanket on board, but it was bitterly cold for them I'm afraid. However they were just *splendid*. One poor girl had got a nasty cut on her head from a piece of wreckage and fainted, but we made her as comfy as possible. Of course the boat was *crowded* and one could not move about at all. We put out 'sea anchors' to keep the boats' heads to the sea, and let ourselves drift, the current taking us in the desired direction. Soon after dark, the lights of a steamer appeared, so we burnt flares to attract her attention, but she put out all her lights and cleared off; she evidently thought we were a submarine and suspected a trick (I believe the Admiralty have issued orders accordingly, so as ships may not go to any promiscuous lights, as the enemy are up to all sorts of dodges). So two ships had gone by and no rescue. It was rather disheartening but we were not downhearted yet by any means. I had to lie up in the bows, looking after the painter which was joining our boat to the next one, as it kept parting and coming undone. It *was* cold as I was so wet. I shivered all night and most of the next day, even in a hottish sun. The night dragged itself through. Sleep was out of the question; we made the women as warm as we could and gave them all the coverings in the boat, but I'm afraid they suffered a lot, but they bore it like Britons and never complained once. The two kids rescued were both in our boat, one was a little French girl about 6, in the bows with me. Poor kid, I tried to keep her warm, but she kept on asking in a plaintive voice, 'where is the big boat which is coming to help us?' It was awfully pathetic, as one could only say it was coming soon now. Dawn at last came, we had a dry biscuit and a sip of water each. We had two kegs on board, but the stopper had come out of one so only one was filled. The other boats were in an equally bad way for water. Early in the morning, we hoisted a sail in our boat, and tried to tow the other three along but it was not much use and we made slow progress. About 9 o'clock, I suppose, we sighted a ship on the horizon. So it was decided that we, having a sail, should go after it alone and try to hail it. We sailed away, fearful bucked at the chance of a rescue, and we tried to cut her off. She must have been able to see our sail but she sheered off eventually and disappeared. Another chance gone! And one or two began to lose heart, though I must confess that all the time I felt confident that something would find us, provided the weather held and we were not swamped. It subsequently turned out that this ship was actually at the time being chased by a submarine, so of course could give no attention to us. We forgave her then, though at the time it was not blessings we called down on her head!

Heated discussions now took place as to what was the best thing to do. Some were in favour of each going our own way and trusting to being picked up and telling the rescuing ship that other boats were still afloat. Others were all for sticking together, chiefly because only two boats had sailors in them, the other two only passengers and stewards.

All the sailing about and going off on our own and returning to our comrades after our fruitless mission of course took many hours and the sun was now bright in the heavens. 12 o'clock. We all tied together again, lowered our sail and had a rest, just allowing ourselves to drift. The chief officer then said he was going off in his boat to look for help and the other 3 were to stay together. So off they went with our blessing and fervent hope for success while we stayed on. Night began to fall and we rearranged our boat and made the ladies more comfortable than they were the previous night. Watches were told off to look out for rescuers and look after the boat and the rest made snug(?) for the night. You must remember that all this time we were filling up odd moments with baling out water, rowing and generally trying to keep afloat, so we were all quite tired enough, though of course had lots left in us yet. It was now the second night after the tragedy.

I know I was just dozing off, though it was almost impossible to sleep in that crowded boat and of course we were bobbing up and down like a cork the whole time, when someone shouted out 'Ship ahoy!' Imagine it, how we all bucked up once more. It was quite dark and we fervently hoped this ship would not treat us like our friend of the previous night. She seemed to be making straight for us by her lights, but the thing was to attract her attention. We burnt a red flare in each boat (these are of course kept in water-tight compartments in each lifeboat) and rowed in her direction. Great speculations as to what she was, a sailing ship? a cruiser? a liner? Impossible to tell of course. As we got nearer we all gave three yells (we were ahead, the other two boats following some way behind) and burnt more flares. At last, after about 20 minutes she loomed up out of the darkness. 'A destroyer', said some Mr Knowall in the boat, and then an unmistakable English voice hailed us from her – 'Hallo, you fellows, we've got the other boat all right; come along the starboard side will you.' And so we were rescued. It was just 7 o'clock, I think, so we had been about 30 hours in boats, not so very long, but quite long enough so we all thought! Our rescuer proved to be H. M. S. *Mallow*, a mine sweeper. They had heard nothing of the *Persia*, but the chief officer's quest had been successful, and they had seen his flares, picked them up, and he had of course told them whereabouts we were and they came straight for us. They *were* good to us. A good meal for all, clothes and every possible attention; no one could have been kinder. I could have cried with relief; and to see those poor women and children looking more or less happy again, at any rate relieved beyond words at being rescued was a sight for the gods. We were soon accommodated in hammocks and got some much needed sleep. They sent wireless messages off at once, and these must have been the first news of the loss of the *Persia*.

The *Mallow* was just out on her own, hunting mines and submarines, so we were lucky indeed, as she was keeping no particular course, but wandering about anywhere, and just happened to meet the chief's boat by a mere chance. We made all speed to Alexandria, a wireless having been sent off there for the despatch of another boat to look for any more possible survivors.

We reached Alexandria next day (January 1st) and were taken on board *H.M.S. Hannibal* where again they were more than good to us. We must have presented a sorry spectacle, dirty and bruised in many cases, many with cuts and wounds caused by wreckage, looking a trifle worn and haggard I expect, but none the less happy at our rescue. We went ashore and made the more immediate purchases necessary for our comfort, and stayed that night aboard the *Hannibal* and came ashore next day and put up at the Savoy Hotel, where we have been ever since. We are more or less clothed and in our right minds now, and everyone has been more than good, but I fear the mental and physical results of all we have been through are beginning to make themselves felt now, though I think everyone is remarkably fit under the circumstances.

I will conclude with a few disjointed remarks on circumstances connected with this awful business.

No one saw the submarine, though one officer on watch on the bridge saw the track of the torpedo for about the last few yards, but she had struck before he could give any orders. She was struck amidships, just under the funnels, bursting a boiler and killing, I'm afraid, all the engineroom staff who were on duty at the time.

Only one boat was lowered in the orthodox way. The chief cut away three, and the second officer two more. These latter two however, full of passengers and crew, were caught by the davits as the ship heeled over and were swamped.

I'm afraid nearly all the first class passengers (there were only 14 I think, saved out of about 80, and only one lady 1st class passenger) were caught on the port side when she heeled over and were carried down with her.

The behaviour of the ladies was just priceless; they bore their sufferings wonderfully and did all they could to help. There was no panic on board, but the whole thing was over in 5 minutes and gave little time for thought. Some people had marvellous escapes. Two second class passengers, sisters (one married with a little boy) when she was struck went to opposite sides of the ship, the unmarried sister having the child in her arms. All three went down with the ship and came up again *side by side* in the water, though they were on opposite sides of the ship when she sank. They were all three rescued. As the ship heeled over a huge blast of ashes etc came out of the funnels, just as they were level with the water and several of the rescued were *coal* black, including the chief officer who also got a nasty knock on the head from one of the funnels.

All the Christmas mails for India, China, Aden, S.E. Africa and Egypt went down. Terrible isn't it. No one saved a thing, except what they stood up in. The sensation of walking solemnly over the side of the ship into the water is indescribable. For myself (and others tell me the same) I felt no fear, more annoyance than anything else; but I know I should funk it now; everybody's nerves seem to have gone a bit. It seemed so deliberate but it was the only thing to do of course. I'm afraid a great many people didn't leave the ship or jumped too late and were drowned.

The engines kept going to the last and when she was lying on her side, the propellor was racing round, half out of the water, splashing up the water to a tremendous height.

The chief engineer on hearing the explosion went down to the engine room to turn off the steam, and was last seen disappearing into a cloud of steam. A very plucky thing to do, but it was hopeless and he was never seen again.

The captain was not rescued. I saw him on deck, just before she sank, tying a lifebelt on to a lady; he had not got one himself. He must have gone down with the ship.

Fortunately she was an empty boat as regards passengers. Only about 80 first class and not so many second. The horrible part is the number of women missing and children too, but I think that all it was possible to rescue were rescued.

I hope I never go through such a terrible experience again. A pal of mine, one Fisher of the India Army, summed it up by saying 'it was worse than any attack' and I think he's right.

I have tried to give you a comprehensive account of this awful business. Please forgive the many literary shortcomings but it's a hard thing to write about, but I know you would like to know all about it, as I don't suppose you'll get much from the papers.

2 January 1916

The survivors' chief concern was the worry and distress of their people at home, as is evident from this undated letter to Nell.

Savoy Hotel,
Alexandria.

Darling Child, I've just got your gorgeous wire; I can't tell you how glad I am that you know definitely now that I am alive and well. I sent off that old cable as soon as we were landed, & I've been wondering & wondering if you saw anything in the papers before you got the cable. If so I'm afraid, dear, you must have had an awful shock, but never mind, old thing, it's all over now, I know. Darling girl, isn't it a blessing I managed to get away, though Heaven knows I never expected to. I was a long way the last to be picked up in our boat, & the others too as far as I could see, as we moved away just afterwards because we could see no one else in the water. Oh, it was awful, darling, & the whole time I was thinking of you and thanking God I hadn't got you with me. We are all agreed now that the Govt should not allow women & children to travel in these dangerous waters, unless it is absolutely essential or the boat is suitably escorted . . . I am sending you by a separate registered envelope an account of it. I'm afraid it's a poor account, but it has the merit of being first hand and true. But for heaven's sake don't let any paper get hold of it, as they would no doubt work up my poor bald statements into a blood & thunder yarn & make good 'copy' out of it. But I don't want that done. And will you please send it on to mother or have it typed and send her a copy, as I thought one account would do for you all, as you must be clamouring for one; I told mother I was sending it to you & you would send it on to her.

Oh Nell darling I have been thinking about you such a lot. Why can't I hear from you? But I'm afraid that's impossible, as I don't know how long we are going to be here, or anything. We have got no orders yet. When I think that I am one of 150 saved out of over 500 I wonder why & wonder why it all is. I had a struggle to save my life, but I suppose it was fore ordained that I was to be saved, so there it is. But I am saved, so dear dear child we can comfort ourselves with that & only hope & pray that the poor women & men who were drowned met their deaths painlessly & quickly; I know they met it bravely. You know how much I admire the women of England, don't you. Well, if possible I admire them more than ever now. They were just splendid in the boats, and the only first class lady passenger who was saved (Mrs Pen-Gaskell; she was in our boat) was absolutely wonderful, though her mother was missing. Isn't it just too awful to think of all those people who were a moment or two before alive & laughing & joking & a short 5 minutes later were all struggling for life & she already drowned.

I'm sorry, dear old lady, to harp so much on this one subject, but you will forgive me, won't you; I'm afraid the mental strain, now one can look back on the whole tragedy, is rather great, & one keeps on involuntarily recalling incidents.

We have been here two days now & have been busy buying some kit. Dear girl, I snatched up your miniature out of my cabin, & had that in my pocket. But of course it was ruined, though the *frame* is all right! I am sending it back to you. I also had your cigarette case in my pocket but that was done in too. You see ½ an hour in the sea water would ruin anything. Besides the above, & my pipe, also my watch which I was wearing (ruined of course) and my life, I saved nothing! All my little trinkets, silver cigarette case, flask & things in my attaché case, all gone! You see I was wearing my *best* khaki ashore at Malta (I had written you a long letter on leaving Malta, dear, to post at Port Said, but I'm afraid it's past posting now) & my cigarette case was in that. I used to wear my old green stuff with badges on the sleeve, you know, on board, so that's what I was wearing at the time. Everything else was lying about the cabin. Your little photograph in the green case, my little leather case with lucky beans & mascots in it; patience cards, everything, all gone to blazes! No real value, but a lot of sentimental value that can *never* be really replaced. Fancy that old box you & I packed, all gone down to the bottom of the Mediterranean! I have bought just the bare necessities of existence as I don't know what they will do with us now. I think they will send us out to India as soon as they can, but probably not for a week or two.

He goes on to describe the weather, 'Raining hard here, with intermittent thunderstorms & the streets are mostly flooded' and Alexandria itself, 'a much bigger place than I thought':

> Hundreds of soldiers everywhere, & the hotel full of staff officers & their wives. I fancy there's a good deal of 'At the Front' talking done there, some way from any front! Australian & New Zealand soldiers are here too, in their felt hats and look very smart. Motor cars & lorries everywhere, & any amount of nurses, ambulances, & I've seen a lot of V.A.D. uniforms too.

He lists the things he has bought 'to carry on with' but reverts again to the disaster:

> . . . Government will of course compensate us for our losses but there are some things that nothing can compensate for. You remember Capt Lyell on Charing X Station? He was saved, I *am* glad, for his girl's sake too. . . . I'll write some more of this later, darling, & send it off tomorrow –
>
> Jan 4th. I'll finish off this letter this morning, darling, and then go out & post it. The *Egyptian Gazette* has long accounts of the show this morning . . . I must try & send you a copy, though I expect the home papers have got it all in. Reuter's wires have been full of nothing but the *Persia* for the last few days . . . Dear Child, I *was* glad to get your cable last night; it relieved everyone too, because they all knew for certain that either our cables had arrived home or a list of survivors had been published. . . .
>
> The *Mallow* which picked us up did us most awfully well. They had cocoa & brandy for us all, & food of course. How pleased we were to be safe again! Everyone was sort of worked up & could hardly believe we had been rescued. The full sensation of the tragedy didn't strike us till now, & I think we all feel it more than ever . . . I know I had a fearful head that night, & one's nerves were all over the place & everyone jumped about 3 feet in the air whenever a door banged or anything! The *Mallow* is a little mine-sweeper, very fast, & specially built for anti-submarine warfare . . . The crew were awfully good to us and they swore by their skipper, a young lieutenant about Paul's age [27]: but they said he was awfully good & didn't care a damn what he did. . . . We came home at a tremendous pace, 15 or 16 knots, & she is only a little tiny boat so she fairly shook with the vibration. We got into Alexandria about 3 o'clock, having fairly eaten & drunk the poor old *Mallow* out of everything fresh on board. But that night an S.O.S. signal came in by wireless, so off she had to go again at 11 o'clock that same night with no fresh provisions, only biscuit & water! She was out 2 days, I don't know what after, but she found nothing. They couldn't get into communication with her for 24 hours, so we all thought something had happened, but she turned up all right eventually. Good

heavens, if the *Mallow* went down I believe I should cry! So always keep a warm corner for her in your heart, won't you, old girl; I know you will. They are the very finest fellows in the world, are the British Navy, & the Germans haven't got a chance as long as there are fellows like that against them.

He had sent his mother a one word cable – 'Saved' – and wrote to her briefly on 1 January.

Just a line to say I'm all right & landed safely. You have probably heard by now we were torpedoed & sank but some of us were saved . . . I don't know what we are going to do, but will write a full account later . . . I expect the censor will see this so I won't say much. Much love to all and *don't worry*. I cabled you today.

And again, at greater length, on the 3rd:

I hope you got my cablegram saying I had been saved from the poor old *Persia*. I sent it as soon as I possibly could . . .

Well, now it's all over I can only thank God I was saved. I went over the side into the water just before she sank, & was not picked up for about ½ an hour. But I'm right as rain now, though feeling the mental & physical strain somewhat. It was a terrible thing & I really think I have had enough of the war by land and sea . . .

He goes on to record his losses with a brief account of what happened:

It is too awful to think about. Poor Jack Lodwick is lost I'm afraid, & Col. Swiney, & we are only 11 officer survivors out of 30 or 40 [He is possibly referring to the losses in France as well as those from the *Persia*]. We landed here & are now staying in this hotel at the P & O's expense, of course . . . We are all awaiting orders. I expect they will send us on to India soonish: I am not keen on crossing the Mediterranean again just yet!

Don't worry about me. I'm quite all right now. Dolly Lyell & I are sharing a room here. He is very well. He was rescued in another boat & when he saw me he said he felt so relieved he didn't know what to do. I can't tell you how overjoyed I was to see him. Of course none of us knew who was saved & who wasn't until some hours later.

I hope poor old Nell wasn't too worried. I cabled them too, & of course, if they got my cable first,before the news, they must have wondered what I was raving about.

I suppose we shall get compensation for our kit. It *is* an expensive job, refitting entirely. Thank goodness I hadn't much on board, still one has collected several little treasures in the years gone by, & they are all gone! Also several things I had carried all through the campaign last winter in France & which I valued very highly in consequence. Never mind, I have got my life, & am more than content with having that. I will write again when I know what they are going to do with us.

However, he wrote before that, on the 7th.

I hear there is a mail going out tomorrow so I will just drop you a line to send by it, though in these days of submarines there seems to be a pretty good chance that it will never reach you. However, I'll risk it. We are still here as you see and have got no orders yet. All the ordinary passengers are going on to India on the 9th in the *Medina*, but they are evidently not sending us on her. In any case Dolly Lyell & I will in all probability rejoin the regiment which is at present at Ismalia on the Canal. . . .

As far as I know none of us men survivors are a penny the worse for our somewhat frightening experience & we are rapidly recovering physically & mentally. Sometimes I have awful daydreams about it & the whole thing comes back with a rush while one is driving or walking along, but otherwise I think my nerves are slowly but surely regaining their normal state of calm. . . .

Last night we dined the officers of the *Mallow*, our rescuers: awful nice chaps. The skipper, one Roberts, lived at Chobham & knows Guildford well & confesses to having been in love with Betty Neville once! So if any of the girls meet Betty they might tell her that a former flame of hers rescued us & we owe him much more than we ever can repay.

Alexandria
13 Jan 1916

Dear Mother,

Just a short note to say I am very fit & well. Dolly Lyell & I have practically completed our kit now & we leave here tomorrow for Suez & rejoin the regiment, which is about 8 miles from there. . . .

How weird it is having every blessed thing brand new from one's skin outwards! And I do hate new things so, and had got awful fond of a lot of old things I had before. It's an expensive job too, especially here, where the price of everything is ruinous. I think a Tommy's cooker might be useful out here, if the methylated would stand the heat: you might ask.

16 Janauary 1916

Dear Mother,

Just a scribble to say I have arrived safely with the regiment at last. We had to ride out on camels & horses & reached camp about 6 last night.

Everyone was very nice and pleased to see us again, & there were various congratulations on our escape. We are in a sort of grove of palm trees, an old Bedouin settlement, with a few old mud huts belonging to sheiks, one of which we use as a mess. Close by is the reputed spot where Moses struck the rock; at any rate there is a constant supply of water there which, strange to say, bubbles up in the highest part of the ground. Otherwise there is a sandy waste on all sides & two miles behind us lies the gulf of Suez, as brilliant blue streak, up & down which we see the tramps & liners going. A P & O outward bound passed by today so I expect she has landed some mails at Port Said, so I *may* get some letters from home tomorrow; I'm longing to hear as I haven't had any letters since I left!

However, when the letters began to arrive, they gave him some concern. He wrote to his mother on the 16th:

I got two letters from you this evening, one dated Jan 3rd and one 6th. I'm most frightfully sorry I was the cause of so much anxiety, it must have been awful for you. How often have I worked it out & worked it out & finally came to the conclusion that no news could have reached you till Sunday & that my cable *must* have reached you before as it was sent off about 4 p.m. on the Saturday. Then yesterday we got the *Observer* of Jan 2, with a very scanty lot of news about it, (but what there was was very pessimistic and alarming) but that on the whole bucked me up, because I deduced from that as there was little news in the Sunday paper there must have been less or none at all in Saturday's & so my cable must have got home in time. Then your letters came today – the first I have had since I left home & that settled the whole show. I *am* sorry about it all, I wish I could have wired earlier in the day but I'm afraid it was impossible.

How nice & kind everyone seems to have been & I hear dear little Babs came & sat with you all Saturday. *Do* thank her from me most awfully & say how frightfully I appreciate her ripping thoughtfulness; it was sweet of her & just what she would do.

Poor Nell; but I've had no letters from her yet. I suppose everything will go wrong for a bit & I shall get them all eventually.

I can't get over your letters, it's made me feel quite rotten in a way – it's brought it all back so vividly & made me feel fearfully sorry for you all at home. Don't listen to anything I say though about making me feel it all again, I was more delighted at getting your letters than over anything else for years. You must of got my account of it from old Nell now; I *do* wish I could get a letter from her, but perhaps I shall in a day or two.

Really people have been most awfully sweet in wiring & writing, they are most awfully good to us I must say. Yes, I know you would thank God in church about me, and thank you for doing so. I'm afraid churches are at a premium out here, though of course one does't need one on such occasions really.

I heard from Ben & Mrs Stack too this mail, but I expect there are heaps of letters knocking about somewhere.

I'm most awfully fit & well now, & have suffered no ill effects.

How splendid old Nell seems to have been; isn't she a little dear, so gorgeously self-possessed and calm. I am proud of her.

Goodnight, Mother, lots of love and apologies for all the anxiety. Best love to all,

from your loving son,
Ted

The careful Gertrude had noted on the envelope: 'Message to Babs'.

Naturally enough, in spite of the reassurances in that last letter, the sinking of the *Persia* continued to haunt him and he would suddenly revert to it, as in a letter of 31 January when, after writing about his possible return 'to the country we started out from (a roundabout way of putting it but there are censors about)' and 'a ripping little picture of Nell', he goes straight on in the same paragraph:

Jack Lodwick poor fellow was next to me on deck, directly after the torpedo struck. We were trying to shove our lifeboat clear of the ship's side as the boat was heeling rapidly over to port and ours was a starboard lifeboat. Of course it was useless & I never saw him again. But I know he was seen throwing chairs and tables overboard, to help people in the water and doubtless several people owe their lives to him accordingly. What happened to him I don't know, as she went down soon afterwards & I met no one who saw him in the water. In any case he was the coolest and bravest of men & died as game as anyone & I'm sure none of those who drowned suffered very much. I think he must have been taken down with the ship. Poor old Lodwick, a *great* friend of mine whose loss I shall ever deplore, and one of the very best that ever lived, both as a soldier and a gentleman.

He was also concerned by the publicity that his proud mother was giving to the event. In a letter dated 22 February he writes: 'I say, isn't that *Persia* letter of mine going the rounds rather a lot? Bee D[udman] seems to have shown it about all over the shop. Please don't, I only wrote it just to let you people know at home.' He had to accept the fact that his adventures were of interest locally – 'I got a Godlaming paper today with some trash about me in it' – but at least the family had their share: 'I was glad that some publicity was given to the fact that you have five sons serving but I draw the line at photographs!'

However he appreciates that his mother must feel some pride and concern, and in another letter, after saying once again, 'I say, I hope that *Persia* account has not become too much public property. My dear mother I did nothing at all really in the water: you all say too much,' he goes on: 'I enlose a letter from Calcutta which may interest you, but please don't let it go outside the family, will you. I wouldn't send it only I know it will please you to know that by a *very* simple act I have apparently brought pleasure into someone's life, but evidently she exaggerated her story a great deal or *he* wouldn't be so enthusiastic. Please send it on to Nell, will you, as I said I would let her have it; but please take the letter with a large pinch of salt.' This letter was one he mentions in his diary:

Thursday 3 February 1916

A belated mail, I got 30 letters! (including 9 bills and receipts). Letters from Nell (3), Bellows [Nell's sister] (2), Auntie [Nell's Aunt 'Dody'], Heather Hickie, Paul, Ruth, Rosamond, Mother (2), Mrs Bobby, Mrs Guy Mainwaring, Gladys [Nell's sister], Ben (2), Cruikshank, Jack [Nell's brother], Spider and one Bonnand of Calcutta who has married a Mlle Derogaz whom I knew on the *Persia*.

This could be called the understatement of the year and was not strictly true as he did not meet Mlle Derogaz until they were both in the water.

Although M. Bonnand wrote with heartfelt thanks that 'But for the marvellous manner in which you rescued her, at great risk of your own life, she would never have become my wife,' Ted dismissed his saving of a fellow passenger as 'a very simple matter; not worth the fuss that was made over it.' The Bonnands thought differently and Mme Bonnand, writing to thank him for a photograph of himself which he had sent at their request said: 'I have taken the liberty to write on it: "Captain Berryman who saved my life" – I hope you will not mind. I bought a beautiful silver frame, a frame worthy of the man, and have put your photo in a prominent place of my drawing room, upon my piano.'

His fellow officers were of their opinion and Fred Fox wrote to Ben:

I wonder if you have really heard the true yarn of the *Persia*, I don't fancy you have, so I am going to write it down here in just a few words. A certain officer after jumping overboard a few seconds before the ship sank saw a woman floating face downwards, and close inspection discovered she still had room for a few more pints of salt water, so he took compassion on her and towed her about for 20 minutes and eventually got into a boat about ½ a mile away – I daresay you can guess who it was and I feel quite sure you will feel very proud of a member of the family who can do a thing like that, anyhow, those of us who know about it, and there are not many I am sorry to say, recognise that the Huns haven't got much of a chance so long as we have lads like this to see the show through. It's no good asking Ted about it, as he will of course say it was nothing, or a lie, but I got most of it out of him by degrees & you can take it from me that he gave up 80 per cent of his chances of getting to that boat simply to save someone who he had never even seen before, because she was of your sex. It doesn't sound much here & I am afraid I am no good at descriptions but when it is a matter of everyone for themselves it takes a bit of doing.

Although it was the policy of the Garhwalis *not* to put in names for medals, on the grounds that the soldier concerned was only doing his duty, both the Colonel and Major Fred Lumb wrote to M. Bonnand, who replied: 'My wife and I appreciate greatly your suggestion that I should write to the secretary of the Royal Humane Society in London a short graphic account as to how my wife was heroically saved by Captain Berryman . . . who swam with my wife with one hand only, the other was occupied in holding her up for fully ten minutes.' He wrote as requested with the result that in due course Ted was presented with the Society's medal for saving life at sea.

The version that Ted was later to give to his children when they wanted to know why there was a solitary blue ribbon on the *right* breast of his uniform was different and even rather ungallant: 'Well, you see, she was so fat I thought she was bound to float and the safest thing to do would be to hang on to her!'

EGYPT 1916

Oddly enough, Dick was also on his way to India and on 15 January he wrote to his mother: 'Tomorrow we should be in Alex . . . I wonder if I shall see Ted, but I expect he will have gone by now. . . . The dog is very fit & popluar. I call her June.' This sounds as if the dog were a very new acquisition and from later references to 'Susan' – 'I expect [she] does enjoy a basket, very kind of you to give it to her' and to some puppies – 'It *was* good Ben selling that puppy' – we can assume that Dick had been ordered East in a hurry and had taken one of the litter with him, leaving the rest and their mother at the family dumping ground – Delaford. The family knew well that Gertrude did not like dogs – but these were Dick's!

He landed at Alex and found that Ted had 'gone off somewhere – Suez I suppose – No letters have arrived at Cox's . . . Everything is an awful muddle.'

The brothers did meet and Dick's lack of letters is explained. 'Those asses Cox' had sent them to Ted, who also banked with them, and this continued to happen to both of them in spite of repeated redirections and explanations; all part of the confusion of the war and the upset of the mails which they disliked so much and referred to so frequently. 'The English mail is late again this week,' Ted wrote on the 24th, 'not due till Wednesday. What a difference from France, where you got letters every day . . . but we mustn't grumble or we'll never finish off the show.'

They each reported home on the other. Dick wrote reassuringly, '[Ted] is very fit and seems none the worse. He seems to have had a good long swim & dragged that woman along with him! He hasn't a camp bed & slept on mine & enjoyed a very good sleep he said. Wasn't it nice being able to meet?' and Ted wrote by the same mail: 'I went over to Suez & saw Dick on Saturday & stayed the night with him . . . he was awfully fit & well. I was awfully glad to see him. June is in great form & was very fit.'

They obviously enjoyed their time together, going shopping and sending weekend cables at 3*d* a word to say that they had met. Dick paid a return visit to Ted who wrote enthusiastically:

Awful fun last week: Dick came over on Friday to stay the night, bringing June with him. She was in great form and was a great favourite with the mess. I think Dick enjoyed the visit though of course there is absolutely nothing to do here, but I'm glad he's had a chance to meet some of my pals in the regiment. He missed the boat back to Suez on Saturday so had to stay another night for which I was very glad. Just after he had gone a letter came for him from you, addressed from Cox, Alexandria. . . .

Dick had enjoyed it. At the end of one his staccato letters written on 2 February he says, 'Yes, I took those shirts & have sent them to Ted. I was over for two nights staying with him & enjoyed it awfully. Their camp is much nicer than ours, much cleaner & so nice having trees about. I went for a long ride all down by the Gulf and picked up some lovely shells that I must try & send you.'

It was at about this time that Jane and her friend Chubbie opened their cigarette shop in London, and both brothers expressed their concern. Ted wrote 'Yes, I hear Jinny has started her shop. I haven't the foggiest idea where it is or what it is or what sort of show it is, but I am inclined to agree with you & Ben that it doesn't seem hardly the job for her. However, as I say I know nothing about it, & only hope it is all right.'

Dick was not quite so disapproving. 'I hope Jane's cigarette business will be a success, but I trust they are giving her and Chubbie a commission as well as 30 *s*, if not they should bargain for one.' He is reassured by the fact that 'Paul seems to have arranged & scrutinised matters all right.'

In fact the business flourished. A later letter refers to '17 The Arcade' as a 'great rendezvous' – but this is just an example of the family's concern for one another and the responsibility the older brothers felt for their sisters and the younger boys. There is scarcely a letter from either Ted or Dick which does not mention Topher, now a Tommy in France with the Middlesex regiment, and the possibility of his getting leave. 'I do hope old Topher manages to wangle a few days leave, he certainly deserves it,' wrote Ted on 4 February, and Dick, 'glad that Topher is all right, after some scrapping', comments that 'Paul is lucky to get leave, I suppose he's glad to get the *Malaya*, it must be a good job as she's a big ship.' He was also glad to hear that Wiggs, Ben's fiancé had been home and had an idea for Jane before she took on her cigarette shop: 'I would suggest Jane goes on the stage, why doesn't she write to Evelyn & get her advice. She knows her address & it's quite a good profession!' Nothing came of this idea but Evelyn continued to crop up from time to time in Dick's letters. She was apparently the sister of a friend of his in Assam.

Meanwhile Ted was still suffering from mail going astray.

4 February 1916

Very many thanks for two letters from you both [herself and Ben] which have been to Bombay and back. I got no letters from Delaford by the last mail except one from Ben saying you had got my account of that show from Nell. I can't think what happens to all my letters, I got 21 in a bunch yesterday from India, England & all over the shop . . . I also got that letter case with the horseshoe in it; I was firmly convinced that had gone with my other treasures but I'm most fearfully glad I left it behind now.

In his next letter he admits that he might be inadvertently to blame for the confusion in his mail.

What a muddle I appear to have caused by all my various cables & letters! I cabled Nell rejoining 'here', meaning Egypt, not Alexandria as apparently everyone seems to have gathered from the cable. Of course I couldn't say exactly where they were, though I own that 'in Egypt' would have done better than 'here' & made things plainer. . . . However, I expect you know by now where I am!

In fact, after giving various addresses: 'The Garhwal Rifles, 20 *Indian* Inft Bde, 10th *Indian* Div, I.E.F"E", Egypt' and, of course, 'Cox's', he settled for 'The Garhwal Rifles, c/o India Office, Whitehall, London' as they get out here just as soon . . . and it doesn't matter where the regt goes, they reach me just the same, so it saves changing the address. Still I should ask the India Office when they should reach there so as to catch the weekly mail.

He seems to have been particularly unfortunate with regard to Nell's letters – 'No letters from Nell this week; isn't it sickening. I suppose they've gone to Kamskatka or Timbuctoo. Hopeless.' However he received a good many from friends and relations congratulating him on his escape, and parcels containing a varied assortment of things to replace his possessions lost in the *Persia*. He writes at various times to thank his mother for 'that ripping flask you sent . . . it's very much admired and envied by all my friends', and later, 'thank you most awfully for the ripping parcel I got today. Everything in it was just lovely. The attaché case is too priceless & exactly the right size & shape an' all. Tommy's cooker, kettle & refills all arrived safely & are most welcome. The little packet of nail scissors etc just the thing and the writing pad & pencils extremely welcome.'

He also received 'a ripping wrist watch . . . but with nothing to who it was from. Anyhow whoever sent it, it's a gorgeous watch. I

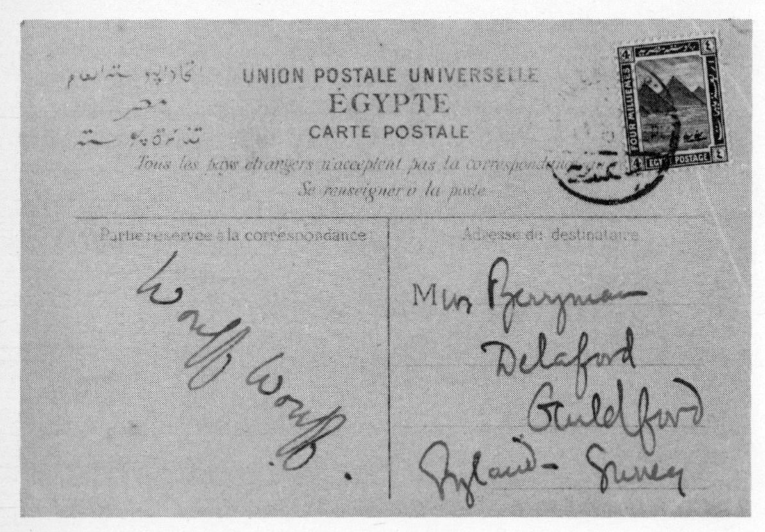

Postcard from Dick to Gertrude, 1916

am spoilt with all these ripping presents I get, really people *are* good to me.'

After a further complaint about the mysterious dearth of Nell's letters – she wrote to him every day – 'No letters from Nell, isn't it weird, her letters always seem to go astray . . . it's sickening to expect letters & then get none', things look up and the mystery of the watch is explained. Just before re-embarking for India he got two lovely parcels from her and several letters – 'It was she who sent me the lovely watch; wasn't it ripping of her; too sweet I think; I am a lucky person to have so many people who are so ripping to me.'

This does not, of course, prevent him from asking Gertrude to send him things. Soon after he had rejoined the regiment he asked for 'a dozen rolls of film for a "vest pocket Kodak autograph pattern" as I have bought one off a chap out here, but can't buy any films for love or money in Egypt. Bunchie has my other camera still, but I fancy Dick has that, or has asked her to send it to him. Please send me a packet of china tea (we get such muck here) some chocolates (Nobby Clarke suggested these!) & a cake is never unwelcome, in fact I haven't seen one since I left home! Also a tube or two of Swan Fountain Pen Tabloids.'

Dick also had his requests to make. Having bought a collar and some ribbon for June he asks Gertrude to send him a round collar for her 'as I am sure I cannot get one out East.'

In fact he was trying to arrange a transfer to enable him to stay in Egypt. He wrote to Gertrude on 12 February (after saying in a previous letter from Cairo where he had had three days leave, 'I'd like to be stationed here'):

I am probably leaving the hospital for a field ambulance. It's not absolutely settled yet but I will cable you about a new address. . . . I was over at Ted's yesterday seeing about my transfer. I saw Ted & his pals. Ted seems quite cheery & very fit & I hope to see him again soon. I hope Jane & Chubbie have found a good place to live in London. I am glad Topher is all right. I heard from Evelyn the other day, she *has* been a success in her show at Wigan. She sent me some cuttings & the people there seem to have been dotty over her. When you get my cable or any news of a change tell Jane to write & tell her will you.

At first it seemed that he would be successful. Ted wrote 'Dick was here for an hour or two this last week, trying to work an exchange into a field ambulance. I hear by a roundabout way that he's managed it, but I don't think he's actually joined up yet', but ten days later he was writing 'So glad Dick enjoyed himself. I hear he has sailed for India in a hospital ship, but have heard nothing definite from him. He bought me a bed in Cairo & sent it across but it was never found this side of the Canal, so I don't know what happened to it. I have had several searches & so did lots of people but we never found it.'

The rumour that Dick had sailed for India turned out to be correct although there had evidently been a certain amount of confusion over his departure.

British India Steam Nav. Co. Ltd.,
T.S.S. *Neuralia*.
3 March 1916

Dear Mother,

I suppose you think I'm dotty. All those cables. But at the last [minute] that F.A. stunt was washed out, so I had to come on here. Only the waterproof has arrived. No boots or distemper pills. June is a dear, tell Ben. Frightfully fond of me and can beg perfectly now!

Ted will be coming out soon. We are due in Bombay tomorrow & we've heard no news since we left Egypt, so goodness knows what may have happened, for all we know peace may be declared. I hope there will be some letters for me at Cox in spite of all the muddles.

Karachi
9 March 1916

Arrived here yesterday. Hot as blazes. Very many thanks for your letter & 2 of Ben's at Cox in Bombay . . . I expect your next lot went to Suez after my cable. But I had arranged an exchange & was stopping on when the blighter I had changed with cried off. . . . Write to me c/o Cox Karachi.

Ted was indeed on his way out to 'some destination in the East, probably the same place I started out from' and, possibly thinking of the long gap in news that a three week voyage entailed, had made several comments on the war and family news before he left.

Paul's lucky getting such a nice wack of leave. I'm awfully glad though as he really has had so little during the war & certainly deserved some. His new ship seems to be the complete buzz.

Yes, I saw the Zepps had been lively again: it seems strange we can't give them a warmer reception. I see 'planes have been over Ramsgate & Broadstairs too, I hope Ruth's all right, but they don't seem to have done much damage.

Ruth, nursing at Broadstairs, had had the excitement of seeing the planes come over, but, as Ted said, they had not done much damage. He had had a letter

. . . from Jinny who seem mighty pleased with her new job. Not many customers as yet but I suppose it will take time . . . I should *hate* it myself but she seems to enjoy it which is a good thing.

Fancy Wiggy being a temp. captain. Heavens how these new armies *do* get promotion. I've no doubt they deserve it but it's rather bad luck on us regulars isn't it. We haven't had a single officer promoted – except in the ordinary course of events, as if it were peace – since the war began.

So glad old Topher's keeping fit & unhit through all that bombardment. Did he ever get his second Christmas hamper I wonder. What a lot of people seem to have written to you about me. Only I don't know a lot of them to speak to, and I assure you I've *never* heard of *quite* half of them!

So awfully glad to hear Jim is looking so fit, & I do hope he is now quite well again. Topher must have been having a rotten time lately poor chap. How I sympathise with him. I do hope & pray he comes through this all right. There seems to be a lot going on everywhere now & the Russians seem to be helping our Baghdad campaign a lot. What splendid fighters they must be! We owe them a lot in this war.

Yes, I am afraid taxes will be heavy after this war. I don't think I've chosen a very good time to get engaged! Never mind, Nell is such a dear that I would do anything for her.

Like Dick, he wrote again at the end of a 'very monotonous voyage', wondering what had happened while they had been at sea.

S.S. *Muttra.*
9 March 1916

This is a beastly dirty little tub; all the officers accommodation is aft, so we get all the smuts & dirt all blown back on to us, & I don't think any of us have felt really clean since we started. She is only a very small boat & the men are rather like the proverbial sardines, but seem quite happy . . . doubtless the prospect of getting near their own country has something to do with it.

We haven't the foggiest idea what's going to happen to us on landing . . . I certainly hope we stop in Bombay a day or two . . . Dick left Suez in a hospital ship just ahead of us . . . there's a good chance of seeing him.

Tomorrow, 10th, is the anniversary of Neuve Chapelle. What a lot of water has flowed under London Bridge since then, & what a lot of things have happened. Having been all this time at sea & having no wireless on this rotten old tub, we have of course had no news . . . since 28 Feb! We left during rather a critical period on the Western Front, the big German offensive in Verdun, & we are of course fearfully keen to know how things have been going. And any fortnight during the war is bound to have something big happening in it.

And in a P.S. 'I do hope old Topher's all right. The eau de cologne you sent me has been a perfect Godsend on board. The cake was much appreciated. Also the China tea.'

And so, eighteen months after they had left for the war in Europe both Dick and Ted were back in different parts of India, for the time being.

INDIA, SPRING 1916

Ted's hopes 'for a day or 2 in Bombay' were not realized as they disembarked on 12 March straight into the train to Kohdwara, the railhead two marches from Lansdowne, so he would not have been able to meet Dick in any case. On the 20th he managed to find time to write a long letter to his mother.

Thanks most awfully for 2 letters from you, which I got yesterday. The mail turned up 2 days ago as a matter of fact but they had done up all our letters in little packets, & everyone was so busy here that they were chucked on one side, thinking they were papers etc. for the men, till somebody opened one & out fell a lot of mail letters! I got 15 altogether, including 5 from Nell.

I must tell you about our various receptions. We had a great one at Agra, all the civil & military population crowded on to the station, & the men were all drawn up in a line & a great speech was made, extolling our exploits & generally laying it on pretty thick. We were there 2 or 3 hours & it was frightfully hot, so we were all quite ready to drive off to the club afterwards where a huge lunch was served. Nice cool drinks & general festivities. You see Agra is the first city we came to in the U.P. [United Provinces] so they saw fit to give us this welcome. I must say it was very gratifying & I think a good thing as it showed the men that at any rate their efforts & sacrifices were very much appreciated. We then got into the train again & came on. At the station where we got out we had another reception, more speech making by the big bugs of Garhwal and a jolly good firework display in the evening. The people were very enthusiastic & gave us a right royal welcome. The general gaiety was somewhat marred by one of our men who shot himself during the night. He had been flogged early in the war for sleeping on his post when a sentry, and he evidently couldn't or wouldn't face his friends & relations on his return home so chose to commit suicide.

We marched up to Lansdowne next day & got yet another reception! All the station turned out, bands, breakfasts & everything en route, & an address on arrival & a big lunch in our mess afterwards. There are quite a lot of people here really, considering, so they made quite a good show. It's very sad to think how few of those who started out have come back, & I'm afraid there are some big gaps in the officers' ranks. Only 6 of us have come back out of about 26 who started; not all killed, of course, some have got jobs or gone sick, but the majority will never return I'm afraid. I suppose these things must be and indeed the name the Garhwalis have made has been dearly paid for, so we who are left have a special mission in life to see that . . . the name & fame they helped to bring Garhwal are never forgotten. . . .

I'm living in Lyell's bungalow, where Ben & I lived in 1914, & everything is brought back very vividly in consequence. We *did* have good times then, & I realise more than ever now what a perfect blessing it was having old Ben out here & what perfect times those were. I don't think I ever thanked her enough for all she was & did then. . . .

We have been divided up into two battalions again but whether they have anything up their sleeves for us I don't know . . .

I haven't heard from Dick at all; I wonder where he's got to . . .

Dick, of course, was in Karachi but characteristically making plans to be somewhere else. He wrote to Gertrude on 17 March to say 'we are opening a hospital for people from Mespot. I expect we individuals may have to go there to replace men who have been there some time. I shan't mind going, but I will never believe I've got to go until I get there.'

He is rather annoyed by the fact that they are allowed to wear mufti so he has had to buy some – 'Isn't it rot with all that stuff at home!' He also wishes he had brought out a car as he has had to hire a motorbike to get about on. Obviously answering a letter of hers he continues: 'Ted didn't tell me much about that woman he saved. She was crying out I'm dead I'm dead and Ted said no you aren't and dragged her along. I'm sure he ought to have a medal. Yes, it must be lonely at home. I expect you are glad of the dogs to keep you company!'

23 March 1916

. . . No mail this week but I daresay a letter will come Saturday . . . I have sent that gold watch home by a man who is sailing shortly, can't think why I ever brought it out. Hope it arrives safe. No more now.

His letter on the 30th was longer but in the same jerky style, as much answering hers as anything.

Fancy Moss turning up, he is a nice man & a great friend of mine in Assam, and of course you remember how I went to Northampton to see his sister Evelyn! Jane has written to me & told me he had been to see them, & had been awfully kind to them. They seem quite comfortable in their shop . . .

There is tons of fighting now isn't there, but we don't get much news. I hope Topher has had some leave & is having a good time at home. I wonder if Rosamond will like the farm as much as London, has she tried it before?

I am glad the puppies have good homes now. June is very well & quite happy & very popular with everyone. . . . I haven't got the pills yet, or the boots. . . . You seem to have had a muddle over Aquascutum! Did you look up the advertisement in the end!

I have written to the authorities & told them this is not at all what I want, & I am now exactly in a similar position to what I was in before the war, only drawing less pay! Would they kindly transfer me to a sphere of a more active nature . . .

Karachi
6 April 1916

Many thanks for your letter (March 5th) . . .

The snow at home has been awful by all accounts. I am glad France does Jim no harm, he only takes drafts over, doesn't he. . . . The Zep raids were awful, weren't they, but I suppose everyone was awfully pleased they shot that one down in the Thames. . . . Topher seems to have had a rotten time, I do hope he found his pack. . . .

Then, either referring to a photograph or a description from Gertrude, he inquires, 'Why Jim in gaiters & spurs? Where's his horse?' and goes on to say that he is riding again and has 'a mount or two' in the races in the following week and ends the letter in his usual disjointed fashion:

Evelyn tells me you sent her a postcard saying I had gone to Bombay. Many thanks.

I've heard nothing yet so far about my application for a move.

Best love to all
your loving son,
Richard

I had a photograph taken here. You shall see my moustache. Please send a big photograph to Mrs H.C. Laws, Dumduma, PO. Upper Assam.

and on the envelope: 'Please send a photograph to Mrs A. Grey . . . Eastbourne.'

Ted was fretting in Lansdowne. 'I feel an awful *slacker*' he had written in a letter on 15 March, just after they had returned, 'while all the others are fighting etc . . . but one simply has to do what one is told. Being adjutant I *must* stick to the regiment as there is such heaps of work to do after a campaign like this.' He consoles himself with the thought that 'you & all at home need not have any anxiety for me at the present at any rate' but on 7 April he writes despondently: 'I'm afraid I've got most awfully behindhand with my correspondence, I never seem able to deal with any. I get out of the office so late and absolutely brain weary that I don't feel inclined to do anything & certainly not in the writing line. How I hate it all but I'm afraid it's got to be done.'

The thought of Nell cheers him up.

I've had an enlargement made of that little photograph of Nell, the last one she had taken, with her hair up. It looks perfectly sweet and it is the only big one I've got of her. Everyone seems to have heard of her up here anyhow lots of people have said to me they've heard she's very pretty and nice in every way, & people to whom I've shown her photograph are always quite overcome . . . What an awful time poor old Topher has had, it's a shame he can't get any leave, but I suppose there are big things just coming off so they simply can't spare anyone. . . .

I have begun sleeping on the verandah, it's gorgeous; but this won't appeal much to you at home with your snow & blizzards, will it! I do hope some real spring weather has begun now – how the troops in France must have suffered. . . .

Excuse a hasty scrawl Mother and tell the others I'll try & write next week; I'm most awfully sorry about it but I simply can't cope with the situation. I'm very fit & well & going strong,

14 April 1916

Dear mother, many thanks for your letter of March 15th. We got an English mail very unexpectedly last Sunday, they still seem very erratic. . . .

Then probably in reply to something she had written about Topher's lost pack (we never know if he found it):

We do indeed seem to be losing our kits rather frequently. I heard from the India Office & they say the whole question of compensation for kit lost in the *Persia* is 'under consideration' so I suppose we shall get something out of them eventually.

Never mind about the camera [the one he had had to send back from France in 1915 and which seems to have been at one time with their friend Bunchie and at one time with Dick], keep it till I get home again: meanwhile I've got one to go on with & all those films you sent me too. . . . By the way, please let me know how much the films cost, & the attaché case, also the notebook Ben sent & send the price along. . . .

So glad Topher is optimistic about the war; he ought to be in contact with current rumour certainly; anyhow it shows the right spirit is abroad in the army. What terrible fighting there is going on round Verdun. It's ghastly to think of all those literal heaps of dead men; of course from the Allies point of view nothing could be more favourable but it all seems such a useless waste of life somehow. . . .

Yes, I get cheery letters from Jinny; she seems very pleased with her job. Nell too writes very happily . . . So glad to hear Ruth is getting her job at Guys; and I expect she'll be glad to get away from Broadstairs & sea planes & things. . . . I heard from Dick a day or two ago; he seems rather bored, but his motor bike should keep him occupied.

Dick had his racing to keep him busy as well.

Karachi
14 April 1916

. . . We had the races on Monday & yesterday. It's difficult to get a mount here as too many 'pro' jockeys come up . . . however I've had a couple & rode a winner yesterday. It wasn't my fault I got a bad start, the starter shouted & frightened my horse . . . and he had turned clean round before I could stop him. Luckily I got him away at once & caught up the others very soon. I didn't hurt myself when I fell off the first day, my fault for not seeing the saddle was properly put on. I'm sure you would have loved to have been there!

Best love to all,
your loving son, Richard

Tell Topher I think I'm quite a good hurdler racer, I've not done much before.

Karachi
19 April 1916

Many thanks for your letter. The *Sussex* sinking seems to have upset a good many letters . . . anyhow yours arrived . . . There's no one else to send a photograph to yet. Did I say Mrs Laws, Ben's friend in Assam – she wants one! I don't want them out here.

Ted had not been so lucky.

Lansdowne
19 April 1916

I'm afraid this week's mail must have been lost in the *Sussex* as none of us who have just come back here have got any letters. Isn't it a shame. One sort of hopes one's own letters would roll up all right.

We are still very busy here; I have a little less office work thank goodness, but I have lots of parade work, which I like far better & it's out of doors anyhow which is a blessing. . . . I wonder what they are going to do with us eventually & if they're going to keep us up here now.

I haven't heard from Dick lately, I wonder if he will be able to get an exchange into something he likes better. . . . Has old Nell been able to get up to Guildford yet? She said you had asked her but she couldn't go. I do hope she manages it soon; she's such an awful dear & I want you to get to know her frightfully well. . . . Any news of Paul & Topher? I do hope the latter is having an easier time now.

Lansdowne
27 April 1916

Rather curious this week, we got 2 mails, 2 days running, it was very nice especially as we had gone for a fortnight without mails owing to the *Sussex* show. . . . I got nine letters from Nell in 2 days! I also got the Pink papers all correct & the weekly *Times*, thanks very much. Yes, aren't the French magnificent at Verdun, and all the time our so called ministers are squabbling about conscription. Disgraceful isn't it – what must our allies think, who are putting all their strength into the war & we are still debating whether we are to or not. So glad Jim has got his second star, it will buck him up. . . . Any chance of his getting to France soon? And old Topher coming home on leave is ripping of course, it's quite time he did.

Dick's mails were also erratic.

Karachi
28 April 1916

I've had 3 letters from you one after the other, mails all funny I suppose. . . . You might tell the Aquascutum people that my coat has arrived. Goodness knows where the boots are. . . . You know I have the pills by now, but thank goodness June keeps very fit (tap wood) & everyone begs me to leave her with them if I go. Popular at all?

I'm so glad Jim has his second star, I must drop him a line. I think I'll see if I cannot get my third now. I ought to easily.

I wonder if you've had Topher home lately. I hope so & I hope he had plenty of money to have a good time. I wonder what Paul's rank is. Ted says your mail to him was evidently lost in the *Sussex*, but mine were all right. Luckily I sent your letter to me to Ted, so he got some news. We correspond quite frequently nowadays. . . .

We are just going to get patients in now. As a matter of fact the hospital is only just ready, it's been a business getting everything shipshape.

Ted was still harping on the mails when he wrote on 11 May:

How erratic the mails are these days to be sure, as after going a fortnight without one we get 2 again this week, another being due today. . . . I had some nice long letters from Nell, who seems very fit & is working hard at the Gloucester V.A.D. hospital 3 days a week, a very good thing too, I think, & I'm most awfully glad she's doing it. . . . I think Bunchie was the other person to whom I wanted you to send a photograph. I must send you the money for the other ½ doz I asked you to get last week. I hope to hear today that Topher managed to get his leave all right. He deserves a whack if anyone does. . . . I had a nice long letter from Ben last mail. She said the East called her a lot these days & seems to be getting on well with her job of addressing by machinery! Yes, it's a sad place now is Lansdowne, a shadow of its former cheery self, so many gaps & so many new faces, which one almost resents, they seem almost to be trespassing. The sadness is tempered somewhat by pride in having given so many of our best & bravest from so small a population. Things are settling down more or less now, & I've not *quite* so much work, still I'm always pretty doggo by the end of the day.

Lansdowne
12 May 1916

I heard from Nell yesterday, & she was delighted at the prospect of going to stay at Delaford . . . I'm longing to hear how she got on, both from you & her. I hope she was nice & behaved herself!

It appears that Topher's hopes of leave had been dashed again: 'What awful bad luck Topher not being able to get home. . . . Poor boy, I do hope he gets his leave soonish as he must be wanting some badly.'

As a soldier he has some pretty cutting things to say about the politicians at home.

It absolutely beats me how the Government hangs on, it's only the loyalty of the people that prevents them getting up & having the whole lot out of it for a set of incompetent muddle-headed self-seeking curs. . . . How Germany must laugh at us, & what a show we are making before the allies who are putting every man into the field with not the slightest hesitation.

What a terrible show that Irish business was; why can't they hang that beast Casement straight off for high treason; surely a trial in the case of a man like that is a mere farce & quite unnecessary. He's a self-proved traitor, caught absolutely red handed, & should be shot or hanged without ceremony . . .

And with a sudden change of feeling:

Gorgeous & fresh on parade this morning & there is a lovely clear view of the Snows today, a thing we haven't seen since we've been back as it's been so hazy.

Dick, having reported earlier the arrival of the boots, wrote briefly on the same date. He nearly missed the mail.

I expect to hear next mail that the gold watch has arrived. I expect that wretched book is in my dispatch box which is locked & I have the key!

It is bad luck on Topher his leave being stopped. I hope the girls and all got home for that weekend.

I got the *Cordwalles Chronicle* all right. Most interesting & I also got a letter from Paul. Thank him when you write.

Jane also wrote saying she had seen Evelyn.

We are getting wounded in now & expect some from Kut soon.

Best love to all, sorry it's so short a letter but I've left it so late.

A week later he writes: 'We've had some of the people in who were wounded & shot up in Kut. Very thin and dilapidated poor things. . . . I wonder if poor Topher ever got any leave after all. I shall hope to hear how the Easter party went off in your next letter.'

Ted, too, was eager for news from home.

Lansdowne
18 May 1916

I am longing to get the next mail as it should tell me about Nell & her stay at Delaford. She was hugely delighted at the prospect when she last wrote. I do think it's bad luck on old Topher not being able to get away on leave; every letter you write seemed to say he was on the point of starting but was stopped at the last minute. He certainly ought to come home for a bit now.

Dick, in his next letter, was still puzzled by the non-appearance of the gold watch, 'those people should have arrived by the time you wrote', and had comments to make on home news: '. . . I wonder if Jim has got to the front yet, anyhow it's nice to know he's a useful officer & can't be spared. . . . Has Susan's nose turned pink then, it was quite black. What a shame it is Topher getting no leave yet, I hope he gets home soon. I am so sorry the dove is dead, I shall miss it when I get home again.' He ends with a particularly Ricardian request: 'Send me my photographs of Nan, Cicely, Bunchie & Sybil.'

By the time he next wrote Ted had evidently received his longed-for account of Nell's visit to Guildford.

Lansdowne
26 May 1916

So glad dear old Nell had such good times at Delaford & that you all liked her so – I hear from you all and you all say such ripping things about her that I don't know how to thank you enough. She is rather a dear, isn't she.

Poor old Topher, it is bad luck on him about his leave; it surely is time they gave everyone a whack of leave now.

How's Specs these days? and how does he like conscription! I suppose he's been roped in with the rest of them. Few good things have been done by the Government since the war began & this is certainly one of the best of them. . . . Yes, Kut was bad luck & *such* bad management. However it's no good criticizing an effete and dispicable system; I fancy the British public will not stand much more of this, & then the politicians will stew in their own juice.

Dick also reported that 'I hear we ought to have been in Kut if it had not been for some foolish mistake. But you never know.' Apparently there was still no news of his gold watch but he did not seem unduly concerned.

Karachi
2 June 1916

I think that man must have run off with my watch! Hasn't it turned up yet? What a shame it is Topher doesn't get leave, I hope he has had it by this time. Bad luck Ben not being able to get away, now Wiggs is home. Yes, I do hope they hurry up and shoot Casement. Many thanks for the message from Susan. June sends hers to all.

Ted wrote by the same mail. It is good to know that they do pay for some of the postage on the things they ask for:

I have told Cox Bombay to send you £4 for all the odds & ends you sent, many thanks for all the trouble you took & I hope the money turns up in due course. How sporting of old Fielding to send you a cask of cider; I expect they'll be asking you to go down & stay there before long; I hope you will be able to manage it.

I haven't heard from Dick for a long time, but I wrote yesterday. I was thinking of getting a few days leave & going to stay there . . . yes, I certainly said he could have the camera; I have got a little vest pocket Kodak which does me quite well.

Poor old Topher, I do hope he's got a bit of leave by now. Yes, Jim certainly might keep you informed of his movements! I wonder if he's gone out yet, as he has been more or less on the point of going these last few days hasn't he. So glad old Wiggs managed to get home; awful glad for Ben's sake; she said his nerves were all wrong, so I've no doubt a few days at home did him no end of good. . . .

So you're saving daylight! Splendid I think & thoroughly practical; I wonder if it will carry on after the war. I don't fancy India will worry its head much about that sort of thing.

I do hope you managed to get away for your weekend with Mr Hunt; I shall be very anxious to hear how you got on and how he is these days.

Charles Hunt was an old college friend of their father's and a former headmaster of their prep school, Cordwalles. Gertrude appears to have an exciting time. Ted wrote on 15 June 'My *dear* mother, what adventures you have had with Mr Hunt; that taxi wheel coming off might have been much worse; how lucky you didn't turn right over in the ditch. His vicarage sounds lovely & I am glad he was so pleasant.' Dick's reaction was more light-hearted: 'You did have adventures going down to Mr Hunt's, that wheel coming off must have been funny, his place sounds awfully nice. I always like the idea of old country vicarages.' There is something rather nostalgic about this; Dick had, of course, grown up in similar parsonages.

At this time he made one of the oddest and most difficult 'please send' requests of the war.

Karachi
9 June 1916

. . . You might send me (don't get excited or flurried about it) my ventriloquist doll as there are crowds of kids here and I'd like to amuse 'em one afternoon. Stick him in a strongish box & send it by mail. I expect the man in that express luggage shop near the station will tell you the best way, or write to the Eastern Express Co (can't find address) they are as good as anyone & they have a depôt in Karachi. Put in the box too, some of those white shirts of mine with R.B. on the front and also my blue uniform. . . . Ask Jane to send me some new songs if there are any. There is some money of mine still knocking about. She has some anyhow.

He continued to write about his watch: 'That man never sent my watch yet. Hope he hasn't run away with it! Trust he has only forgotten', and rather wistfully about Evelyn who had apparently written to tell him that she had been to tea at Delaford:

. . . I am so glad you like her.

It is dreadful about Kitchener. We heard the day after; I wonder what everyone at home thinks about it. . . . It is very hot here. Always is they say before the monsoon breaks. Ted says he may be able to get down here next month. I've told him we'll be delighted to see him. . . .

Did Evelyn sing the other Sunday, doesn't she sing well? She liked you awfully.

Ted was more affected than Dick by the news of Kitchener's death. By the same mail he wrote:

Please excuse a rotten letter, but we have just heard of the tragedy of Kitchener's death in the *Hampshire* with the whole of his staff. It seems to have completely knocked us all over here; personally I feel very much the same as I did when I first heard about the *Titanic*. Isn't it ghastly? the one bright figure, the one proved patriot gone. The creator of England's mighy army that has done & is going to do so much. . . . why couldn't he live just long enough to see his life's work – for so I think we can call K1 & K2 & all the rest of them, however many there may be – crowned with success.

What a full week this has been. The big naval fight, of course, occupied all our thoughts at the beginning of the week: a magnificent show wasn't it, despite our heavy losses, for it seems as if we fought against tremendous odds at first. I can't quite make out how long the *Malaya* was there . . . at any rate she seems to have had her baptism of fire & I do hope old Paul's all right.

Ted wrote wistfully on 22 June:

I wish we could hear some more news about the naval battle; we heard a good deal at first, but since then things have been very quiet and we are all anxiously waiting Jellicoe's full report. . . . What a splendid victory it was & how proud you must be that Paul took part in it. I don't suppose he's been able to tell you much about it as yet.

JUTLAND

Ted's concern must have been to a certain extent assuaged by a six page letter from Paul dated 21 June 1916:

Dear Ted,

I have been trying to get a letter off to you for ages now, but have never succeeded somehow, but I am going to settle down to it now. It was *damned* good of you to send me that cable – in fact I was more pleased with that than anything else – *really* – 'cos the amount of bluddy boofaced pessimists there are knocking about after our stunt simply make me sick. God! they were awful. You know what the B.P. are – & the damn press criticizing the various officers an' all – what the hell does a bloke fugging in an office know about tactics & things like that – yet they sit down & write a lot of bosh which of course is read by the B.P. I'll just give you an extract from the *Aberdeen Free Press*:

> 'Owing to the undoubtedly crushing defeat which the Navy has suffered off the coast of Jutland . . . our faith in the British Navy – "as the sure shield and defence of our Empire" – has been shattered once & for all to dust & ashes.'

Can you imagine anyone writing like that. This fellow as a matter of fact was arrested shortly afterwards – but let off – I should have tortured him.

> *Daily News* '. . . Defeat in the Jutland engagement must be admitted . . . But in face of yesterday's news the demand for the return of Lord Fisher to effective control of the Navy must again become insistent.'

The only paper who really did well was the *Morning Post* – which I am sending to you – *priceless* it was – especially the leading articles – s'matter of fact they were hard to buy during the day which is something in the B.P.'s favour. I am also sending you some other papers & enclosed is off the back of the Daily Mail – Just like those bluddy Yanks.

About the action – somehow when we were out, units – like myself – had no idea the Huns were out at all – in fact we were doing what is known as a 'dummy run' on our own Battle Cruisers – you just raining & laying the guns etc – when I suddenly saw them open fire & then splashes falling round them, Coo! I said – We're off – and in the next five minutes my turret was firing at the Huns. It put the fear of God into you at first to see these bluddy great shells falling all round – & the light was so bad for us – you could only see them very indistinctly – but still we all blazed away merrily & one could see hits on them now & again. The bluddy awful sight was seeing our ships going up & steaming over the place about 5 mins afterwards – and seeing *nothing* but a few bits of wreckage and a man or two – poor devils – We were all in the thick of it for about 2 or 2½ hours and giving just as much as we took – and we were at a devil of a disadvantage on account of the light. Then the Hun B.C.'s took us into the High Sea fleet – & then there was trouble – but their shooting got frightfully erratic & they must have wasted 1000's of rounds – there was a bluddy tornado of splashes all round us – I should think at least 5 or 6 Huns were concentrating – Still we weren't hit more than 8 times – of course all this time no Jellicoe as yet – until I had it passed through my turret – 'the Grand Fleet is deploying into action' – God – you can imagine my relief! – the most priceless sight I've ever seen – then they opened fire – only for about 20 mins though & the Huns got cold feet – their firing went to Hell & they turned & off out of it with the whole of us after 'em. Then it became mistier & dark – time about 11 p.m. & I never want to go through a night like that again – the most ghastly scene you can imagine those destroyer attacks – our destroyers on their Fleet, but it was so damn hard to tell what was happening – except you could see these frightful flashes & *noise* going on & then a whole ship go ↑. They were bluddy fine our MBD's that night, we didn't fire at all – it is not a thing that is encouraged i.e. big ship actions at night – the reasons being obvious – and next morning we somehow lost touch with them – they had gone in – because they hadn't very far to go – and naturally they know where their minefields are more accurately then we do – so we steamed up and down over the scene of action for about 8 hours – but nothing more was seen – I daren't tell you any details because I am certain they would be censored – but I can tell you it's practically certain we got 5 of their capital ships – i.e. Battleships & 2 B.C.'s – at least ½ a dozen light cruisers – & they haven't many of them either – & 20 destroyers. Then there [are] several who must be badly damaged – We could see that for ourselves.

The great thing seems to be that the Huns obviously get cold feet when they are fired at – or else they had no ammunition left – & they don't seem to have the guts either – And the opinion seems to be that they would not come out again in a hurry – I don't think they expected anything that time – but they were caught.

Of course I've lost heaps of pals – but that's the way they all wanted to die! – so . . . ! It was a nasty jar about K[itchener] & of course there are heaps of rumours about spies etc – but I think that's impossible – besides it was much too rough for a submarine – even his destroyer escort had to go back on account of the weather – That little fellow Stewart who was in the *Gloucester* with me was in the *Hampshire*. He was the navigator.

Comic things happened when the sailors of different ships went on leave after the action. In several places they got boo-ed and at a certain place the soldiers turned their backs on them – in fact there were damn nigh some riots – and it is supposed to be a fact and I quite believe it that two men – the pink-faced pessimist type – have been killed by bluejackets ashore – just taken aside & flopped out. When we went on leave the following Monday there were boo faces down to about Edinburgh – & then things began to liven up a bit – It's awfully hard to say whether Balfour was right in publishing what he did so early – but then until Jellicoe had seen everybody – Destroyer Captains etc – he couldn't possibly tell how many had gone – & the B.P. are always asking for the truth about our losses – & they were told straight out. The Huns were bluddy marvellous – they had our losses – naming the ships too – in their papers on Thursday evening – God knows how they knew – They had the *Warspite* wrong though.

Well they gave us some leave – I got 4 whole days at home – too damn short really, but I managed to see most people I think – making Jane's shop and the Club my H.Q.s. I went home on the Monday night to dinner & went to town next day till Thursday night. I saw *all* the 5 super priceless sisters & on Thursday night we had the usual family party at a Box – 'Mr Manhattan' this time – 5 sisters, Jim, myself, James, Chubbie & Sheina Kellie – of whom you have doubtless heard. The missing link was Nancy, & no one can make out why she was not there. I lived at the rate of about £2000 a year at that time and Stilwell had to come up to scratch again – which he did very nobly – but I find it damn hard to save any money you know. I do save some – but then I blow it and *more* during any leave I get – naturally – & have nothing to show for it – but I wouldn't stint myself for the world – taking any of those sisters out anywhere & giving them a good time – & Chubbie & the like. I met heaps of pals too – survivors from various ships – whose yarns were *most* interesting. Everyone at home was awfully fit and well, & it was marvellous how they all gathered together from their different jobs. Jane & Chubbie are doing damn well at their shop & it is a topping little place & a regular rendezvous for the Wouff-Wouffs. It seemed to be *packed* all the time I was on leave, & they both enjoy themselves thoroughly – going out to dinners & dances an'all. Jim was very fit too – & very keen to get out to France – he seems to be fed up with this knocking about at home doing nothing – so I should imagine. Mother was as young as ever – you might just notice a few more grey hairs, but nothing else & of 'mud' there was none.

I should have liked to have seen Nell but hadn't a chance – we had a slight F.F. some time back – a correspondence F.F. and an exchange of photographs. That *is* a topping one of her – the side face on – she also wrote to me after the stunt too. Course I had masses of letters – but have managed to square 'em all off now – thank goodness.

A damn good stunt the other day – H.M. suddenly blew up North and came on board us to inspect the damage an' all. *We* being the first ship to which he came, so naturally he was more interested – absolutely informal no blazing of bugles or anything – just a good look round – ½ our ship's company were on leave too, so they never saw him. He shook hands with us all & spoke a few kind words. Then we yanked him into the Ward Room & he signed the mess photograph – quicky taken out of its frame for the purpose – 'Course we are frightfully proud of ourselves – particularly as being the first ship for him to see after the action – we got knocked about a bit you know.

Drew is up here fairly close and we have been interdining a good deal lately. He asked after you & sent his chin chins next time I wrote – so here they are. I am having quite a good time where we are now. There are some damn fine tennis courts – presented to the Fleet by Lady Jellicoe's Father, old Cayzer – & I play there most days. One Hillyard of tennis fame is a Lt Cmdr stationed here – & I somehow get mixed up in setts with him – Coo – but it's encouraging. Then there are several people whom I know knocking around – chiefly N.O. wives – and one gets asked out to dinner etc – what sort of time are you having at Lansdowne – rather dull I should imagine – what are the prospects? I thought I should have seen Topher when I was on leave but his leave seems to be so inconsistent – he keeps saying different dates – Dreda has got a bumper purse for him when he gets back so he ought to thoroughly enjoy himself. Well I must go and have a drink after this epistle – Cheerio cockie and damn good luck to you,

Yrs Paul

INDIA, SUMMER 1916

Ted did not receive this 'huge long letter' until the end of July and on 30 June he wrote to Gertrude: 'I'm longing to get this next mail, as it ought to have your first news of the naval battle; as far as one can make out there was a feeling of depression at first, but it seems to have changed since, now that more & more details of the German losses are coming out. I sent a cable to Paul congratulating him; I wonder if it ever got to him.'

When he next wrote, on 5 July, it was to say he was thankful to have definite news of Paul 'as of course we had seen long accounts in the papers in which the *Malaya* had figured very prominently & I felt sure she couldn't have come off scot free.' He goes on to lecture her quite severely:

I was rather grieved at the depressing tone of all your letters from home this week. I *cannot* . . . see anything but the bright side. . . . We can't win this war in a day & we've got to suffer losses . . . I know it is ghastly to have to sit at home & just wait & you know how tremendously I admire you all at home & your splendid pluck & I know what a tremendous help your behaviour is to the men who are fighting; but all the same I think that Kitchener's death & the naval battle – it was . . . a splendid victory – seem to have cast an unwonted gloom over the whole country; 'a black week' Rosamond called it.

Things seem to be moving on the Western front don't they, & every day brings more news: but I'm afraid this will rather tin-hat poor old Topher's leave if he hasn't had it already.

Then his tone changes:

Yes, you & I would get on well strafing the government wouldn't we. This war ought to be run by soldiers & sailors at the head of things . . . Funny Specs has not been roped in . . . Has he tried conscientious objection yet!

and, as if to make up for his earlier severity, he ends his letter:

Well, keep smiling as much as you can, won't you all at Delaford; I know you will, because all you dear people at Delaford have been *just splendid* in this war, & you excite my wildest admiration & enthusiasm. And I love you all.

At about this time Ted sent home Sir John French's farewell order to the Garhwal Brigade. 'The only brigade in the Indian Corps that got one from him; he gives us his personal thanks you notice, which is a great compliment. Please keep this amongst the family archives.' He also encloses a picture of a bureau as he wants Ben to get something like it for Nell and reports 'I've written to Ruth to tell her to get herself a present, something *really nice*, when she starts at Guys; anything up to 3 guineas or so I'm quite ready to give.' Two months later he is writing 'Glad Ruth's pleased to have got what she wanted; I expect I shall hear next mail what it is.'

Writing on 25 June he says he has only lost one mail so far 'the *Sussex* one . . . Nell numbers all her letters to me so as I can tell if any get lost, & I've got them all except the Sussex ones, so I must have got yours too.' He animadverts on the English tin helmets: 'I don't think they are very becoming do you? They seem so flat and broad brimmed; the French ones look so much neater and nattier.' He is glad that Mrs Quentin (Bunchie's mother) approves of Nell and wonders where Bunchie is now. On 7 July he is commenting on more news from home. 'I had letters from Nell of course and Jinny also; the latter seems most awfully fit and cheery, & she apparently has great times at the shop. What a meeting place it has become, & I quite agree in wondering where we all used to meet in the old days! Jack Fielding is up at the front line now with his battery so has begun soldiering in earnest.'

In a later letter he comments, rather unkindly for him, 'Apparently Mr & Mrs Fielding are very depressed about their son in the Gunners in France; I wish they would take an example from you; for you have so many more to think about & yet you never show anything; you're just splendid and I'm very proud of you.'

Dick's letters are, as usual, much shorter. He, too, is relieved about Paul, 'I never thought the *Malaya* had so many casualties. I am so glad Paul escaped,' and, of course, wonders about Topher's leave. 'I am writing to him & you might send him on my letter,' and on 23 June writes a short letter, even for him.

Many thanks for yours & the *Bystanders* & *Tatlers*. I will expect the camera. It has not arrived yet. You must excuse a short letter as I have left it so late & I must catch the mail. Blow that man for not sending the watch. But I saw a friend of his t'other day he says he is sure he will post it in the end. Hope he does.

You say you must go to bed, it's long after 11.30; it's not really, it's 10.30 isn't it?

Both brothers wrote home about the possibility of meeting. Although Ted's proposed visit to Karachi had to be postponed because of Dick's temporary change of occupation, this in itself was to provide an opportunity.

Dick, relieving someone on leave, was serving on an ambulance train, crossing and re-crossing the Sind desert. On 10 July he writes:

'Lor the dust and the heat. . . . The water (you won't believe it) which you have your bath in gets so hot from the sun, that I can only just sit down in it. I am wondering if I shall see Ted this time. We go to Amballa & it's not far from him. I've wired him & he might possibly come down. . . . We stay a day. There are 120 wounded natives on board. Of course they don't mind the heat, but some Tommies just from home the other day had a rotten time of it. You ask Ben, she did the journey in the cool & clean part of the year!

Ted also wrote of the possibility of a meeting:

Sirhind Club
Amballa
18 July 1916

I am just down here for a day to meet Dick, who is turning up tonight in his old hospital train; even if he's absolutely punctual I shall only see him for a few hours, as I have to catch a train back tonight to make certain of getting back to Lansdowne tomorrow. I came down yesterday and arrived here about 5.30 this morning. A good deal hotter than Lansdowne of course, but not unpleasant, very muggy & sticky as usual in the rains. But it's an amusing little jaunt & ought to be awful fun seeing Dick this evening. I rather fancy it's his last trip in this train. The Lieut. Governor of the United Provinces is coming up to Lansdowne on Sunday . . . so we are having parades & lunches & dinners for him, so that's why I have to hurry back.

In their next letters they both reported in their own characteristic ways on the meeting.

Thursday 20 July
On the old train still

Ted came down this time to see me at Amballa. His old C.O. was very stingy & he could only be with me a very little while. However it was awfully nice seeing him & he looked very well. . . . He had dinner with me on the train and we biked about Amballa on my old mo. bike. Ted was sitting on a cushion at the back. His train went at 2.15 that night. I was so glad to see him though & I hope he'll be able to get down to Karachi.

Lansdowne
26 July 1916

I had great fun at Amballa & saw Dick for a few hours. I arrived one morning at 5.30 as I told you I think, 'cos I wrote from the Club there. His train turned up punctually at 6 p.m. and mine went off again at 2.30 a.m., so we had about 8 or 9 hours together. We talked hard the whole time of course, & rode about on his motor bike. He rode it & I sat on behind & took the salutes! We had dinner on his train, and after that went for a spin round Amballa, quite a long way out into the country; it was hottish so very pleasant flying through the air like that. We got well out into the country and then sat & talked on a bridge; the place was just like England in the moonlight & might have been, except for the croaking of the frogs & various other Indian night noises. Then we came back & sat & talked in his train until it was time to go. He was awfully fit & well, & I thoroughly enjoyed the trip, even though I was only away about 2 days. His train is quite comfy, electric fans an' all, but I should think it was jolly hard to keep clean on those desert journeys.

He goes on to describe the parade for which he had had to hurry back.

The Lieut. Governor of the U.P. turned up last Thursday. We paraded for him at 3 o'clock, all four regiments up here, & at 3 o'clock exactly it came on to *pour*, great sheets & streams of water, no ordinary shower. However as we were there we stayed & of course, being only in thin drill kit, were soaked to the skin in less than 2 minutes. At 3.15 the L.G. turned up, mackintosh'd an' all, but as he stepped on to the parade ground he said 'I can't stand this' & flung off his Burbury, & came on in his morning coat & beautifully creased trousers! Seeing us standing there in this awful downpour was too much for him, & of course in 3 minutes he was a drowned rat! *Soaked* through & through; jolly sporting of him, as his kit must have been ruined, whereas our khaki drill of course doesn't matter, being washable. Well, he inspected us all, & presented some medals to men who had won them in France, & we marched past him & then the parade was over, at 4.30, so we had been standing in this appalling downpour for 1½ hours! I've *never* been so wet, or seen anyone so wet as the L.G. was! However we all went on to the Club, where there was an At Home for him, of course we changed for it, & you would never have guessed we were all the same people as had been on parade. . . . I should think it would be a long time before he forgets his visit to Lansdowne.

Of course, not all the native troops had been able to return. Some had been taken prisoner in France and one of them had apparently managed to write a letter which was probably published in the papers. 'What a splendid letter that was from our prisoner of war,' wrote Ted while he was waiting for Dick to come to Amballa, 'thanks awfully for sending a copy, we were all most interested. I suppose they get a Hindustani speaking German to write for them, & I think they treat our men fairly well too. Thanks awfully for sending the food etc, they do appreciate it don't they. I rather agree with you about the war being over this year. Isn't Verdun *wonderful*.'

There is plenty of news from home. Ted writes 'I had a long letter from Rosamond last mail, she does seem to enjoy her farming I must say. Isn't Ben going on the land too? I have an idea she said something about it'. Both brothers are delighted to hear that Paul has shaken hands with the King. 'Getting in with Royalty at all?' says Dick, and goes on to comment on an exciting motor accident evidently reported by Gertrude and philosophizes 'I wonder there aren't more really, except I suppose so few people drive nowadays, isn't petrol 2*s* 10*d* a gallon or something?'

Topher's lack of leave, of course, is a continuing story. 'I do hope he has had it by this time,' writes Dick, 'but I suppose as long as the big push goes on no one will get any. Pathetic indeed his nearly crying when he got your letters.' And, by the next mail: 'I do hope old Topher is all right. Really the Officer casualty list is so big what must the Tommies be. Jim seems to be a useful man nowadays. I expect he'll get his star before I do!

'What splendid news about Jim!' Ted wrote by the same mail. But he was not referring to promotion:

I *am* glad & will certainly drop him a line. But I can't get hold of her Christian name at all; I don't think I can ever have heard of it before, Sheina is it, or Sheima; anyhow that doesn't matter, very much. Yes rather I've often heard you speak of her as Miss Kellie in your letters & Dryden often seems to have gone to dinner there. I'm most awfully glad, for old Jim's sake, the very best thing in the world that could have happend to him; & I'm so glad you're glad. The war has proved prolific in family engagements hasn't it. Can you send me a snapshot of her, or anything, of course I'm longing to see what she's like. I haven't heard from Jim since I came out & I must say the news came as a great surprise to me.

However, in his letter of 3 August he writes about something very different:

A sad letter this week, for I have seen the awful news of poor Wiggs' death in the papers; I only saw it 2 days ago, the first time it was published in our papers out here. It's impossible to express adequately one's feelings on these occasions – common enough alas! nowadays – and words are of so little use. I suppose poor Wiggs' time had come; his luck didn't hold, and indeed you want all your luck to see you through the fighting now going on; the best you can hope for is a wound, that is the biggest luck obtainable. I have written to Ben, but I'm afraid it was a halting sort of letter, but it is so hard to write on these occasions. Poor Ben, my whole heart goes out to her – one of the best that ever lived – in her bereavement, and if anything I could say or do would give her one grain of comfort, it is hers and wholly hers. I feel I haven't expressed the depth of my sorrow, but it is deep enough, in all conscience. It is very much there, but it simply refused to be framed in words.

Dick also wrote, in the middle of a short letter: 'How dreadfully sorry I am to see poor Wiggs is killed. Poor Ben I *am* sorry for her. Ted sent me a wire asking if I had seen it, as we don't see the papers till a day after he does. The initial was J instead of I, but it must have been the same.'

Both brothers continued to express their concern for Ben, but meanwhile, life goes on.

Dick had finished with his train – 'Don't imagine that inquiry which you may have seen about in the papers of a train going across the Sind Desert refers to mine. I was much more careful!' – & expressed relief that the gold watch has at last arrived safely. He is looking forward to the arrival of 'Harold'. 'I am glad you remembered Harold's book,' he says, 'how did you find it?' and 'many thanks for tidying Harold up.' Harold, of course, was the ventriloquist doll. He also thanks his mother for sending 'that photograph to Evelyn; thank Rosamond too.' One presumes Gertrude knew what for! He has wired for his dress clothes and is also expecting Ted's old camera. 'Then I shan't be able to get any films for it.'

They both refer to news of a wedding. 'I didn't know Betty Neville had married,' Ted writes. 'Who to? I remember Roberts of the *Mallow* was an old flame of hers;' while Dick comments briefly: 'Rather, I knew Betty Neville. Who on earth married her!'

On 10 August Ted writes: 'I've been thinking a lot of poor Ben this week; I do hope she's all right; I know she'll be brave, but there is so little to be said or done, isn't there.' He has some regimental news to report: 'Nothing much doing up here. We have just got orders to raise a third battalion of Garhwalis, I suppose they have done so well that they want to make more use of them. We, both the 1st & 2nd Bns, are giving some men each to form a nucleus, but no officers have been appointed yet, & the thing is very much in the embryo stage at present.' In his next letter he reports that 'Our 1st Bn is off to Quetta shortly, as a sort of garrison for the place I suppose & also probably to make room for the 3rd Bn here. No more news about the raising of it yet, but I suppose we shall get some shortly. . . .'

He writes a short extra letter by the same mail.

Lansdowne,
Garhwal, U.P.
18 August 1916

You know that picture of Neuve Chapelle in the Academy this year, the Rifle Brigade & 39th clearing the village; well, the Colonel has very kindly given me a framed artist's proof as a wedding present (a bit early perchance!) & is having it sent direct to me c/o you; so will you please send it on to Nell when it comes; it'll probably be a biggish thing, so please let me know how much the carriage is, & I'll send it to you. If you want to have a look at it, open it before you send it on, only I think she ought to have it. Our men are very much in the background, it's nearly all Rifle Brigade, but it's quite a nice thing to have.

When he writes again he has had two letters from Gertrude with more details about Wiggs.

23 August 1916

Terribly sad about poor Wiggs, I do hope old Ben is getting along all right: poor girl, I am most frightfully sorry, but words are useless to express what I really feel. . . . I know she will be brave, but it is a terrible blow for her. The Queens seem to have done awfully well, as far as one can gather from the meagre mention that is made of regiments in the papers, but at what a cost! Fancy only 200 men coming out of the fight. . . .

23 August 1916

I wrote you a line this morning, & now the mail has come in & I have just got your letter dated August 2nd . . . many thanks. Also the enclosures about Wiggs; pathetic reading but how splendidly he died, and what a general favourite he must have been. Thanks most awfully for sending them; I am so vastly relieved to hear he died quickly; I knew he must have died bravely.

I heard from Ben too . . . poor child, but she is wonderfully brave & wrote splendidly; I feel as if it would take me years to get over my sorrow for her.

So glad Ruth is going in for war work as apparently the demand for nurses is tremendous now. And Ben too, the very best thing she could do, & what a splendid nurse she will make.

He has happier news of Ben's friend Alix, now married to Nobby Clarke.

Alix has I believe arrived in India; I saw her name down in a list of passengers arriving at Bombay yesterday. I must see if I can manage to go & see them in Simla if I can wangle the leave.

Writing on 31 August he reports that 'Jack Hogg has got command of our new 3rd Battalion, he has come from the 9th Gurkhas, & arrived a day or two ago. We had a brief F.F. about his people in Camberley. I had met him once or twice before, but didn't really know him.' But the real news of this letter is the fact that Dick is leaving India. 'What about Dick going to Marseilles! As of course you must have heard from him by now. I got a hurried line on the 24th saying he was sailing the next day. I fancy he'll be rather pleased, as he was rather sick of kicking his heels about in Stationary Hospitals and I don't think the Government were doing him very well.' Then, unconsciously echoing Dick's telegram to Ben in September 1914, 'What about being alone in India!' he adds, 'I feel rather lonely out here now he's gone, even though he was such miles away & I only saw him once for an hour or two.'

BROTHERS-IN-ARMS

Dick had at last got what he wanted – 'something of a more active nature' – and he wrote to Gertrude on 25 August: 'I meant to write on the mail boat today as I've had orders to go to Marseilles. It's been put off (this morning) so now I dunno' when I shall leave. I've cabled you to write to Marseilles. Must catch mail.'

As usual, there were delays.

Karachi
1 September 1916

Sorry for such a hurried note last week, but I thought I was off. There has apparently been some difficulty about transport . . . I have orders to report to Marseilles & know no more. Anyhow it may mean a lot of leave later on, & perhaps . . . I can get across to see you all, spurs & everything complete. Poor Ben, it is dreadful for her. I do hope she is better.

I am glad Topher is all right. Nuisance about my dress clothes, I'll have to have them sent back now.

Harold has arrived & has been quite a success.

Ted wrote a long letter on 6 September, commenting on the war news:

. . . The general opinion seems to incline towards the Germans retiring either voluntarily in order to shorten their line, or because they will have to weaken their western front on account of Roumania's entry into the Arena. . . .

I say I hope you were all right in the last big air raid, 13 Zepps they say, & only 3 managed to reach London . . . but the rest seems to have penetrated over Eastern & Southern counties & I do hope they hadn't got as far as you. . . .

He refers to Dick's delayed departure, Ruth's Red Cross work and then goes on:

What great news about Jim! I don't know whether to send a cable or not on the 8th, as it doesn't seem quite certain yet. I must wait for the next mail which should be here on the 8th . . . and even then I'm afraid it'll be a trifle late in arriving.

Dick's reaction was cooler.

Taj Mahal Palace Hotel
Bombay
10 September 1916

. . . Jim & Sheina were married yesterday then, of course I won't dare meet his father-in-law, as he's the old IMS col isn't he, who said I dressed up so. Bit awkward meeting Sheina (s'pose I call her by her Christian name) too. She used to skoff didn't she?

Even Ted was critical of the apparent confusion over dates for the wedding. He wrote on the 9th, 'So Jim's to be married today, that appears to be the latest fixed anyhow. So I'm sending him along a cable, & I hope it gets to him somewhere near the right time. I'm most awfully glad he's getting married – the very best thing for him', but on the 26th he comments 'How typical of Jim all the wedding arrangements seem to have been, so mysterious an' all at first, & then asking lots of people!' and in another letter of the same date he writes 'I also had a short note from Jim saying he was to be married on the 9th . . . he seems to have done things in a typically erratic way as usual, & made up his mind on the spurs of various moments.' But on 3 October he writes, quite bitterly for him: 'So Jim & Sheina were married earlier than you expected, & consequently my cable which I knew would be late enough in all conscience for the 9th must have been truly late for the 6th. However I don't suppose it matters very much.' This is still rankling when he writes to thank her for the paper with the account of Jim's wedding. 'I see they got "many & valuable presents". Nell wrote & said she had chosen a cigarette box for Jim, but she didn't describe the trickiness of it. . . . Yes, that cable you mention was from me, a trifle late for the wedding I'm thinking.'

This, of course, was only a temporary annoyance and did not affect in any way his good relationship with his elder brother. He is glad to hear there is a possibility of Jim's being posted to India, but does not count on it too much. 'Jim wrote to me about his coming to India scare, but I've heard nothing more, so presume it has gone the way of most scares,' and Dick, by now in France, wrote: 'Jim seems to have had a nice quiet wedding. I wonder why they want to send him to India, I dare say he'll like it, & Ted will be pleased to have him near. Mrs Berryman going if he goes?' After yet another 'please send' ('a lanyard thing one carries a whistle on round your shoulder. I want a *red* one as that's what medical people have in the cavalry. No good unless *red*') he suggests 'If Jim would like one of those teapot, sugar basin & cream jug sets complete from Harrods £2.6*s*.0 I'll give him one. Ask Mrs Berryman what she wants. I'm not very rich but I expect Dreda is saving up something for my leave isn't she? She generally does collect for us I believe.'

Whoever eventually paid for it, presumably it was Gertrude who had to see about buying it.

Nothing came of Jim's 'scare' of going to India. There was some talk of his getting a job with the Portuguese army which would have seemed a good idea as he spoke Portuguese but, although he seemed on the point of departure from England several times – 'I wonder if Jim's gone yet,' Ted writes at the end of November, 'as you say these "final leaves" are often anything but final' – at the beginning of 1917 he at last sailed – for Hong Kong.

Meanwhile Dick's return to Europe had been attended by the delays and confusion that seem to be part of his peregrinations. In his letter of 10 September from Bombay he writes cheerfully: 'Of course you need never now have bothered about my clothes. Such a pity, but Cox have instructions to send them back to you when they do arrive, & how annoying forgetting that coat. I would have liked tails as well anyhow.' After referring to Jim's wedding he goes on: 'I was sorry to have to leave June behind, I have given her to rather a pet of a girl . . . I dunno' what I shall do here all tomorrow. Spend money I suppose.'

In one of his letters of the 26th Ted says: 'For all his cables & hurried orders I believe Dick only left on the 18th after all; . . . You will have heard by now of course what his orders are more or less, & I suppose he's going to join a field ambulance, probably a cavalry one, with the Indian cavalry, or he may be going to an Indian cavalry regiment as a doctor.'

In this same letter we have the first mention of a 'British warm' that had been left at Delaford.

> By the way you know that Jaeger British warm I had in Gloucester, a big double breasted one, with leather buttons, light colour, belonged to someone who sent it to us? Could you send that out to me, as I want if for Delhi, unless one of the rest of the family have bagged it meantime. Jinny would know the one I mean, & I expect you all do. It's an awful nice one, & I hope it's still available.

By 13 October Dick had arrived in France.

Off to the front tonight with no one to see me off! Please tell the girls 'Mr Martyr'! I am joining a cavalry regiment, but do not know which yet. On the back of this is a list of luggage which will arrive some old time. Do let me know where Topher is. No one ever sent me his address. . . . Thank Jane for the combined k f & spoon.

The long suffering Gertrude could expect to receive: 1 black uniform case, new; 1 uniform case, old; 1 small tin uniform case in crate; 1 green canvas lunch basket; 1 large basket; 1 small case, leather, empty; 1 small bundle of sticks; 1 tent; 1 box of cigars; 1 bed.

He has some compunction about all this. In his letter of 23 October he wonders 'if all those boxes have arrived yet to load up the overloaded house. Jim's are there now I suppose. You will be boxed in when all mine arrive.' He has given her an address to write to: '104, Indian Cavalry Field Ambulance, France' and on the 18th he wrote:

That address I gave you yesterday is all right, as I hear tonight I am to be permanent. I'm quite pleased as it's a good job & later on I'll get a regiment if I want one. I want some breeches. There should be two pairs arriving soon from Karachi. Send me the new pair will you, as I only have one pair here & I've bust them already.

I can't get any leave yet I fancy. We can go to Paris, but I want to save up my money for home. Tell the girls at last I've heard a gun fired in anger in the distance; but I've not been in any battles yet.

I'm longing to hear if Topher is anywhere near & if I only had his address I might find out & if he's anywhere near I could hop over & see him.

and, of course – 'Could you get me an acetylene lamp like you sent Topher.'

Meanwhile Ted, left behind in India, was writing long letters, commenting on the war – 'Sept 26th: What *are* the Greeks doing! They are fools indeed & they've fairly let themselves in now by their silly vacillating policy hitherto, & serve them jolly well right.' And he also refers to family and friends and quotes letters from Nell, chiefly about her war work and the bureau he had given her.

In August he had asked Cox to send Gertrude £12 to pay for it – 'It sounds a lovely bureau but Nell doesn't mention it in her letters, so I suppose it hasn't turned up. Apparently she has been wanting one for years, so it's rather a lucky shot of mine.' But on 9 September he is able to write: 'Nell has got her bureau & is mighty pleased with it; old Ben made a splendid choice apparently' and in another letter of the same date he reports that Nell has sent him a photograph of it '& seems delighted with it'.

Nell was working hard in her hospital. There was talk of moving her elsewhere but nothing came of this and she was working nights, a fortnight at a time, which he thought was a good idea. She was 'still very busy "house maiding" as she calls it in her hospital. She sometimes writes & says she's had a real hard day, I hope they're not over-working her there; but she seems very cheery & happy enough.' And on 3 October he writes: 'Nell writes very cheery letters still & seems delighted with the bureau. She is still hard at work at her old hospital & tells me she went in for a Red X exam in September but didn't think she would pass, but I expect she did all right.' Whether she did or not, no one now knows.

He is, of course, continually concerned about Topher, writing on 9 September 'so glad you have good news of Topher, & I'm glad he's well behind at present, at any rate. Fancy feeling the effects of gas 9 miles away!' and on the 26th 'So glad you get good news of Topher; yes, he's bound to be popular & I expect he does his job well too. I should think they'd open leave again before Christmas.'

One of the friends he referred to was Julian Yeatman – 'I do hope Julian Yeatman's all right; I thought I saw his name in the paper. . . .'

On 21 September he writes, for him, a short letter, referring to many different subjects.

I got no letters from home this week . . . so shan't be able to answer any letters, having none to answer!

Such wet weather all this last week but today was perfect . . . and a magnificent view of the Snows . . . it's clouding over again now though, . . . I *am* so sick of the rain.

The regiment goes to Delhi in November sometime . . . sort of guard over the Viceroy, same like our detachment at Simla is doing now. . . .

Not much news from here, same old hard grind. The 3rd Batt. is going strong now, but the 1st Batt. haven't left for Quetta yet, so we are rather squashed up here.

The news from France is good isn't it, our men are wonderful, & what a wonderful thing this new armoured caterpillar car of ours seems to be, & what splendid work it has done. . . .

And, at the end:

My lady friend of the *Persia* & the C.O. & one or two others made a great fuss about that show & today to my surprise I got the bronze medal of the Royal Humane Society, but I'm sure it's far too much for what I did.

A letter from Ted dated 28 September contains a very awkward 'please send' request:

Just a scribble to ask you to send my sword, as we shall want them at Delhi. It's in a brown scabbard, & has a *black* sword knot on the hilt. It has a rifle pattern hilt, i.e. with a bugle device in it, something (only something!) as per picture. It is made by Hawkes, you'll see his name on the blade. I think it must be up in your room somewhere, as I know I left it at home when I came on leave from France one time.

You'd better insure it perhaps, & take the number on the blade in case it's lost. P'raps Cox would send it out for you.

While still in Lansdowne he writes about the Hindu Festival of Deshera:

We're having [a] holiday now as it's a big Hindu Festival which lasts ten days. But Holiday only means that parades are off; I spend hours in the office daily as usual. Today is the big day, when they cut off the heads of 50 or 60 goats, & 2 huge buffaloes as a sort of sacrifice, a ghastly sight, & they will always ask us to go & see it. I suppose I must go, as I'm commander for a few days as DB [Col. Drake Brockman] is away on a staff ride, & I expect they'll be expecting me. It's pouring with rain, but they said wet or fine. I *hate* the show, it's so barbarously primitive & bloodthirsty & a horrible sight as you may imagine. It's 1.30 now, so I must trot off. Hope you manage to find my sword & coat warm, unless someone else has bagged the latter.

At last he is able to write, on 25 October, 'It must have been ripping having old Topher home, & for such a long leave too. From all accounts he thoroughly enjoyed his leave.'

Dick, after his unexpected departure from India, is still trying to catch up with his mail. On 23 October he writes, 'There must be some gaps as you only say Topher enjoyed his leave & never said when he had had it or for how long.' He hopes to be able to 'wangle a drop of leave' himself and would like to get it at the same time as Paul, if possible. He goes on:

What a rag eh?
I heard from Ben poor old thing, she still seems very sad.
I hope my breeches will hurry up. I've only one pair of them over.

After saying he doesn't think he wants any clothes he goes on at once 'I expect I'll be wanting some sox soon.'

Gertrude had evidently been offering to send him clothes – perhaps in an effort to clear the house a little, as he writes later: 'It's not my B. warm at home, I've got it here!' He asks for 'a pair of gauntlet gloves (soft gauntlet part) size 8 I'd like them. Warm & waterproof' and writes a letter that is almost all 'please send':

1 November

Dear Mother,

Would you mind sending me some loofa sock things for boots. Say 2 pairs size 10 for gum boots, 2 pairs size 7, 2 pairs size 8, & you might send me some of those funny things you just shove on you toes under your socks like I used to see you send Topher.

Best love to all,
your loving son
Richard

By the way I'm a Capt.

How good for Ted getting that medal.

Please send me that Balaclava hat that is knocking about somewhere.

You might send me one of the linings for my tin hat 6¾. It's got sort of rubber buffer arrangements . . .

30 October 1916

The lamp arrived and is a Godsend. Just in the nick of time. As I had actually that moment run out of candles. Thanks awfully for it. The glass was smashed but that doesn't matter & such elegant furniture would be rather out of place in a dug out.

I've left the billets now and am up with a party just behind the lines digging roads etc. How the girls will be amused to think that at last I am at the front. However it's not very dangerous here only an occasional shell goes over. Our guns all round make a lot of noise, & it's a nuisance at night to have your candle put out by an extra big bang. It's absolutely rotten weather & the mud is awful. I shan't be sorry when I go back again. I'd like some candles & a writing block about this size & some envelopes . . .

Best love to all

Ted, writing on 24 November, comments, 'So Dick has arrived safely in France and has gone up to the Front. What a very typical letter he wrote! I must drop him a line. I wonder if Jim's gone yet . . .'

He was obviously wishing he could be more actively engaged. 'I *hate* the idea of this sort of stunt during the war,' he wrote to Ben from Delhi, 'but as we've got to do it I suppose I may as well make the best of it . . . . It was a guest night tonight, & they played 'Tonight's the night'. How it reminded me of that cheery evening last year, somewhere about this time too!' And his diary, from the end of August onwards, is more a record of 1915 than of the current year.

Sunday, 27 August 1916: Col Hogg arrived to command 3rd Bn. – Y. M. C. A. tent day at Sneedhams Green, 1915! – Nell saw me for the first time, but I never saw her!

After recording little more than 'Wrote Nell' on the succeeding days he comes to

Thursday, 7 September, 1916: Davies' tea party at Sneedhams Green a year ago today where I first met Nell.

Sunday 10 Sept, 1916: Wrote Nell (170) Dance at Broadsground this time last year & I first spoke to Nell!

Friday 15 Sept 1916: Wrote Nell (176) My first lunch at Broadsground this time last year!

Wednesday, 20 Sept 1916: Wrote Nell (181) Tea at Broadsground with Nell last year!

Thursday, 21 Sept 1916: Wrote Nell (182) – C.O. gave me R.H.S. bronze medal today

Friday , 6 Oct 1916: Nell put her hair up a year ago today.

Sunday, 8 Oct 1916: Wrote Nell (196) – Over to Cheltenham in the car last year, came back with Nell.

He does record the battalion's move to Delhi:

Friday, 27 Oct 1916: Left Lansdowne 8 a.m., arrived Kohdwara 4 p.m. . . . Hot march & men tired. Entrained 9.30 & off at 10 p.m.

Saturday, 28 Oct 1916: Arrived Delhi (Kingsway) 8 a.m. Nothing ready in camp, as tents had arrived but no poles! Camp near Durbar polo grounds, between them & Kingsway Station. Familiar ground of the Durbar of Xmas 1911. Wrote Nell (213).

Sunday, 29 Oct 1916: Pitching camp all day. I went up to Viceregal Lodge

3 or 4 times to see about guards etc as the Viceroy turns up tomorrow. – This time last year! THE happiest day of my life – Wrote Nell (214).

The camp is described in greater detail in his letters.

Delhi
3 November 1916

We each have a great big tent, about the size of ½ the drawing room, and with weird furniture & carpets, a boarded floor & electric light it is really very little different from living in a house, except there's only one room, of course, & it's very dusty just at present. I use my small manoeuvre tent as a bathroom, & as I have always used it to live in entirely hitherto, I am beginning to wonder now how I used to managed to do so!

We are camped on familiar ground, this camp being near the old polo ground used at the Durbar. But of course things have altered a lot since then & really the only things left are the main roads which were laid out at Durbar time & which have been kept up. All the pomp & magnificence of the Indian chief's camp and all the miles and miles of tents of course are not here and the place is hard to recognise.

9 November 1916

We have settled down fairly comfortably now, & have 2 nice big tents for our mess. . . . The C.O. and I share a car, on hire, between us, & it is almost a necessity to have one, as we are three miles out of Delhi . . . I had my first driving lesson today, & hope to become quite a chauffeur by the time we leave here!

He writes more frankly to Ben.

Delhi
10 November 1916

. . . D.B. & I share a car my dear! A tinpot American invention called a Chevrolet, a sort of between-a-overland-and-ford. But it goes quite well, 4 Seater, self starter an' all. But can you imagine a C.O. if you please not having a car of his own! Why, everyone here of official or social standing has one, & he has to *share* one (on hire too!) with a junior captain! However I suppose I must play up to him. He is learning to drive but is a perfect fool at it as you may imagine, & thinks he is competent already in 2 lessons! Wait till he gets on to some windy roads and some traffic. I am learning too, of course, & we should have some fun out of it.

He is concerned by news of yet another sinking. In the same letter he writes:

What about the *Arabia* being sunk. Awful isn't it, but I see they saved everyone thank goodness. My friend Mrs Proctor was on board poor woman, but I suppose she's all right. Did I ever tell you, the day before she left Lansdowne I heard quite by chance she was going down the hill next day, and as I couldn't possibly find a minute to go & see her, and as she was a cheery soul & I liked her, I just scribbled a note, wishing her luck etc. She wrote back a hurried line of thanks, & afterwards I heard . . . that she was ever so bucked at my note I and [another friend] being the only two men in the station (she had many friends) who took the trouble to say goodbye. She was feeling rather wretched at the time, her husband having just gone to Mespot, so I'm glad I did that little thing. Funny how these little efforts count for so much sometimes. Her husband poor man must have been having a rotten time; because when she came out last year she booked a passage on the *Persia*, & changed it, but he sailed from Egypt to India just then and on arriving at Bombay he heard about the *Persia*, & didn't know for 2 whole days she wasn't on it. And now this has happened, but she's saved I sincerely trust with the others. . . .

He also wrote to Gertrude about the *Arabia*.

Delhi
16 November 1916

. . . What about the *Arabia* being sunk; but what a mercy they were all saved. My friend Mrs Proctor was on board . . . I'm afraid that week's mail must have gone for good. I wonder if some rugs I was sending were on board. . . . Heaps of people here now, as all the Army Headquarters people are down from Simla, & I suppose before long one will be sucked into the vortex, one simply has to do all that sort of thing here, as ours is a social job more than anything else, & soldiering is really a secondary thing. The war touches India very lightly, except in cases of regiments who have lost so many good fellows, & there are few who haven't. But the general population of India is very little affected by it, & the same old life goes on just as before.

Bitterly cold down here now. I hope the British warm turns up soon, if it is still in existence.

The news is good again isn't it. Funny, I got pink papers & the *Daily Mirror* weekly edn (I like that, it gives you such a comprehensive view of things when there isn't much time to read) but no letters last mail. I *am* glad Topher's C.O. can say such nice things about him; splendid, & you must be awfully pleased.

Splendid as this was, Topher's circumstances were to change unexpectedly for the better.

THE SINKING OF *TYNDAREUS*

On 11 November, 1916, Topher wrote to Dreda.

Dearest Dreda,

Ever so many thanks for your last letter. We are still back for a rest but go up again on Tuesday worst luck. My dear, yesterday I met old Dick, hooting at all! Apparently we have been quite near each other all the time, when we were up in the trenches. His lot have been ordered back suddenly. And the lot that took over from him were the 18 Middlesex, and they told him where I was, he motored over yesterday to see me. He was looking fearfully well & in a very cheery mood. We had tea together; he is pretty good at French, but his accent makes me laugh. We had some good laughs together. He went in to see my C.O. and asked him if he could take me as his groom (because an elder brother can claim a younger brother if he wants). The C.O. was awfully nice & told him to write to him putting in his claim and he would do all he could. So with any luck I may go with him, what fun eh, but mum's the word. I wish I had met him up the line. I can't think how I did not, because he was quite near me, sickening isn't it. But it was fine meeting at all. He has grown a moustache, a very nutty one. He thinks it is better than mine. He hopes to come in again this morning. I hope he does . . .

Our T.O. is on leave, and is going into the shop to see Jane. I have written to her telling her so.

Well dear no more news,

best of love,
yr loving brother,
Topher

Dick wrote briefly to his mother about this meeting and other matters.

Sunday, 12 Novemver 1916

Many thanks for your letters & the parcels, but no breeches yet! or socks. The loofas, paper & canteen are here & many thanks for all. I expect you'll hear Topher & I have met. It was nice being able to see him & I think he was pleased too. He looked awfully fit, but most anxious to get out of his job & I am doing my best for him.

I am out of the danger zone at present, but may be off again. It's very nice down here, quiet & nothing much doing. I went to tea yesterday with a countess & was very much struck by one of her daughters. The money has come, many thanks for it.

What a pity I didn't know about Wiggs before. Ben has written & I could easily have gone & seen where he is buried poor boy. However if I go up again I will go & see at once.

The lanyard is very smart. And very many thanks.

Must post this.

He wrote at greater length to Dreda the next day.

My dear Dreda,

I believe I owe you a letter don't I? Many thanks for yours, write sometimes & give me any news. My dear I've just come back from the front & am now safe again! Who do you think I saw the other day – Topher! He was awfully pleased to see me I believe & of course we had a huge *buck* & he told me all about his leave & so on. What a nice little moustache he's got, you really ought to tell him to go steady with it. He admired mine awfully & now he's going to try and train his like mine! Poor boy, he's gone up again today I believe but I *may* be going up again in a day or two, so we must have another F.F.

Of course you can never imagine the state of the country up there, you'd never believe it. It's no good trying to describe it, I can't understand how anyone ever lived up there. There really isn't room to walk between the shell holes & of course the mud is the limit. It's so dangerous too. The shells keep dropping around you as you ride up & one might easily drop on one & give one a nasty blow. Oh lor too, the air fights & bombs dropping at night, I am sure it must be worse than that Zep raid you had at Guildford. I hate the moonlight nights as the Bosch always come then, 'sterrible. And the guns going off all round you all day & all night, & the big ones each time rattle the whole place, & the other night just as I was passing water into an old shell case before getting into bed, bang! goes a huge gun, out goes the candle & there was I in the dark, wondering what was going to happen next! 'Tis funny being back here again & everything is calm & quiet. A comfortable bed with sheets & clean plates & cups to eat & drink with. On the whole I like the other best, one's doing more, but enough's as good as a feast & for the men it would be better to do 3 days in the trenches than a month making roads & railways up to just behind them.

I went to tea with a Countess yesterday. Bow wow, and one daughter most fascinating, fair hair done in a huge chignon, & dark brown eyes, ripping figure & plays the piano so nicely. Please send me 'The only girl in' etc. to give her to play. Her aunt is the richest woman in Paris, so I'm all for it. The girl is about 18.

I must write to Topher.

Write to me again soon if you have time.

Best love from Dick

His next letter to his mother was as short as usual.

18 November 1916

Dear Mother,

I got the disc and gloves all right. Open my luggage when it comes & have my field boots looked after. Get Capon to put an ordinary shoe tree in the front & stuff the legs with paper. There are some films in the camera that want developing. Dunno' what they'll be like.

The breeches have come but the others aren't mine & in case you send that British warm, that's not mine either!

I got the *Bystander*.

Believe I'm off again . . .

So his next was shorter still.

XX Deccan Horse
B.E.F. France
1 December 1916

Dear Mother,

Just a line to say address as above not as I put last time. Tell Ben & Dreda I wrote them the same. Euh isn't it cold,

yr loving son
Richard

He had achieved his ambition: Doctor to an Indian Cavalry Regiment.

12 December 1916

Many thanks for the parcel with woollie, chicken, socks & sweets. I've taken off my present woollie & put on yours, much nicer, it does not take up so much room. I'm awful glad of the sox, [his spelling varies] those other 2 pairs you sent me are most useful. Always worn with the field boots & spurs.

I hear from Cox my keys were never sent! However they should be on their way now & I hope you'll be able to open the boxes & get boots buttons etc. Should you not get them almost as soon as this, write to Cox & ask them if they have received them. Lesley Roberts may want those buttons soon. One of the keys does for 2 boxes that little tiny tin suitcase & one of the others. The brass one opens the red & black tin box, the big new one, the big new box. I hope everything arrived as per the list I sent you. Will you have that fishing reel cleaned & oiled a bit; also the box-spurs. Has my evening dress etc returned, no good coming home if it hasn't. I do hope everything will be all right in the boxes & not gone bad or anything.

I'm going over today to see if I can hear any news of Topher's arrival.

Snow yesterday. 'Sawful.

And in a P.S.: 'There's some lace in one of those boxes. Keep care of it & don't let anyone bag it. Its for a girl I know.'

Another letter makes one wonder just how Gertrude sharpened pencils. Probably with short, decisive strokes of the pen knife to a very sharp point:

14 December 1916

Many thanks for your letter with the pencils, somehow or other I could have told anywhere they had been sharpened by you, I shall be sorry when I have to resharpen them . . .

Paul sent me two papers today. I heard from Karachi that June is very well & looked after by a nice girl I knew there. Don't forget about that lace, I know if the girls see it they'll want it, and it's for Cicely!

There are two rather valuable platinum & pearl rings about somewhere, I would like you to give them to the two girls who you think have behaved best during the past year!

And, in a PS: 'If you could get a *real* dough cake sometime, have it put in a good box & sent out. Pay all postage on anything out of that £5. It's a shame to make you pay.'

His next letter is undated, but would seem to fit in here.

. . . Have you mixed Topher's and my feast up. 'Cos we aren't together yet! I've no idea if he will be transferred or not. I shall probably be alone for Christmas, & if he's near I'll try & get him allowed over & he can mess with me. . . . I've written to Jane to buy me a saddle, that bit I wrote about isn't there I think. But there may be another, very rusty when I saw it last, it's a curb with a snaffle combined. Please get that out somehow if it's there. But you say nothing about my things or keys. Have they come yet? I've written to Marseilles about them to see if they ever started. I've just remembered! What flowers grow between now & March or April? I'd like

to plant some around my hospital & make the place look nice. Don't sunflowers grow nowadays. . . . Also I wondered if any of these working parties of lovely ladies would like to make a red cross flag for me. Any size, the bigger the better. You might send along seeds or bulbs or whatever if it grows during the next few months. No desperate hurry. You know the woollie hasn't arrived yet. . . .
PS In one of the boxes you'll find a tunic with dark leather buttons on, & two little brass buttons on the black tabs. Please take them out & send them to Lesley & Roberts, 16 George St, Hanover Square.

20 December 1916

Many thanks for your letter & that pack of cards. Most useful as the ones I had off last year's Xmas tree are very dirty. I want Lesley & Roberts to have the *leather* buttons, never mind about the tabs.

So glad the keys have arrived at last. I managed to wake them up at Marseilles . . . Fancy 20 soldiers to tea, what a business. Get the photographs in the camera developed for me. Do you want any more money?

The new Government seems to be going to do things all right.

It was about now that Gertrude decided to make a new will and she wrote to her sons about it. Dick and Ted responded in characteristic fashion.

XX Deccan Horse
B.E.F. France
2 December 1916

My dear Mother,

I wish you wouldn't please give me such shocks. 'Read this first' you said & it promptly began all about your will, I imagined the second letter was all going to be about some awful illness you had got!

He answers the second letter in the same paragraph:

What fools Cox in Marseilles are. The keys were delivered to them I believe, anyhow I've written to all concerned & I hope they will turn up. And when they do I think I'll have those field boots sent out. Would you mind packing them up securely & sending them. I may as well use them. . . .

Where did Topher say he was, I haven't heard from him lately, but he must be resting again now. They don't seem able to decide about Jim. I expect he'll like Hong Kong – only the first 10 days of the voyage are rotten, they are quite safe when once past Port Said. . . .

Ted sounds very swagger in his new tent. I wrote to him yesterday. . . . You'd better send me a Xmas pudding as everyone seems to get odd things & I must put up a show, but you needn't bother about sending anything else. . . .

The Countess' daughter seems awfully bucked with the music. Tres Charmante & elegante or something. I saw her for a sec yesterday.

Then, in an abrupt PS:

Of course I quite agree with you that the girls should first & foremost be provided for.

Then about Holmwood. I think that it would be simplest to put Holmwood together with everything else, & divided up as you suggest. I don't fancy I should ever live at Holmwood, much as I would like to, & taking everything into consideration it would be best to put Holmwood in with the other things, & put me in with the other boys.

My idea has always been that provided all the girls don't marry, the unmarried ones will live together somewhere, or at any rate have a small house, with as much of the nice furniture that you've got in it. Then we unmarried boys will always look on that place more or less as a home, i.e. if we are working abroad. I'd hate that furniture to be lost. Anyhow Holmwood would be too big for them

Ted, of course, did not get the letter till much later, and he answered it on 30 December:

Very many thanks for your letter last week, which I got sometime ago, & I'm afraid I've been some time answering. . . .

I haven't done much this week. I had a very homely Christmas with a family called France; he used to be our bandmaster, but got a commission when the war began; very nice & Christmassy & I quite enjoyed myself. . . . Frederic Villiers, the war correspondent . . . was giving a lecture here, & happened to mention the regiment in the course of it, so I thought I would ask him to dinner. After many adventures, thanks to a hired chauffeur, who deposited us in the hedge amongst other things, we eventually managed to get here, ½ an hour late! However he was fortunately used to these little contretemps, and I think he quite enjoyed his dinner, as we were all in mess kit, and he was in a regular star-turn war correspondent lecturing kit, khaki & a loose cloak & field glasses etc, just like he is in his pictures. It wasn't a bad lecture, but like all war correspondents he was a bit of a liar, for he described several incidents that I knew from personal experience, & his facts weren't quite accurate. However, of course that's part of his business, & he was very interesting to talk to.

The Somme films have been here this week too, & I went to them one night. I think they are rather *too* good, & recalled horrors that one has so far managed to forget; but otherwise they were splendid. I arranged a special matinée for our men one day & they thoroughly enjoyed it. Last night I dined with Ricketts (you remember him in the Hockey XI at Sandhurst I expect) and went to a concert given by the Wiltshires next door here, quite a good show. Today the Wilts have had their sports, & I have just come back from them; quite amusing.

Your letter was chiefly about your will; and I quite agree that it is much better to face these things out & discuss them from a family point of view.

First of all let me tell you that I quite agree with the principle you are working on, that the girls should be provided for first . . . I think it's best to tabulate my reasons:

1. The boys are all provided for, except perhaps Topher . . .

2. In educating us boys – *thereby enabling us to get a start in life & to fend for ourselves* – a great deal of money must have been spent. This initial outlay would correspond to any income the girls will get, on whom so much money has not been spent originally . . .

3. *All* girls can't get married, & one simply *must* take that into consideration. A spinster with – say – £120 a year can at any rate live by herself or with another friend and a girl with £120 a year if she gets married at least has *some* income to help things along.

4. If you provide more for the boys, it would mean less for the girls, of course, & that would mean *someone would have to give tham a home if they didn't marry.* So, if you gave the girls less each, in order to give the boys more, & *if* none of them married, it would mean that one of us would have to give them a home, & would therefore spend the little extra – so very little we got, by their having less, in keeping them. So why not let them have it straightaway? Don't think I'm hard or cruel, as I know any of us would be only too delighted to keep any of our priceless sisters . . . but what I say is, let the girls be provided for first, & then let the boys have anything that's over, which, after all, is what you suggest yourself.

So if it means selling Holmwood, well I say sell it, because I do think the girls have first claim. I'm not sure about Topher, he is the only difficulty I can see. I rather think he ought to have some capital *reserved* for him, so he can start a show of his own when opportunity offers, even if it means cutting the other 4 boys down. As I say, after all, we have had a good start, & it's our job now to watch our own interests.

Them's my sentiments, but my dear mother please don't think of dying yet! You have lots of years before you I hope and we can ill spare you just now. But if you frame your will on these lines, I at any rate shall be fearfully satisfied. Must write to Ben now. Lots of love & wishes for 1917 – will it see the end I wonder?

yr loving son
Ted

Although he appreciated meeting old friends, such as the Ricketts mentioned in this letter, Ted found life in India's winter capital remoted and unreal. Soon after he had arrived he had written to Gertrude:

Delhi
24 November 1916

. . . Nothing very much going on here. I have been busy calling on everyone, & found most of them out so one has been able to get through a good deal . . . The army Hd quarters people come down en bloc from Simla, knowing each other already, so one is really rather out of things till you get to know a few people. I went to a big show at the Delhi club last Saturday, but didn't know a soul, though the place was crowded with the . . . cream of Indian society, such as it is. The C-in-C was there, in uniform, so I expect we shall get orders to wear uniform always like we did at home. At present you wouldn't know there was a war on, so little is India affected; we go on just the same, no food, no petrol or other restrictions, all amusements the same as ever, no lights to worry about, you can have as many as you like! Only the awful gaps in the regiments show what India has done, & it's only the Indian army that really knows there's a war, the vast majority of the Indian population being absolutely untouched by it, for the fighting races from which the army is recruited form of course only the smallest fraction of the total. . . .

I'm still without a horse; it seems absolutely impossible to buy one here, and horse flesh is very scarce. . . . We have been very strenuous these last 4 days . . . bivouacing & battle fighting, all day & all night. A whole brigade of 4 regiments is out in training about 4 miles from here & we had to take out 500 men to do enemy to them, so you can imagine we had lots to do. However it was a very pleasant outing, but as I say strenuous. Our first two camps were in a ripping place, by the banks of a canal, just where it leaves the Jumna river, & the canal man has built a bungalow there and made the place awfully pretty and home like. . . .

I am acting as 2nd in command now, being the next senior left in the regt [the C.O. was on leave] but am still doing adjutant as well. My time as adjutant is up next March, so I may as well carry on till then. . . .

He is very pleased to 'have got some pictures of the Tanks. I simply couldn't picture them to myself before, so we are very glad that some photographs have been published at last. They must indeed be awful things to see coming along and there seems to be no escape from them.'

Now he is beginning to find his social life easier as he gets to know people and meets many old friends.

It's awful nice meeting old friends like Rickett [his fellow hockey player from Sandhurst days] & they are most awfully kind to me, & I have been round to several 'pot luck' meals with them whenever I get bored with the mess, which is pretty often!

The Ricketts took him

. . . on a regular trippers trip, round some old tombs and forts and things. . . . I must say these old places are most awfully interesting even to one so un-archeological as I, but they are so redolent of the past & the magnificence of all these old oriental things, & they are now all ruins & fallen to decay. I must say it makes you think a bit when you look round and see nothing but ruins all round for miles & miles & you wonder if London & all the splendour of modern Europe will one day be like this. I don't see why it shouldn't. I have no doubt these old Kings of 1300 and thereabouts never imagined for one moment that even in such a short time as 600 years all their palaces and cities would be ruined & deserted, a mere object in life for sight-seers.

As he gets more involved he has less time for such philosophizing. On 19 January 1917 he writes: 'I have had really quite a busy week & have met a whole lot more people lately which I always think is a good thing, don't you. . . .' He had lunch with the Cruickshanks, 'Mrs Cruickshank being a very old friend of mine; you may have heard Ben speak of her as Molly Ormsby [daughter of a Colonel Ormsby of one of the Gurkha regiments in Lansdowne], & I knew her awful well. . . . Ripping meeting old friends like that again.'

He also met a number of old friends from even earlier days.

I went to a dance on Wednesday . . . And oh yes, I must tell you I met a Mrs Mackenzie who used to be Dorothy Massey at Camberley years ago; I didn't remember her much, but I expect you or the girls would. . . . She rattled off all our names without mistake or hesitation, and asked after everyone, & of course we had a tremendous Camberley F.F. . . . Awfully nice meeting an old friend so to speak, though we didn't actually remember each other. . . .

At 'a very cheery evening' he 'had another Camberley F.F. with Mrs Mackenzie; she's awful nice & a general favorite.' And, answering a letter of Gertrude's – 'thanks for the note about Mrs Dot Massey John Mackenzie's skirts! I'll remind her about them when I see her this evening. She wears weird clothes nowadays, always very *smart*, but she's so frightfully thin and requires very careful dressing I should imagine . . .'

He also met several friends from his prep school, Cordwalles.

. . . I met one of the Metcalfes from Cordwalles . . . he is asst. Private sec to the Viceroy & rather a nut in his way . . . we never recognized each other till we were introduced. The last time I saw him was singing a duet with him at Cordwalles, & Mrs Mason drew me with my coat tails flying! You remember the picture I expect in Mr Hunt's dining room. . . .

. . . I met a fellow called Miles . . . he was at Cordwalles with me & I remember him well when he said so, but I shouldn't have known him if I had met him casually. He is a baronet now! . . . And Lady Miles is also a very cheery little person, & we had a tremendous F.F. . . . Rather funny Metcalf & Miles & me all meeting here, & none of us had met since Cordwalles days!

. . . A regular Cordwalles dinner 'at the Miles'. . . . Metcalfe & I were there, & Ricketts who was at Stoke Poges next door, you remember we used to play them at cricket & footer. I wish you'd look up the Cordwalles Chronicle of 1897 & see how we fared . . . & if any of us made any runs, especially Ricketts, who swears he was playing for Stoke Poges & made a lot! *How* we talked & rattled up the past; Miles . . . remembered being a robin in the acting when Metcalfe & I were an old man & his wife & we recalled a thousand and one incidents long forgotten. I loved it all. . . .

There was 'a fair amount going on in the Christmas week, a travelling company . . . a dance at the Club, a variety entertainment and some regimental sports'. He has some shooting to try to 'bag a peacock for Christmas' but only got a hare and a partridge and 'a day in the country, which is always pleasant'. Gertrude has evidently sent him a Christmas pudding: 'I hope it turns up eventually; it will be equally welcome whenever it does; I'll warn people about the 6*d*!'

As well as the regular dinners and dances there were a number of more military occasions. 'The Viceroy gave away various medals & decorations to Indian troops at Viceregal Lodge last Tuesday, quite a good show but *rather* long & boring, as there were 200 recipients of medals! However it was a gay scene & lots of colour.'

There was a lot of colour on another occasion too. At a regimental guest night they had an exotic dinner 'served by our cook, who is really an artist. One dish was sort of cutlets, made of paté de foie gras, each cutlet being cased in a different coloured sauce, green, pink, blue & all colours! Most alarming to look at but no one is any the worse for eating them I fancy.'

He plays a good deal of tennis with a family called Bingley, and has lunch and tea with them frequently. Mrs Bingley 'had been working at the Guildford Red X hospital . . . She seemed to know you.' Later he writes 'I told Mrs B you remembered her quite well, I thought it best to! She is nice and homely & the kid Barbara (aged 14) is an awful dear.' 'I had some "flapper" tennis with Barbara Bingley & a small friend staying with her. I think they had a day out & seemed to thoroughly enjoy it. Nell will be getting jealous! But I don't think she need worry her pretty head much.'

He asks Gertrude to get Nell some gloves for Christmas and comments on news of the rest of the family. 'Poor old Dryden hard at work again in the bank. How I *hate* the idea of her being there.' He is sorry that Rosamond has hurt her thumb and hopes 'the dear person' will be better soon. He also hopes 'that Wiggy's things have been settled amicably by now, it seems strange it can't be done somehow & poor Ben must feel it frightfully. I'm relieved to hear she is so much better.'

Jim had evidently met the barber from the *Persia*, and Ted comments:

How amazing! I should think he did remember me, cos I had my hair cut in harbour at Marseilles & he made a special favour of it . . . because every man arriving overland by the boat train always demanded a shave & he never had time to cut hair. He was a fool – he was the man who said 'chuck him overboard, he's a goner' about a pal of mine called Fisher, who was only just rescued in time, having been sucked under when she sank, & so was pretty well done in & collapsed when pulled into one of the boats, but the barber's remark speedily brought him to life again!

On 26 January he writes:

From your letter I gather Jim is now definitely going to Hong Kong – is presumably well on his way there now. I wonder if he's pleased or not or if he'd rather go to France. He enlisted so early in the war, that it seems curious he should go so far away from it when he does go anywhere.

He was delighted to hear that Dick and Topher had managed to meet in France:

. . . Poor Topher must find it very rough as a Tommy & I expect he would like a bit of a change now and get a commission . . . I expect they are getting a rum lot in the ranks now & I expect all his friends are scattered about for various reasons. . . . I can't understand how Topher has managed to join Dick, as Dick is with Indian cavalry & there are no Europeans in the Indian cavalry except the officers; but perhaps things are a little more elastic in France, anyhow it's awful nice for them both.

Dick, in fact, was a little dubious about it. He wrote just before Christmas saying that he had heard from Topher:

I am glad to hear to expect him to come soon & he won't have to do that awful transport job again. I'm afraid he'll find it a great change as there won't be half so much to do. I dunno whether to have him as my servant or not. He'd have to clean my boots & call me in the morning & cook my dinner! Of course we could go for rides together & have some fun.

Topher did not manage to join him in time for Christmas. Dick wrote on 28 December:

You could have said anything you liked about the lace, I'd liked them to have seen it & envied it. Yes they are silver with moonstones, those rings, I only said platinum & pearls for a rag.

Think I can borrow Gerard Thomas's car when I'm at home. Must have one . . .

Your dining room stunt sounds as if it was most popular. Don't fag too much about the flag. I don't see why you should have to pay for it.

I am hoping to see Topher any day now.

But it was not until 16 January he was able to write:

Topher is here at last & I think he likes it better than his other job. We go out riding together & I fancy it will work all right. I hope so anyhow. I got a nice saddle from Jane at last. . . . Snowing & freezing like blazes I hate it & long for the East again . . . Jim gone & must be nearly there by now. How lucky he is . . .

But was he? Jim's battalion of the Middlesex Regiment sailed for Hong Kong on board the *Tyndareus* which went the long way round by the Cape – presumably to avoid the submarines in the Mediterranean. The *Cape Argus* of 12 February reported:

One of the most glorious episodes of the war, away from the actual fighting fronts has just been revealed by the publication . . . of the following telegram – 'The behaviour of the Battalion of the Middlesex Regiment, on board the steamship *Tyndareus* after the accident to that ship, there being a large quantity of water on board, and the ship apparently sinking by the head in a heavy swell, was most praiseworthy, and equal to the *Birkenhead* tradition of the British Army in the same spot. It was only due to this that no lives were lost in the boats . . .'

The following message has been received from his Majesty the King: 'Please express to the Officers commanding the Middlesex Regiment my admiration of the conduct displayed by all ranks on the occasion of the accident of the *Tyndareus*. In their discipline and courage they worthily upheld the splendid tradition of the *Birkenhead*, ever cherished in the annals of the British Army. George R.I.'

An unknown reporter really went to town on this one. In an article headed 'The Gallant Middlesex' he wrote:

The Battalion of the Middlesex Regiment, which narrowly escaped going down in the Steamer *Tyndareus* off this coast last week, awoke this morning to find itself famous. The Steamer *Tyndareus* was about to call at Table Bay for fuel and supplies. The weather was fine and the majority of the soldiers were watching another transport which was coming along behind when suddenly a terrific shock was felt and the boat began to fill with water at a great rate. It was a critical moment for everyone on board. Panic or confusion would have resulted in a terrible disaster. But the men . . . behaved like heroes. All must have realised their danger . . . for the steamer could be seen to be going down by the head and threatening to take the final plunge at any moment.

The men responded to the commands of their officers as briskly and orderly as on parade . . . with death apparently staring them in the face, they burst into song and cheered each other by joining in popular tunes. Boats were lowered . . . and all were got off, down to the favourite dogs. . . .

His Majesty King George . . . compares their conduct . . . with the behaviour of the heroes of the *Birkenhead*, whose exceptional coolness and bravery aroused the enthusiasm of the whole civilised world, and caused the then King of Prussia to have an account of the incident read to his troops on parade as a splendid example. . . .

He goes on to explain that the *Birkenhead* was also rounding this coast when she struck a reef:

The soldiers and sailors, realizing the danger, sprang to attention at the word of command as though on land and in safety. There was no confusion, no panic – the *Birkenhead* . . . went down by the head . . . with her stern high out of the water, just as the *Tyndareus* is reported to have been. . . . The great and gratifying difference . . . was that those on the

Tyndareus were saved, whilst the majority on the *Birkenhead* were drowned. They stood to attention to the last . . . and met their death like the brave men they were, without flinching. . . . And the coolness and discipline displayed by the officers and men of the *Tyndareus* still survives.

A fact which adds lustre to the incident is that the men of the Middlesex Battalion were not old and seasoned soldiers, they were many of them . . . fresh from civilian life. That they should have so quickly become impregnated with the highest traditions of the British Army and of the distinguished regiment to which they belong, is a wonderful proof of the great qualities of the British race.

Jim's account of the incident is altogether more prosaic. He wrote to his wife Sheina, on 21 February 1917 from Garrison Officers, Mess, Wynberg:

I don't think I ever gave you a description of what happened the night of the accident. Well, we were all at Mess when the bang went off. I was going to say when the explosion occurred, of course everyone jumped up and grabbed a life belt – somebody started. We were all out and up at our boat stations in about two minutes, and the men were all in their places – my boat was 207. I had 50 men, a couple of Chinamen and one or two of the crew – a huge volume of water was splashed up over the ship, and dead fish were found lying all over the place. The old ship started going down a bit by the bows, but she did not do any nasty lurching which was a mercy. There was a fairly big sea running and bright moonlight. We were in sight of land, and there were two ships in sight also. The men behaved splendidly, and no one seemed to fuss at all. The boats were got along without any flurry and we all started climbing and clambering down rope ladders – I got down the last of my lot, and the boat was pretty full by that time. I had been twice down to my cabin to get one or two things – I got my revolver and field glasses and the greatest godsend of all, a hundred cigarettes – I also grabbed a letter which I had written to you which I posted directly we got here.

We pushed off from the ship, some of the boats were already away, and some had been picked up by one of the ships that was standing by. One was a hospital ship all lighted up with red and green lights and the other belonged to the same line of steamers as our ship. Well, we started away, and the waves looked very different from the small boat, huge great mountains that seemed to be going to swamp our overcrowded boat any minute, of course there was no chance of rowing as the men were too crowded, and none of them knew much about it, then lots were sea sick, and the boat started filling with water, so we had to bail her with helmets and caps. The fellow of the crew we had with us did not seem to know much about it, so I had to take charge, and I knew less. We got along fine at the start and got near the hospital ship, but unfortunately we got on the wrong side, and it was impossible to get the men up, we pushed off quick or we should have been smashed to pieces. Of course I did not know how to get round to the other side, what can you expect from a comic soldier? I now know how to do it – so we had to let her drift, well she drifted down towards the other ship and again we got on the weather side, people shouted and gave directions but I couldn't work it, so we drifted away again. Then with the four oars we had out we managed to keep her head to the current, which is what we ought to have done right away, but how was a d— land lubber to know? and we started to drift towards the ship again. We were about ¾ of a mile away and the men were a bit down, and between you and me and the ink pot I didn't fancy our chances, but we got there. We got round the stern somehow and got alongside and all got aboard safely. We were out for about 4 hours, so some of us were pretty cooked.

The accident happened about 10 minutes to 7, we were away about 7.30 and got aboard the other ship about 12. There were still some boats out so we hung around to see what could be done, then we signalled to the hospital ship, and counted the men and found not a single man missing. We hung around till the next morning and saw our old ship still afloat and a cruiser and another trying to get a rope aboard to tow her. We started back to Cape Town and got in about six o'clock and they brought us straight here, so there were no casualties at all. We even saved the dogs.

Gertrude kept a copy of this and the cutting from the *Cape Argus* with her copy of Ted's account of the sinking of the *Persia* in a large brown envelope on which she had written tersely: 'Letters from my ship-wrecked sons'.

'MESPOT' 1917

Ted's British warm and his sword were a recurring theme in his letters. As early as 2 December 1916 he was writing:

Thanks awfully for sending off the sword & coat. What awful nonsense it seems doesn't it not being able to send arms by post. But it was a bright idea to send it through Cox, because if they can't do it, I shouldn't think anyone can. The coat is badly needed, as it is bitterly cold here in the evenings & mornings, & I only have an old British warm which is warm enough but very shabby. . . .

What a brain wave you had in the middle of the night about my sword; yes, it's a good thing to put a little vaseline on as a sea voyage is always apt to rust them, though mine is a plated hilt so shouldn't rust.

He had either forgotten, or was too kind to remind her, that it was he who had suggested sending it by Cox in the first place. He thanks her again in a later letter 'for sending off the coat & sword; the latter seems to have caused a good deal of bother; so sorry'.

On 16 December he wrote, after describing the manouvres and his meetings with old friends, '*And* the coat has arrived all safe & sound, yesterday; thanks ever so much, it is *most* welcome,' but it is not until 5 January that he is able to write: 'I hear from Cox that my sword has arrived in Bombay safely, so I ought to get it up here soon now, after signing about a million papers & forms. Thanks awfully for sending it.' Nearly a month later his sword still hasn't arrived: 'My sword hasn't turned up yet, but Cox is retrieving it from the customs & various other obstacles & says he is sending it along very shortly.' On 18 February he reports that 'my sword has arrived, but I haven't retrieved it from the rly. station yet, & now we are just off, I suppose I shan't need it after all.'

He had begun this letter with his comment that 'Jim has really sailed, & Hong Kong is quite a good place I believe,' (not knowing, of course, that Jim had got no further than the Cape of Good Hope) and referring to Dick and Topher:

I can't quite understand . . . but I suppose many things are possible now that one never thought of before. . . .

Please apologise to the family for my not having written much, but I have been frightfully busy these last few days. . . .

. . . I am under orders for Mesopotamia, & we shall probably start about the middle of next month . . . But please don't worry, mother, I'll be all right & will take great care of myself. Conditions out there have improved out of all knowledge, & now ice & electric fans & magnificently equipped hospitals are the order of the day, & they are sparing no money or trouble to make no mistakes *this* time. It is a picnic compared to what it was, & though I expect there are many discomforts still, & there simply *must* be on a campaign like this, yet it's ever & ever so much better than it was and not a bad place at all. Of course I'm awfully excited & pleased at the prospect, & I do hope it won't add too much to your anxieties, which must be heavy enough. Don't worry to send me anything, as things must be hard enough to get at home. A few sort of lemon drops are good things to suck when one is thirsty I'm told, & water sterilizing tablets might be useful, & possibly a little eau-de-cologne with menthol in it to make it cool. . . .

The news from Mesopotamia continues good, and I suppose there will be big things doing in Europe soon now – this submarine campaign seems to be the chief danger at present . . . I hope it's not making things too unpleasant for you at home.

He reports on his sword and then goes on:

Better stick to Cox for an address, as I don't know what Brigade or Division we'll be in. . . . Address letters *very* carefully as I hear they still go astray a lot out there. Lots to read will be welcome I should think. . . . Must run over & post this now, as the mail goes at 5.45 tomorrow morning. . . . Perhaps a little aspirin or quinine wouldn't be out of place in Mespot if you are thinking of sending anything along but please don't worry to send parcels, as I 'spect we'll get all we want out there under the improved conditions.

Best love to all & wish me luck,
ever yr loving son,
Ted

There was the usual time lag between first receiving orders to go and actual departure and, although he was naturally busy during the day, he managed 'to get out of an evening generally. I dined with the Bingleys last Monday . . . they had an amusing book called The Hospital A.B.C. . . . get one & send it to old Nell if you can, it will amuse her. Some of the V.A.D. people drawn in it are, we came to the conclusion, exactly like Maggie Davids, as of course Mrs Bingley knew her too . . .' He thanks her for 'a shower of *Sketches* & *John Bulls*, and also *Fragments from France*, Part 3, which has kept the mess in roars of laughter as the saying is!

Thanks awfully for them; but I'm not sure that Bairnsfather isn't a wee bit put to it now to find a funny subject . . . he'll have to take care not to overdo it. . . . He really is good when he is good & wonderfully true to life.'

There was some official entertaining too:

The commander-in-chief is coming to dine in the mess tonight so we shall all be on our best behaviour. My bath an' all is ready just now, but I can spare a minute or two yet. . . . There are some Red X delegates in Delhi now, Swiss people who are touring all the allied countries looking at prisoners' camps. One of our fellows . . . is looking after them . . . & he brought them to dine the other night. They talk English & I didn't air my French on them, though some of us tried! The Russian Consul in India, one Tomanoffski, also came to dinner. He was all through the big Russian retreat at the beginning of the war, in Poland, & was very interesting to talk to. . . . I should like the *Saturday Review* sent each week in Mespot. Could you fix this up for me, & let me know what a year's sub is & I'll send it along. I really must change now. Good night, & I hope the chief will enjoy his dinner here!

Continuing the letter the next day he reports:

Last night was quite a success; the Chief is a genial old bird, & quite human; he has an aggressive chin which means business I think. . . . I am so awfully glad to hear good news of Ben. She wrote me a long letter . . . & I'm afraid I've been very remiss in writing lately but this mobilization has kept me fairly busy, & one has a certain amount of friends to see; I am revelling so in meeting all my friends, old & new, after a rather trying 8 or 9 months in Lansdowne, & I'm sure it has done me good . . .

and in a lively PS: 'Fancy old Hall joining up! Yes, of course I know him well; he must be 150 at least!'

On 10 March he wrote:

We have definite orders to leave here on the 17th now, but I have been dining with my pal Reid tonight & he tells me not to be surprised if they are postponed! So what *is* one to make of it all? . . . Isn't the Mespot news wonderfully good nowadays, & tonight I hear they are only 4 miles from Baghdad. But I fancy there will be lots for us to do when we get there, if not this hot weather, at any rate as soon as the next cold weather begins. . . .

I don't quite understand the German retreat yet, but from all accounts it seems all right for us, though no doubt our plans for a spring offensive will have to be modified slightly.

In spite of Reid's caustic pessimism, the 2/39th Garhwal Rifles did leave for Mespot on 17 March. Ted wrote on that day:

Well, we are just off, at last after many false alarms . . . I have had a frightfully busy time these last weeks, and feel quite tired & weary; but I expect the voyage will buck me up a lot. I am giving up my adjutancy; my time is up anyhow at the end of the month, so this is my last day as adjutant, & tomorrow I command a company, quite a new job for me! . . . Cheer up, Mother, I'll be all right & I think we are in for a very interesting time in Mesopotamia. What price the news from Russia! But it seems to be a jolly good thing as German influence has obviously been too much in evidence there lately, and there seems no doubt that the Russian people are all out to do down the Hun, & so have taken the matter into their own hands and ousted the government & the Tsar has gracefully retired. . . .

I have collected a whole heap of new kit for Mesopotamia, thin clothes & thick hats & mosquito nets . . . but the conditions there are so vastly improved that it's really one of the best run shows we have. Haven't we been wonderfully successful, & the capture of Baghdad must have made our prestige thrice as strong after the Kut disaster an' all . . . I'll write again from Mesopotamia I expect, but don't expect much from there as posts are bound to be erratic. . . .

Gertrude was in the habit of writing notes of importance on the envelopes of the letters from her sons. This one was labelled 'Last letter from there before going to Mesopotamia.'

Ted wrote cheerfully on the way to Karachi:

21 March 1917

Just a scribble in the train – I'm afraid my writing is awfully wobbly! – to say we are off at last! . . . We had a great send off by the Wilts Rgt in Delhi, their band played & the men lined the road to the station & cheered us. . . . I had 3 friends to see me off, my friend Reid & one Lamb, & also Mrs Kaye of whom you have heard me speak I expect. Awful nice of 'em to come down & say farewell and we appreciated it awfully. Quite a pleasant journey we've had, though rather dusty. It's the same . . . that Dick used to do in his old ambulance train, all across the Sind desert. I'm afraid you won't hear from me for some time now, as the voyage will take 6 or 7 days I suppose & then there's the voyage back for the letters, so there's a fortnight at least clear gone, & then 3 or 4 weeks I suppose from Bombay, so I should be prepared for 6 weeks or so without a letter. As for letters from you, heaven knows when I shall get any. We have had none for a fortnight, though . . . there is a mail in now, & one due to be delivered in Delhi yesterday, so we just missed that. Still I suppose they'll roll up

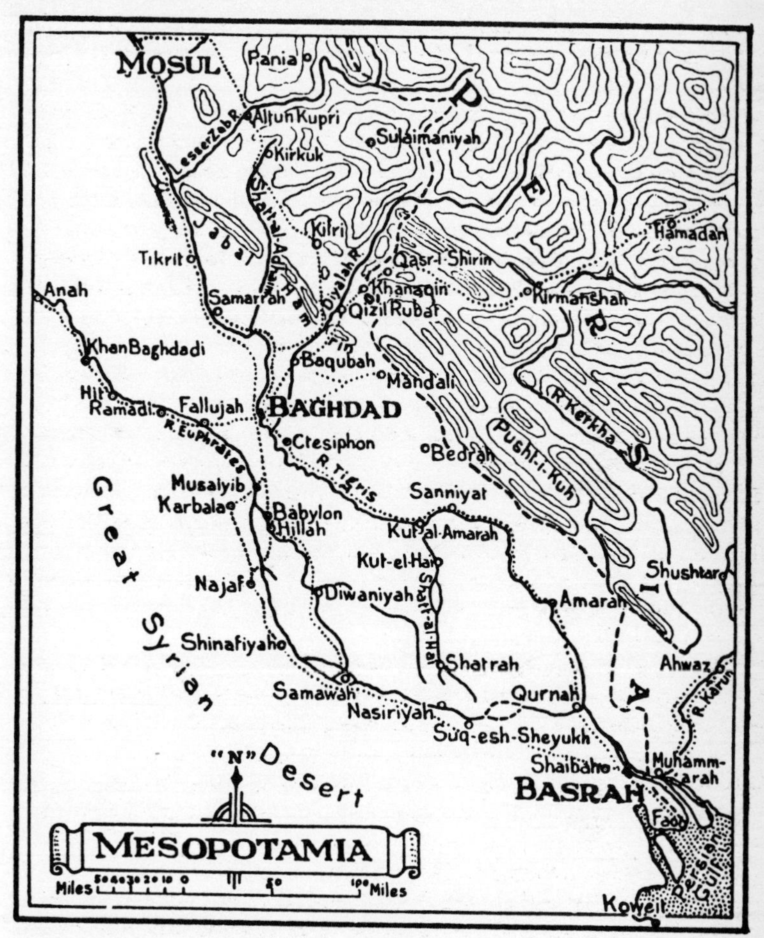

Map of Mesopotamia, from a Christmas card

some old time. . . . Good news from the West, isn't there. And heaven knows how far we've got to march to catch up our advanced troops north of Baghdad!

His next letter was written at sea on 27 March: '. . . I'm sure I don't know when this will reach you as I shan't be able to post it till we land, and I haven't an idea when that will be.'

They were held up for two days in Karachi but he spent most of the time with someone in the D.M.S. whom he had known in Lansdowne and who had shared a bungalow in Karachi with Dick 'all last hot weather, so I thought I had some claim on his hospitality'. He also saw June who was flourishing and a great favourite with the people with whom she had been left:

I don't think they would part with her for worlds. I met them too . . . and a whole lot of Dick's friends. They were all frightfully sorry he had gone, & said some very nice things about him, & he was evidently the buzz in Karachi. I have written & told him about it. . . .

½ the Bn is on another ship, and the other ½ on this one with me. There is another regiment on board & quite a nice lot of officers. They were up Assam way when Dick & Ben were there, & remember them both well. Would you say I was meeting many of Dick's friends lately! . . .

It's a funny little ship; in ordinary times used for carrying Mohammedan pilgrims to Mecca & elsewhere. . . .

We have been three weeks without an English mail, & heaven knows when we shall get it now! We shipped a lot of mails on this old tub at Karachi & it's just possible ours may be among that lot, but I doubt it. All my letters will be censored now of course, so I shan't be able to tell you much. In any case I trust you are prepared for thoroughly erratic mails from me from now onwards, for besides the probable difficulties of writing often, the posts must of necessity be erratic, for they of course take 2nd place to military requirements, though I believe they are wonderful in the way they run the posts – as everything else – out there now. . . . I should like ½ doz rolls of film for my camera sometime, if you can get them, a vest pocket Kodak. I simply couldn't get any in India when we left. Get the freshest you can, ones that haven't got to be developed for months yet. *30 March* We get to Basrah tomorrow . . . & then I expect they'll send us up to relieve the troops that have done all the fighting lately so we shall go pretty well straight to Baghdad. But of course . . . I shan't be able to tell you. Anyhow I'll tell you . . . by saying we have been sent to the place I expected.

I'm going to give this letter to the Captain to post when the ship goes back to Karachi; it may catch an earlier mail than if I posted it ashore. So I'll have to put a stamp on it, but fortunately I have some by me.

No more now, I'll write as often as I can but be prepared for erratic mails!

The mails – the hold ups, the sudden arrival of 'a whole heap of letters', the arrangements made for getting them to England and from England to 'Mespot' – are a recurring theme, along with the heat (by April it was 100° in their tents at midday), the dust ('On Sunday we had a tremendous dust storm . . . the air was thick with it for 2 or 3 hours'), and the news of family and friends.

'What splendid news about old Paul;' he writes on 11 April. 'I *am* glad, & must try and send him a cable. I somehow didn't imagine there was anything in the wind, though he told me he had met a niece of the Conway Gordons . . . & you mentioned her once or twice in your letters.' This 'splendid news' was obviously of Paul's engagement to one Nancy Swan. He is glad to 'hear from the girls that Dick managed to get home after all, & even to get one evening with Paul. But they hadn't seen much of him, especially as they are away from home so much themselves.' He hopes 'those 4 girls managed to get on to the land, especially Dreda who must be so heartily sick of the bank & who really & truly deserves a change. . . . I think it's splendid the way she has stuck to it, loathing it as she must.'

It is not until May that he hears details from home about 'the *Tyndareus* business' and he thinks there must be a letter missing as she mentioned 'Jim having lost only his fountain pen' as if she had written more about it all in an earlier letter. Two letters later he is able to write: 'Many thanks for the account of the *Tyndareus*. They behaved magnificently those men didn't they and you must be proud to have a son in the regiment. . . . Fancy Jim going to Singapore after all; perhaps he'll wander into India from there. . . .'

Ted's letters at this time show concern for the family at home:

. . . I see in the papers they mention the great scare there was when all those officers were recalled suddenly, & rumours of raids & invasions were rife . . . it would not come to anything if they do land, as they would soon be cut off from all supplies . . . But I think you can trust the Navy. . . .
. . . Hope you are all right . . . I don't like these air raids, & I think the invasion scare is no bogey but a very possible reality.

However by the end of June he is able to write light-heartedly (obviously the invasion 'scare' is over): 'Putting up the tennis net!

Shocking war time an' no potatoes! I expected every mail to hear that had gone the way of all spare land and had been dug up for agricultural purposes.'

Gertrude's reliable man of all work, Capon, who had moved from Camberley to Guildford in order to stay with her, was evidently unwell, as Ted writes on 13 June: 'Poor Capon sounds very ill, I hope the baths will do him good; I should like to subscribe towards his treatment, if you'll let me know about it, as he has always done me pretty well when I've been at home.'

Ted has news of other old friends, of whom he met a remarkable number:

. . . Gaskell, who was in Lansdowne when Ben was staying with me . . . Sam Orton is also here . . . and he has been along to see us. Curiously enough the 1/5 Queens are in the same Brigade as we are & I hear the Gabbs are with them – aren't two of them out here – Harold & Desmond? Anyhow I'm bound to meet them soon . . . I wonder if any other Guildford people are in that Battalion.

. . . I met a man . . . who used to be our doctor, one Newland by name; he is in a field ambulance here. Also two of the ships officers off the *Dufferin* . . . the ship we came home in for the Coronation in 1911. One . . . has chucked sailoring & taken up wireless telegraphy. They have a very comfy little wattle & daub mess here & have their wireless going & pick up various messages from all over the place, Berlin & Malta, & sometimes from the Eiffel Tower wireless in Paris, if the weather conditions are favorable, and so they get news sometimes well in advance of official communiqués. Rather marvellous isn't it, especially as the apparatus here is only a travelling one, & can be packed up & taken away in motor lorries & on pack horses & put up somewhere else in no time!

As well as reporting on friends he meets, he comments on news of friends at home: 'I am delighted to hear of Bab's engagement, & I will certainly write. I know Jack Houghton of course well & I always thought he was such a good chap. . . . Wasn't he wounded in 1915?'

Ted was understandably fed up with waiting in the base camp at Basrah while fighting was going on further North – 'It's beastly this sitting down waiting, we did exactly the same in France in '14.' At least they were being equipped with a few things specially required for campaigning in this country, 'coloured glasses, spine pads & helmet flaps. . . . All our men are wearing pith helmets . . .

as they find the slouch hat is not enough protection, even for a native.'

He has time to go shopping in the native bazaar which was:

. . . very quaint and curious. As a rule Eastern bazaars rather bore me; when you've seen – and smelt – one you've seen & smelt them all. But this one is rather different, some parts of it are roughly roofed with planks & mattings & the sun rays sort of break through in between the cracks & the beams of sunlight coming into the crowded streets are really awfully pretty. . . . The streets are full of all sorts of people, chiefly Arabs, of course, in their picturesque biblical robes, but one sees also types of almost any race from Egypt to China; negroes from the West Indies, to say nothing of tommies & officers wandering about. . . . Nothing could give a better example of . . . how the war has affected the uttermost parts of the earth and has dug out people from most unexpected and unheard of corners.

At the beginning of May Ted writes:

We shan't see any of the scrapping this spring as the hot weather is coming on & they don't & can't do much while that is on. . . . I hope you haven't been wondering too much if I've been . . . in all this fighting they've had lately up north of Baghdad; well, anyhow by now you know that I've . . . been sitting quietly at base all the time. However I suppose we shall . . . probably be in time for some of the fun next autumn – if the war isn't over by then!

It is cooler in the evenings and he describes a joy ride in one of the Red Cross launches with a friend and some nurses from one of the many hospitals.

It was lovely . . . the river here is about ½ a mile broad or so, & always full of all kinds of shipping – cruisers, gun boats, transports, fussy little motor boats & lots an' lots of native craft of all shapes & sizes. We went down the main stream a bit & then wandered off up a side creek, which was really gorgeously peaceful & quite *English* to look at, but for the dark palms which came down to the waters edge on each side. . . . I revelled in the pleasure of it all. At one place an Arab sheikh had his residence, & growing all over his verandahs was a lovely climbing rose, pink & in full bloom. Close by was a huge splash of colour in the form of a big cluster of oleanders & it was too much for us, so we landed and made friends with the sheikh by signs & broken conversation carried on in English, Hindustani and few words of Arabic, & came away . . . with huge handfuls of flowers . . . which went to brighten up the wards of the hospital. We came back in the dark almost & the river was awfully pretty with all the ships lighted up.

The weather gets worse, with one or two 'piping hot days' then 'a howling gale with a perpetual sandstorm day & night'. He reports that the Colonel has gone into hospital with a touch of dysentery, thankful to get away from the hot & dusty camp into a nice cool clean hospital. 'He evidently wasn't feeling up to much. I don't know how long he will be away, but these things always take some time to get right . . . meanwhile I am commanding the regiment & unless they think I am too junior I suppose they will leave me in command until he comes back.' The next day, 3 May, he writes 'I heard from the C.O. yesterday & . . . he is being invalided to India, which means he will be away 2 or 3 months I suppose at least, so I shall be in command for some time with any luck, unless, as I say they put anyone else in.'

Ted had barely taken over command when on 6 May he was able to write:

The air is rife with rumours of our marching onto Baghdad . . . I don't think I am giving away military information in saying this, as after all . . . there's precious little elsewhere to go is there! I should like to march up very much, as we should go all over the ground made famous by Townsend & his defence of Kut, and where all the fighting in the attempted relief of Kut last year took place, & where the successful advance was made by General Maude's army . . . recently. . . .

There seems to be a lot of fighting going on in France nowadays, & especially in the air. Germany is evidently very anxious about the Western Front & seems to be doing her utmost to keep us from breaking through. . . . I see Prince Albert [later George VI] has been appointed to the *Malaya* [Paul's ship], so she's evidently a star turn in the fleet.

For once things moved quickly and three days later he was writing from Amara:

We were ordered to move up here at very short notice, 24 hours, and some of us have already arrived as you see & the rest of the regiment is arriving in bits later on. We embarked on a river steamer at 8 o'clock on Sunday . . . It was a lovely cool morning & the trip upstream was most awfully pleasant. We went about 40 miles . . . to a place called Kurnah where the Tigris & the Euphrates join. . . . Kurnah of course is the traditional site of the Garden of Eden, and I fancy all the authorities of any importance have come to the conclusion that it was there or thereabouts that Adam & Eve were domiciled.

Certainly to the weary traveller from the desert Kurnah must indeed seem a garden, for there are numerous palm groves there, & pomegranate trees, & a kind of willow growing along the river bank, and the whole place all round is green with marsh and reed beds which makes things very restful for the eyes after the glare of the sun in the desert.

The Euphrates is a nice clean blue-water river, while the Tigris comes down in a very strong current of horribly muddy water, completely overwhelming the poor little Euphrates and discolouring the rest of the river on its way to the sea. . . . As you may imagine Eve's tree is still shewn to the traveller, or at any rate a tree that satisfies his curiosity sufficiently to say he has seen the tree of knowledge of good and evil. That it is not an apple, nor anything like it, matters not; it is enough to have seen it. . . . In any case, I picked some leaves off it (I am told this is *quite* the thing to do!) & am sending them along herewith. . . . You can . . . shew them to your more credulous friends as the real thing, & leave the sceptics to draw their own conclusions.

From Kurnah they went on by train, in open trucks, travelling all night.

It was awfully cold . . . & at 4 a.m. next morning . . . I had to put on your Shetland woolly to keep warm! Fancy, Mespot on the 6th May & Shetland woollies! . . . We had breakfast by the side of the line, there are no stations of course yet, as the line has only just been finished, & marched out to camp here. . . . Very like Basrah . . . pretty surroundings, it couldn't be otherwise with a great broad river & palm lined banks. . . . The river scene is just as busy as the one at Basrah & innumerable craft of every kind are constantly moving up & down, from monitors flying the white ensign & fresh from the fighting up Baghdad way down to a frail cockleshell of a canoe which some picturesque Arab laboriously paddles across the stream, dodging motor boats & steam launches & battling doggedly against the swift current.

There is a club here, & of course a pretty big permanent garrison, being one of the big places on the lines of communication. Hospitals & store depôts of all kinds abound, & so in many respects it resembles a station in peace time. . . . They have tennis & golf here, & I expect boating parties & picnics, to which the river particularly lends itself. I am very fit & well . . . and am seriously thinking of studying Arabic . . . one feels so handicapped not being able to speak to the inhabitants, not even to swear at them, though possibly this can be done equally effectively in English.

Having got so far they find they have time on their hands:

23 May 1917

Some of us . . . are getting up a pierrot troupe to give concerts to the various hospitals & depots here. . . . We have rather fun, & some of the troupe are really 1st class, especially the pianist who can play any blessed thing under the sun. They have made me stage manager, as I'm the senior in the troupe; you can imagine our difficulties, as we have very little music & each sort of dips into the past & rakes up some songs he knew years ago, hums the tune over to the pianist, & then sings it! . . . Another difficulty . . . the Arab tailors in the bazaar are hardly up to making pierrot costumes unless one of us sits over them & watches every stitch! . . . If you could send me one or two George Robey albums, or those 1*s* albums of the latest songs occasionally it might be useful, though heaven knows where we shall be when they come out . . . by that time the troupe will be much scattered I expect, but we may have another one going.

In his next letter he reports on the concert:

The concert went off all right . . . personally I think a little more 'working up' was required . . . but all the members of the 'Pip Squeaks', as we called ourselves, were very lackadaisical & took things & rehearsals very easily on the 'it'll be all right on the night' principle. However, the sick & wounded Tommies & nurses at the hospital certainly laughed & cheered, & the bosses were most embarrasingly grateful . . . so I suppose it went off all right.

He had to give up the Pierrot troupe as the regiment was moved to a camp two miles away on the other bank of the river with no means of getting across at night for evening rehearsals because the bridge of boats was opened to allow the water traffic to pass. However, it had been good fun while it lasted and he had got to know 'a good few people through it'. The new camp was pleasantly situated in a palm grove running down to the river bank:

There are some lovely walks along the river here, through the most gorgeous date groves, with willows all growing alongside the river. And pomegranate trees with the fruit just ripening now & their lovely scarlet flowers. Funny little Arab children play around the villages, & the gardens are deliciously untidy, but lovely & cool & green. Melons & a sort of pumpkin-like vegetable grow here, and all sorts of weeds & creepers; and yesterday we found real live English blackberries, which of course took us straight home to England.

They water their melons & dates by curious old wells, & Persian wheels, where tins are attached to a wheel which revolves in the water, worked by a very ricketty old horse who walks round & round, a very Heath Robinson contrivance, consisting of home made cog wheels and creaking axles.

There were daily bathes in the Tigris which he enjoyed apart from the muddy bottom and the occasion when he lost his signet ring. He had taken it off, as it was always a little loose in the water, left it under it tuft of grass on the bank and forgotten it. Twenty minutes later when he went back, it had gone and, as a thorough search by himself and several of the men achieved nothing, he assumed it had been stolen by some passing Arab. The next morning to his delighted surprise his orderly brought it to him while he was dressing. The explanation was simple 'It appears, as Capon would say, one of our regimental police . . . saw it quite by chance and picked it up, thinking, he said, it was brass! Wasn't it lucky. Very silly of me of course to put it there. . . . I was most awfully distressed at the time & was most frightfully pleased to get it back again.'

He does not seem to have been so lucky with a pair of socks, which appear to have been sent by mistake to the General commanding the brigade:

My dear, *how* we have all been laughing at the idea of General Maude getting a parcel with a pair of socks marked for me in it! A gorgeous idea I think; & my pals have all been ragging me, & say I'll have to go up to Baghdad to have them presented, & all the troops will parade while I step forward & he hands them to me! As a matter of fact I . . . think it's just as well . . . No harm in being on sock-receiving terms with the G.O.C.! tho' I expect his A.D.C. will have most to do with it.

In the same letter, dated 13 June, he writes of his promotion. It was a little complicated but he does his best to explain:

They have made me a Major now, from April 8th. It's acting rank only, but with pay as a major. It's because I am – or was then – 2nd in command, and on *field service* they give you the acting rank of major then – 2nd in command (if you are not one already) & full pay as such, very nice. But when the war stops, or if I leave the rgt for any reason – sick, wounded, go to a job – then I drop the rank & revert to captain; & my successor in the job gets the rank & pay, after waiting 15 days from the date of the vacancy. That's why I had to wait till April 8th, 15 days after sailing from India. Previous to that I had been 2nd in command since last September, but as we were not on F.S. no promotion was admissable, see?

He also thanks her for 'the cutting from the paper about the Indian

Army; most interesting, & though it all seems so long ago now, still it's nice to know one's little bit has not been forgotten. I suppose things were rather bad just then.'

He is obviously thrilled to be in command, even if it is only temporarily. In his next letter, on 28 June, he writes:

> We are very busy training still; work from 5 a.m. to 8 a.m., then no parades are allowed – too hot – by order till 5 p.m. So we have lectures etc in huts, & the men bathe or sleep or mend their clothes (economy 'mend everything', make everything last twice as long as you do generally, is our watch word out here) till it's time to parade again. They are all as keen as mustard, & it has been a tremendous pride & pleasure to me to have been in command of the Battalion now for 2 months, short as the time is. I feel I have a slight say in the matter of its training, & I am prepared to stand or fall by its behaviour in action. I must say I have absolute confidence in it; but then that is only natural. I do hope I get a chance to command it in action – it would be a great opportunity, and if only the fates are kind I think I stand a good chance of doing so.

After touching on a variety of other subjects, such as friends from England ('I haven't seen Desmond Gabb yet'), Dick and Topher ('so glad to hear they are flourishing'), the sports 'the Gunners next door' had organised, and food shortages at home, he turns to the war in its wider aspects and looks to the future:

> I fancy we have the Hun fairly 'coopered' in the West now. We have been making . . . small attacks everywhere . . . preparatory, presumably, to making a great big push on a very wide front sooner or later. Russia appears to be going to see us through after all . . . & I think Greece will . . . give us no more trouble. If only we could get America's army into the field. Well, they'll come soon enough no doubt . . . & the allies have far greater & *untouched* reserves to draw on than Germany, who must be wasting all her reserve strength in furious & fruitless counter attacks. Our casualty lists are sadly long as you say, but however great the price it's worth it, beside it's the duty of this generation to posterity & the world at large. Think what future generations would say of us if we failed now. It would only mean a far greater tragedy in years to come for them.

In his next letter, dated 28 June, he writes of 'the men' again, this time in rather a lighter vein:

> We had some swimming sports the other day for the men who, as I told you I think, spend most of their day bathing, and we thought we would encourage them by having a few sports, especially for those who have

learnt to swim here. Our men are not natural divers, & have only learnt a bit here under our instruction, so you can imagine their efforts off our spring board were amusing to say the least of it.

By this time the weather was worsening:

We've had a week of gales & dust since I last wrote. I think I must have told you that there is a special wind out here, which is supposed to blow for 40 days, commencing June or July. It serves to keep the air moving & affords considerable relief to the heat. It is known as the 'Shamal' & blows from N.W. . . . At times it reached almost the heights of a gale & blows with concentrated fury . . . it is accompanied by a cloud of dust which is so thick at times it is difficult to see 10 or 20 yards. . . . Other days the Shamal drops to a gentle breeze and at times – today for instance – it doesn't blow at all, & up goes the temperature in consequence. . . . It's 106° now at 11.30 a.m. & the hottest time is 2 in the afternoon, so I expect we are in for 112° or 113° today!

The Shamal was a mixed blessing but in his next letter he writes of a completely different and rather lovely phenomenon.

5 July 1917

. . . We had a wonderful eclipse of the moon last night, a total one, lasting about 2 hours. I hadn't noticed it in my diary though now I see it is down there. Of course we saw it as soon as it began at about 11 a.m. as the moon was full, and in about ½ to ¾ hour it was entirely blotted out, and only glowed a dull crimson like a cinder, a most impressive sight. It stayed like that for about 2 hours or so & then got all right again. I've never seen such a good eclipse and of course we had a splendid view of it. I was sleeping out in the open, as I always do nowadays, and kept on waking up to have a look at the show.

I've not been very grand these last few days, 'liver' I think the doctor has put it down as; but he has treated me with various dopes & things & I'm ever so much better now, in fact I'm practically well again. . . . No news of my socks from G.O.C.! so I expect he's bagged them himself. However p'raps I'll be seeing him in a week or two, though of course I shouldn't dare ask him about them!

He was being rather optimistic about this meeting. Gertrude's note on the envelope of this letter was 'Just before he went into hospital with dysentry.' His next letter was from 'No 2 British Genl. Hospital, Amara, 11 July 1917: Please don't be alarmed at the address, as it only means I'm here for a few days to get over a slight go of dysentery, & ought to be fit again shortly & back with the regiment, certainly by the time you get this.' He goes on to say that he had felt rotten, with symptoms of dysentery but had not wanted to go to hospital. However as he did not respond to treatment, and it was best to catch 'these things' early, he had gone into hospital and already, after three days, was feeling much better and had been promoted to a diet of semi-solids 'which means custard for lunch & an egg for breakfast & tea.' He was concerned for her worry.

I hope they didn't send any alarmist wires home about me. Dysentery I believe is *always* reported as a 'seriously ill' case, & I asked the doctor here not to be too depressing, but he has to wire home about all officers admitted to hospital – I am thinking of wiring to you also, to say I'm all right, which I really am. . . . This treatment takes 10 days though & by the time that's finished I ought to be quite fit again. So don't worry in the least about me please. . . .

Of course Gertrude worried, to the extent of sending a telegram as well as writing to her doctor son in France. Dick wrote reassuringly:

14 July 1917

Your wire & letter arrived by the same post today. I *am* sorry to hear Ted is down with dysentery. What bad luck & just as he had a chance. Anyhow let's hope he'll soon be well. He's sure to get good attention nowadays, & no one ever pegs out with dysentery. 'Seriously' only means rather bad, it's not like 'dangerously'. Very difficult to write much nowadays. More in a few days. Best love to all. Don't worry.

Yr loving son,
Richard

The brothers' optimism was justified. In his next letter, on 17 July, Ted reported that he was much better:

I am allowed up & today I'm allowed out for a breath of fresh air; I am on a good solid diet, chickens, eggs an' all, I drink whiskey & soda for dinner, & in myself feel as fit as a fiddle. . . . You see, I went on milk & rice pudding *at once* in camp . . . when the first symptoms were apparent, and then I thought it best to come to hospital as there isn't very much doing nowadays. Of course if we had been doing any soldiering, up at the front & all that, I wouldn't have dreamt of coming here, but would have managed to get fit again somehow.

Certainly hospital with its electric fans and supplies of ice was a far more comfortable place than the camp, where temperatures had been up to 118° in the shade with not a breath of air to relieve things. He describes the rather bizarre conditions:

Cases of heat stroke are common among Tommies, but they have little 'aid posts' dotted about all over the place, with a canvas trough full of water, into which you hurl any unfortunate fellow who goes down with heat stroke till medical aid can be summoned. The great thing is of course to bring down the patient's temperature . . . Poor Col Hefferman [the hospital O.C. who had died of celebral malaria brought on by the great heat] went up to 110°; think of it! . . . I hear the regiment is keeping wonderfully fit, despite our men being hillmen & not used to great heat. One man has died of heat stroke & we've had no more cases.

When he wrote again, on 26 July, he had left the hospital, but had not forgotten it:

I want you to write to 2 of the sisters . . . to thank them for all they did for me – the Matron of the hospital, Sister Macfarlane, & the sister in charge of the officers' wards, Rowan Watson. I'd be awful pleased if you'd just drop 'em a line thanking 'em for all they did for me . . . I have told Cox to send you £1 with which I want you to purchase a few odds & ends like shaving soap, acid drops, coloured hankies, and any little thing to send to Sister Macfarlane for her Red X store, where she keeps a few things she likes to give to patients. It will be some return for her goodness to me. You might include a box of sandalwood soap, *which is for her to take for herself* (make sure of this).

Mail is still a sore point. A ship leaving London on 31 May, carrying precious letters and parcels, had been sunk by a mine only sixty miles from Bombay. However, eleven bags for Mesopotamia were rescued, and he received a copy of her photograph in Red Cross uniform for which he wrote to thank her on 1 August.

I like the photograph you sent. *Quite* right, my dear mother, to have something to hand down to posterity: I think you've done your bit splendidly in the war, in many more ways than hospital work, not the least of which is in keeping so wonderfully cheery & always smiling for all your anxious moments, from which I'm afraid you are seldom free. But I trust it is some satisfaction to you to know that your cheery & happy bearing & the way you never allow us to catch even a glimpse of the anxious thoughts that must be always with you, all this I say helps us more than we can possibly say to carry on with whatever particular job we are doing.

Gertrude in Red Cross uniform, 1917

You've been just splendid all through. The photograph is quite good I think; you look *rather* like a Serbian nurse, at least what I remember of their pictures in the paper! But it's a good 'likeness' & easily recognizable. . . .

I got a parcel from you a day or two ago containing some gorgeous soap, films, lemonade powder (most refreshing) & some lemon tablets which I'm afraid had all melted into a sort of paste! & some beef & milk tablets which I hope to try some day. Altogether a most pleasing little parcel (& a bottle of Eau de Cologne, *most* acceptable) thanks most awfully for it.

I remember the well at Carisbrook ~~well~~ (sorry) [Gertrude had written from the Isle of Wight on holiday] & I remember having a drink of the water, *very* cold coming from such a deep well. How I would love a glass of it now! Today is fiendish, a howling gale and clouds of dust settling into a thick layer over everything. The wind doesn't lower the temperature, it just keeps the hot air moving *and* the dust.

For the rest of August his letters mostly refer to the climate 'We are in sight of the cold weather now & haven't got much more of this rotten hot weather to get through. How I hate the heat!', the mails, of course ('I lost one or two parcels from Nell [from the *Mongolia*] which is somewhat annoying. You seem to have got a whole budget of letters from me all together . . . most erratic the posts seem to be. However we've been very lucky so far – tap wood! – losing so few:'), and family. In his letter of the 14th he writes:

I am truly thankful to hear Dreda has left the bank for a far more congenial occupation. Does she dress in that saucy farming rig with gaiters an' all! When I retire & live on my farm I shall have to take lessons from Rosamond & Dreda. I still cling to the idea of retiring as soon as I can (I *can* get £200 a year in 5 years time) & starting something of the sort . . .

He also refers to the family friend, 'Specs', who 'is now a defender of his country & quite time too. However it's his show & his conscience that's got to be worried, if anyone's, if he didn't try to join up before.'

He goes again at length into the complicated subject of his temporary promotion to Lieutenant Colonel. The date of this was 14 May, but it only appeared in orders in July:

. . . I revert to my lower rank in the event of D.B. [his colonel] coming back, or if they put anyone else in command, which is quite likely as I am somewhat junior and there are any amount of fellows in other regiments who are senior to me but who have not got even temporary commands . . . so don't be alarmed or despondent if one day I write & say I've been demoted! I hope I've made that quite plain. It's something to have risen to even Tempy. Lt. Col. in these days when all sorts of odd people get rapid promotion.

He is glad she likes 'Eve's leaf'. It's interesting certainly, but now I hear they think the Garden of Eden was more up Baghdad way! However Kurnah will do very well for the present.'

Writing on 22 August he says the weather is still 'frightfully hot'! . . . We just sit and drip & lose weight all day till evening & long for the sun to go down. But . . . there are people a good deal worse off than us, right up at the front, in small tents & not so many comforts easily obtainable such as ice as we have.' They were now living in big tents, with one of the small tents they had been living in at Basra 'as sort of bathroom, in which the thermometer had registered at 125°.'

He had some unexpected sad news to report from Lansdowne, the regimental depôt in India, to which most of the officers' wives had returned after the exodus of 1914.

Mrs Bobby Reid died the other day, having given birth to triplets, all girls, & doing well I believe. They arrived 7 weeks before they were due it seems, so her death I suppose is not surprising. Poor Bobby, he's awfully cut up of course, & the regiment has lost one of the best & brightest women members. . . . Personally I can hardly realise it; one gets used somehow to hearing of the death of one's men friends nowadays, but it doesn't seem right that people like Mrs Bobby Reed should die.

The other news from India was better – for him, anyway:

I have had long letters from D.B. There seems little or no likelihood of his returning. . . . This means – silly as it sounds – that I shall keep the command till someone else gets it. I mean Henderson, our 2nd in command & on sick leave at home, may come out . . . or some senior fellow in the 39th or any other rgt – they are not particular nowadays – may be put in . . . don't *count* on my keeping it . . . I've got it by a piece of luck & will be luckier still to keep it. How I should love to command it in some fighting, & to see the results of one's efforts this hot weather. For indeed we have been working hard to get the regiment as efficient as possible & in good fighting trim & I should be grievously disappointed if they failed in any way. But I know they won't, I'm confident they wili do their best.

Then on the 25 August he wrote:

on board 'P 93'

. . . I'm writing this on board the river steamer and will try and tell you all about it. We got orders rather unexpectedly to move at 24 hours' notice – none too long if you have a big camp to strike & pack up and heaps and heaps of stores & baggage to pack up & load.

For once it seems the authorities meant what they said and within a day of their receiving their marching – or, rather, sailing – orders, the 2nd 39th Garhwal Rifles were once more on their way to the front.

AUTUMN CAMPAIGN 1917

'P 93' was a paddle steamer, a shallow draught boat with a huge barge attached to each side of it 'filled with stores, rations, men, animals, transport carts, guns, in fact anything & everything that requires conveyance up river'. It was obviously 'a very unwieldy craft' and the river was difficult to navigate owing to its winding course and fast flowing current. The river bed varied a lot in depth and they often ran aground on uncharted sandbanks, but it was never serious – 'a little puffing & jerking on the part of the engines and we are off again'.

In his letter of 25 August Ted describes the embarkation:

> Well, old 'P 93' (one of the latest by the way, cabins, dining saloon, electric light & fans & 'every modern improvement', including a lovely bathroom with a full size lie-down splash-all-over-the-place English bath, gorgeous) came alongside our camp at 7 yesterday morning & we commenced loading her up with tents, ammunition, rations and all the hundred and one things that a regiment carts about with it. Every single ounce had to be manhandled & taken & loaded on the ship from the camp. It was a piping hot day, one of the hottest we've had, & the N.W. wind that had brought such relief the previous day changed to a S. wind, which was just what we didn't want, as this brings a damp & sticky atmosphere with it, & is trying enough to sit still in, much more so to do manual labour in, & very strenuous labour at that! However the men tackled the job with their usual good spirits & by 11.30 we were finished & off up the river.

Their journey was through flat and uninteresting country, relieved every few miles by a small barbed wire encampment consisting of a few tents and matting huts, apparently manned only by a sentry with a fixed bayonet – 'marching posts' where troops not going by steamer rested for the night. Occasionally they passed bigger encampments from Basra to Baghdad and beyond. 'A dreary life this must be for the troops,' Ted comments, 'for they are miles from anywhere, & can only watch the steamers bearing their more fortunate companions up the river to where things happen, or down stream on leave or to some base hospital . . . still L. of C.

must be kept intact, & doubtless we shall all get our tour of this uninteresting duty someday. We reach Kut tomorrow – I trust I am giving nothing away! – and from there go on by train.'

He was very much moved by the thought that, although dull and uninteresting to the eye, they were passing through the country that had been the scene of the fighting during the ineffectual effort to relieve Kut in 1916 and again when Kut was retaken and the way to Baghdad reopened.

On 29 August he wrote to Gertrude from the camp where they were now settled, doing his best to descibe Kut, although he had not seen much of the town itself:

To begin with, we anchored about 2 miles below, where a sort of new Kut has sprung up, consisting of huge dumps of stores & depôts and a hundred & one things necessary for an advanced base. The railway ends – or begins – here too, so in the short time between getting in by ship & going off by train there isn't much opportunity for sightseeing. . . . After tea we strolled up the river bank towards Kut to have a look round. There is really very little to see. A jumble of broken down trenches which might be ours or the Turks', it's impossible to tell which. Barbed wire, bones, & dud shells testify to something having happened round about here, but otherwise the place must be rapidly assuming its former aspect. You see we captured Kut once, then the Turks got it, & then we got it again, so the whole countryside is seamed & scarred with trenches belonging to both sides. The town itself, an ordinary mud-built town – was rather knocked about but has since been considerably repaired. . . .

There is one rather interesting thing here; on the river bank, about a mile below the town, the Germans built a sort of column of Victory or it may have been built by the Turks in memory of those who fell, both British & Turkish in the seige of Kut. I have heard both explanations. It has no inscriptions on it, but at the base are 2 guns captured from the British at the seige. It is in bad repair & will not survive long . . . but it is a curiosity in its way. Close by are the graves of several Turkish officers.

They had travelled from Kut to Baghdad in open trucks along the newly laid line and marched out to the camp about 1½ miles outside the city. Here they were welcomed with breakfast and cold drinks by the other regiments in the brigade, including the Queens, the Surrey Regiment, so Ted once again met many friends, this time from home.

4 September 1917

. . . We lead a strenuous life here, putting finishing touches to our training. It is indeed pleasant to join up with our brigade at last and to get to know our fellow soldiers. I told you I had met the Queens but no one in particular. I met Spens the adjutant & he remembered us all very well from the old Camberley Frimley days. Was it his sister, red haired, who married Harry Harris? (What's *he* doing, by the way, & where's Charley Anderson all this time? pardon the interruption!) I didn't like to ask him, though we had a good talk about most other people.

He writes lyrically about the local fruit, 'Huge luscious water-melons, grapes, & sweet limes, also dates, of course, of which I ate my first fresh one a few days ago,' and goes on to describe Baghdad:

I have of course visited the City of the Caliphs and am much pleased with it. I had heard so many fellows say they were disappointed . . . but I am by no means . . . in fact I think it is a good spot. After all, it all depends on what you expect. It is a typical Eastern town, mud & brick built, with one big main streeet & the usual small winding smelly bazaars, roofed in to keep the sun out (and the smell in!) and lined with the usual rows & rows of tiny little cupboard-like shops. The one big street was made by the Turks by the simple expedient of cutting a wide path right through the middle of the city, irrespective of any private houses or anything that barred the way. As a consequence this wide street is bounded on both sides by mutilated houses. Here you can see half a living room or bedroom, with furniture still in it; & further on a whole house cut neatly in half right down the middle, showing the arrangement of rooms & staircases perfectly! Christian Churches, Jewish Synagogues & Mohammedan Mosques – for it is a most cosmopolitan place – all suffered in the same way, hewn down together if they were in the line of the street, or cut in half or a piece shaved off to satisfy the Turkish street maker. It is a most curious sight, the ends of all these buildings left rough & unrepaired, as if some great giant had taken two long cuts with a huge knife through the centre of the city and lifted out the debris with a spoon & so left the street clear as it now is. The Turks called it Khalil Pasha Street, after the victor of Kut; but it is now called New Street. As an improvement it is a decided success but it was a most ruthless method to adopt. . . .

I went across the river & saw the railway station, the famous terminal of Germany's Eastern aims. There was nothing much to see, a few burnt out trucks, a lot of scrap iron, a cluster of railway buildings inside which there seemed to be a lot of work going on, judging by the noise of clanging & hammering that issued from them.

We breakfasted at the Hotel Maude, (by the way I've never got my socks yet, & I simply daren't go & ask for them!) & came back to camp in a bellum. Bellums here are nice sensible boats, just like sea-side rowing boats, & they row them just like those men in blue jerseys at the sea, only dressed in Arab kit of course – so much safer & more comfortable than the cockle shells of Basrah & Amara!

. . . D.B. is still in India & will not I fancy come out again . . . his time in command is up in November . . . so I suppose I shall keep it for a bit longer yet, & very glad I shall be too. I want to take the rgt. into a show & see how we all get on, so I hope they don't send anyone out to take it from me, though I have always told you to expect it at any time.

11 September 1917

Many thanks for 3 letters which arrived on 6th. They were dated 12th, 18th & 25th July. Yes, wasn't it silly of them to wire & say I was seriously ill . . . I'm so sorry, but I wired as soon as I could to say I was all right. I am absolutely fit again now . . . though I didn't really turn the corner & feel my own usual self again till we'd been here a day or two . . . please don't worry any more about me. I'm taking great care of myself, as if anyone gets ill & is invalided it only means being sent to India, and I should hate that more than anything else, being right out of things owing to some rotten illness and not helping things on a bit.

The strenuous training continued although the hot weather was by no means over – 'every day this month we've had it 112°, far above what it should be . . . but I love the work, being in command as it's all so interesting & such good practice for me; and it is a pleasure to work with such good & keen officers & men as I have got under me.'

He has heard from Jim in Singapore: 'He seems very happy & is by all accounts a very busy man, what with being cable censor & a few other things.' However he seems to have had his usual bad luck with Nell's letters and cables:

I only got Nell's wire after I had come out of hospital as it was addressed c/o Casualties, Bombay, & was sent on by post from there, which seems rather a rotten arrangement. It's best to stick to the regiment always for an address & not try any games. . . . You say something about getting home, but I'm afraid that's clean out of the question. You have to be pretty bad to be sent home from here. However with any luck I'll be home on a month's leave next year sometime, & if the war's over I may get longer.

He ends this letter: 'I fancy D.B. is absolutely certain *not* to come back now.'

17 September 1917

Just a line to tell you not to expect a letter from me for some time after getting this one, as we are off on a straffe, so don't suppose I'll get much chance to write. Please don't worry, I'll be all right & I'll write again as soon as ever I can, but of course on these occasions one doesn't get much time & besides I expect censorship is strict. . . . I am most awfully glad to command the Battalion on this show & I do hope we get a good chance: I have absolute confidence in the Battalion, officers & men alike; so wish me luck & don't worry. Wish I was nearer home all the same so as to communicate with you more often & quicker. . . .

Well goodbye for the present & wish me luck & the regiment too. I never expected to command it in action, & am indeed proud & happy to get the chance.

22 September 1917

Just a line to say all's well. We have had no scrapping yet but have had 4 days hard marching, *very* hard, over frightfully bad & dusty roads. We have come 54 miles, & that at the end of an enervating hot weather & the men not hard & not having had much practice in route marching lately, is pretty good work; hard work anyhow. The dust on the march was *awful*, absolutely indescribable, you really & truly couldn't see one yard at times. It is very cold at night now & still warmish during the middle hours of the day. We only have one blanket each, & our greatcoats of course, & no tents, so it's pretty parky at night, I carry that Shetland wooly in my haversack & find it *frightfully* useful. There are some more troops just ahead of us, & we heard guns this morning so evidently the ball has opened, though of course by the time you get this it will all be over, & a brief reference in the papers will be the only thing the public will know . . . I must keep a full record of all our doings as things & incidents fade so quickly from one's memory if one doesn't jot them down. Well, please don't worry, mother. The regiment is in great form & I'm tremendously glad to get a chance to take it into action. I haven't got the time to write to the others as you may imagine, so will you please apologise, & expect my next letter when you get it.

10 October 1917

Just a scribble to tell you I'm all right after the fighting round Ramadi on Sept 27th, 28th & 29th, which you may have noticed in the papers, though I don't suppose they will make much reference to it. The 1/5 Queens were in it with us, so you may perhaps hear accounts from some of their relations. The fighting is all over now, as we have killed or captured the entire Turkish force here, some 3,000 men, & 2,000 surrendered to us, the

Garhwali War Memorial, Lansdowne, with guns captured at Ramadi

Battle of Ramadi (Sketch by Fred Roe)

good old 2/39th! Isn't it splendid. The regiment had done *awfully* well, though I say it as shouldn't, as I commanded it all through! The G.O.C. the force had been round to thank us & congratulate us & said that we were going to be specially mentioned separately from the others as having done so well. The officers & men were *magnificent*, mother, & I am frightfully proud to have commanded such a splendid lot of men in action, & I know you will be too. The Queens were splendid too, & fought like veterans.

We did a night march on 27th Sept & dug trenches close to the enemy that night, marched all next day till 3 p.m. & then attacked & captured another ridge; dug trenches all that night & next morning advanced over 1500 yards of open ground & attacked & captured another ridge, & a very important bridge which prevented the Turkish army escaping. Also we captured *3 field guns*, isn't that magnificent for infantry, & all by our little selves too! Those guns were knocking us about rather badly at very close range, so 2 of our men got Lewis guns & captured them, alone & unaided. A very nice thing for infantry to actually knock out guns, & then capture them. After that, practically the whole of the Turkish force (2,500 out of a total of 3,000 odd) surrendered to us, the 39th, including Ahmed Bey the Turkish commander & all his staff. We had a good many casualties in the 3 days fighting, during which we came under very heavy machine gun fire at times, & also heavy shell fire. But we fortunately only had 2 officers wounded, & very few men killed. The main point is the operations have been entirely successful, the general & all are fearfully pleased, & Genl Maude has sent us some very congratulatory messages. I, of course, am more pleased than I can say; I knew the men would do well, but they have exceeded my wildest expectations. We have had heaps of congratulations from the other regiments & individuals, & the Garhwalis have more than sustained their reputation. The 3 days fighting were *really hard*, no sleep practically, very hard marching & some good stiff fighting; very very little water, scanty food, but a cheery view of life helped us all along, & now of course you couldn't find a happier crowd anywhere. I'm awfully fit & well, had many narrow escapes, but a miss is as good as a mile isn't it. Too busy to write any more. Best love to all the others.

This letter, written in Ted's easy to read, flowing writing on several sheets of a small writing pad, has some smudges on the last page. It is more than probable that Gertrude wept a few tears of relief, pride and joy that Ted had achieved his ambition so successfully.

This account of the Battle of Ramadi can be supplemented by the messages scribbled in pencil, and in one case, in red chalk, on pages torn from field service pocket books and sent back to the commanding officers:

B coy. 2/39th G 28.9.17

We are holding both banks of the AZIZIYAH CANAL just south of the AZIZIYAH BRIDGE and facing RAMADI 7.45 a.m. C Coy is here too.

R.B.E. Upton Lt.
O.C. B Coy 2/39th.

90th Punjabis

AZIZIYAH BRIDGE captured by Garhwalis & line of road across it held. Have left weak reserve on Shaikh FARAJAH Ridge. Need support for counterattack on AZIZIYAH BRIDGE apparently massing.

C & D Co Queens
AZIZIYAH BRIDGE 7.55 am

To O/C 2/39th G

B Coy (about 100 men) have captured the AZIZZIYA BRIDGE and holding Bank facing East. Supports & ammunition required urgently. Please stop our guns firing on AZIZIYAH BRIDGE.

From o/c B Coy

B. Coy 2/39th. 28.9.17

D Coy & B Coy have captured a village just North of the AZIZIYAH BRIDGE. Also there are 4 guns in the village with their gun teams & horses. We want reinforcements as we have a long line to hold. We also want ammunition. We are digging in North of the Village. There is some cavalry on our left which may be our own.

R.B.E. Upton Lt.
O/C B Coy 8.25 am.

O/C 2/39th G

Captured 4 guns and one m.g. and about 1500 prisoners.

F. Powell Capt
Cmdg D Coy, 2/39 G

Reinforcements if possible. Have dug in all round defence 100 of Asisyah Canal Bridge. 8.36 am.

The O/C 2/39 G

Situation report 11.30 am

I am holding a line facing E marked *red* in the accompanying sketches. The troops in the line consist of a detachment of the 90th Punjabis 2 Platoons of th 1/5 Queens and 2 companies of the 2/39 G.R. I have made over the line with the 1/5 Queens and the 90th Punjabis detachments to Major THOMPSON cmdg 43rd [Gurkhas?] and am closing the 2 Coys of the 2/39 G and coming to FARASAH RIDGE. The enemy has [not?] been seen since 8.30 when all the prisoners were sent in.

Capt, 2/39 G

O. C. 2/39th G 28.9.17

Coys No 1 & 4 halted & dug in roughly on spot directed. 90th, after a short halt, again went forward. They acknowledge their error in having done so & are about to withdraw from their too advanced position with permission of their C.O. Rifle fire smart at times.

F. Powell Capt
Cmdg D Coy

4.45 pm by orderly.

9.10 am 29 10[sic]17
2/39th GR

SAA being sent now. Hope to reinforce you with 2 Coys 43rd shortly. 4 m.g. should have joined you. Have asked for artillery support. 90 P[unjabis] 8.55am.

B & D Coy 2/39th Garhwal Rifles 29.9.17

After advancing over the Aziziyah Ridge Cpt Rogerson decided we had better push on & pursue the enemy hotly. On reaching the far bank of the canal we saw enemy guns about 150 yards from our position on the Canal Bank. C & A Coy then advanced up the canal and occupied both banks of canal & N.W. of RAMADI. B & D Coys then advanced on the village in which the enemys guns were seen. After resisting our advance to the village the enemy capitulated. We captured 3 field guns and a lot of arms and ammunition including a machine gun. We cleared the village and sent forward a party of about 12 men to bring in prisoners who were surrendering further up the Canal. We then dug in all round the village, and are now constructing an all round defence. About 2,000 prisoners have been brought in, including a Turkish Colonel. There are still some Arabs & some Turks collecting loot & rifles, but after providing escorts for the prisoners etc we can spare no more men to round them up, so are firing on them. We have received one section of the Queens as reinforcements and they are still here. We are drawing water from the AZIZIYAH Canal and we have received some more ammunition.
Capt O.C.D Coy
R.B.E. Upton Lt O.C.B Coy
F. Powell Capt OC. D Coy.
Time 11.10 am O.C. 2/39th Garhwalis.

2/39th
B. N. 60 29/9

Cease all firing. Flag of truce with Col Costello going out to meet AHMED BEY.
Dunsford Col
11.45 am.

The Battle of Ramadi was over.

Nell also had an account of the battle, which differed in some details from the letter Ted had written to his mother.

. . . Thirst was our main enemy, & by the second night our men were really done, as they had dug trenches all the first night, marched about the desert the next morning, attacked & captured trenches in the afternoon, & were digging again all that night. Water was very scarce indeed, & had to be brought up to the firing line by night. Previously it had to be brought up in small tanks in motor lorries, as we were miles from the river, & part of the way the lorries were under shell fire, so you can imagine the difficulties to be overcome. It was hot by day too, much hotter than it should be, & what with fighting & marching & digging our men were really done in by early morning on the second night . . . I know what it is to be thirsty now, Nell! Washing, of course, was out of the question & we were pretty sights after the battle.

He describes the advance to the Aziziyah Ridge, which they had been ordered to attack as it overlooked the only bridge by which the Turks could retreat: 'We advanced across this 1500 yards of open ground, under very heavy rifle & machine gun fire, & a lot of our men were hit I'm afraid, but by the greatest luck in the world only two officers . . . Why we weren't all hit I can't think, as the air fairly hummed with bullets.' The Garhwalis then went on alone to capture the bridge – 'This we did in great style' – and next Ted tells her of the capture of the guns:

. . . Then a very rare thing happened, we – the infantry – captured 3 field guns. Wasn't it splendid, Nell dear, it wasn't as if the guns had been knocked out by our guns, divil a bit; the guns were firing at us at 400 yards range – absolute hell it was, I can tell you – & then some of our men advanced with rifles & Lewis guns, shot down the gunners, & then 2 companies charged & captured the guns. A magnificent piece of work, all done by the 39th too, alone & unaided, except by our own rifle fire. Ask Jack [her brother, a war-time gunner] how often infantry capture guns! Not often, as he will tell you. *Then* the fun began; it hardly sounds credible, dear, but *over 2000* Turks surrended to us . . . and the battle was then over, in fact, the whole operation then finished, as there are no enemy left here now, not a single one, as we have either killed or captured them all, & all their guns, & simply tons of booty, rifles, ammunition, kit of all sorts & heaven knows what else. It's been gorgeous, dear child, & all the more so as I know you will be so pleased.

His overwhelming delight at commanding such a splendid regiment, although such a junior officer, comes over strongly in his letters to both Gertrude and Nell. At the beginning of Nell's he wrote:

I *am* so proud, dear child, to have commanded the regiment in such a good show . . . The big general commanding the force came round today & said he was going to mention the regiment specially in dispatches, separately as having done such splendid work! and then laughingly said that he didn't think he would, as we must be so tired of having that said about us! I'm so awfully pleased about it all, 'cos I know you'll be pleased, dear . . .

8 October 1917

Dear Mother,

I haven't really & truly had time to sit down & really write letters lately. Ever since the fighting was over on the 29th Sept we have been more than busy clearing up the battlefield, guarding prisoners, on outpost duty etc, and we've had hardly time to turn round. From all accounts our victory here seems to have caused a tremendous impression everywhere, and the force has received numerous congratulatory messages from the King & General Maude . . . so I am most awfully glad to think the 39th played such an important part in it, and so proud myself to have commanded the Battalion in the fighting. You will have seen references to the capture of Ramadi in the papers, & I expect you wondered if we were there, very much so, & the regiment played a very prominent part & did splendidly – one of our officers [captain Rodgerson] has been given a D.S.O. for the good work & gallant conduct that day – he was badly wounded in the mouth, his tongue being nearly shot away, but he stuck to his job & eventually came back to the ambulance & on the way stopped & wrote down for me a clear & concise account of the situation where he was, though he must have been in great pain at the time. He was very plucky all through & thoroughly deserved his award. I have had a line from him in hospital & he tells me they have sewn his tongue on again & he will get his speech back all right, as of course he couldn't speak a word when I saw him. Our two men who knocked out the Turkish field gunners with Lewis guns have been decorated too; these are what they call 'immediate' awards, given by General Maude in the field, I hope we shall get lots more in due course, as the men thoroughly deserve them. The 5th Queens were with us in the fighting and – being a Guildford regiment – no doubt the name Garhwal will soon be quite familiar there. They are awfully struck with our men, & especially with their work during the fighting, & I expect you may hear something about us in your conversations with various people. The Queens fought splendidly & did awfully well, & please tell everyone so. . . . I owe several letters to the family but I really haven't time to do anything like answering letters just at present. I am most awfully fit & well & love this sort of thing, real soldiering with a vengeance. . . . The Shetland woolly has been more than useful & I don't know what I should have done without it. I carried it in my haversack on the show & very glad I am that I have it with me now.

I am telling Cox to send along £2.15 for Ruth's things, I'm awful sorry, but I had an idea I'd settled that.

The flies here are absolutely indescribable. The Mess (we are messing in a tumbledown old Arab hut) is black, really & truly with them, & at meal times you can't see your food for flies. They nearly drive you mad.

Then in a PS: 'This is the writing pad you sent me in Egypt in Jan. 1916!'

10 October 1917

I hear a mail goes out today, so I'll just scribble you a line to catch it. Genl Maude flew over from Baghdad today to inspect our Brigade & to thank us etc & make the usual complimentary speeches. . . . We are still camped on the scene of our victory, & we move camp tomorrow, right up near the outpost line, so we shall be very much 'at the front'. We are still without tents & sleeping on the cold hard ground. There seems to be a good deal of difficulty in getting things up & grub is rather short at times, but the show is being run well on the whole, & in a few days things ought to be running as smoothly here as anywhere else; one can't expect much, as we have only just captured the place!

I thought of asking old Maude this morning about those socks, but my courage failed – all C.O.s were introduced to him & we shook hands and he asked us how we were etc – He didn't impress me much, he is not the hard, stern, cold conqueror I expected him to be, he is rather the reverse, but this doesn't seem to interfere with his capabilities at all.

Reuter is most optimistic in his wires about France, & we certainly seem to be giving the Boche a rotten time now, & getting the submarines in hand too. Air raids are distressingly frequent, but I see reprisals spoken of, & L.G. seems to have sanctioned them, so I expect by the time you get this some raids will have taken place over Germany. But the war seems no nearer its conclusion. . . .

All our wounded are doing well, I hear, except one Indian officer who died yesterday. He was badly wounded in the thigh, poor man, & such a good officer too. The fortune of war! Well, he died a soldier's death anyhow.

17 October 1917

I got no letter by last mail from you, but I expect I shall get one in a day or two, as everyone is the same, a lot of letters missing still. But you see we are somewhat far away from civilization and the roads are bad up to here, in fact there are no real roads yet: transport is short and all there is is being used for more important things like food & ammunition. However I must say they are doing wonders & we have had 3 mails altogether since we left Baghdad just a month ago. . . . We have moved to another camp, just behind the outpost line & we are now busy digging our new defences. We have got our tents now, which is a blessing, but we are still on 20lb kit . . . but I am quite content with what I've got really, though it means sleeping in your clothes & nothing much in the way of a change. But one gets horribly used to pigging it & everyone is just as dirty as everyone else so it doesn't matter – all the same, if you think of it, a cake or two of soap & some cigarettes are always welcome. . . .

We are all very fit & getting nice & hard – of course this open air life leaves nothing to be desired & I love every minute of it. All the same I long to get home again to see you all once more and dear old England. But as long as I'm here I feel much happier than if I was in India, doing something to help possibly, but not in the line I want. . . .

Since our great battle of the 29th we haven't seen a Turk. They put me in command of a mixed force the other day, cavalry & guns & infantry, & we went out & reconnoitred 10 miles or so in front of our line but never saw a sign of anything, bar a Turkish aeroplane, which must have wondered what we were doing – I also had some armoured cars with me & they went out about 20 miles but saw nothing – a most desert country this, simply miles & miles of sand & low hills – all sand – wherever you go or look. The banks of the Euphrates produce a little greenery, reeds & palm trees, & the Bedouin Arabs raise scanty crops here & there & then wander on to a fresh camp: for the rest it is one howling waste. So you may imagine an army operating here can't go very far from the river, as this is absolutely the only water supply. We were fighting 4 miles from the river the other day & got thirsty enough, & the supply of water to us in the firing line was a very difficult matter.

I had long letters from Paul & Dick last week – Paul is getting married soon I see; & a very sensible thing to do too I think. I see no chance of mine being a war wedding, I'm too far off to hope for anything of that sort I'm afraid. I *might* manage a month in England next summer, but it's doubtful. But the war should be over by then . . .

Two of the Turkish guns we captured on the 29th are being used as anti-aircraft guns here. I have had them engraved with the regiment's name etc, so we can claim them after the war for the mess. They are most certainly ours. . . .

I am ever so fit now though it wasn't till we had been in Baghdad about a week that I really begun to pick up . . . However I assure you that no one could have gone through all that heat & dust & marching & fighting we had in the last fortnight of September, unless he had been absolutely well, as fit as a fiddle & as strong as a horse. I did, so I am, if you follow me! . . . The only thing is a molar in my left jaw, bottom row, is aching like blazes & it has been stopped once but wants looking to. I don't want to have it out, or else I could have it done here, sitting on a biscuit box, & letting a shoeing smith from a cavalry regiment pull it out with a pair of pantomine tweezers or something equally painful. So I have shoved in to be allowed to go to Baghdad where there is a real dentist. There isn't much going on now, and though I hate having to go away for a day or two, still I feel it will make me much fitter to do my work properly so I think it's the right thing to do. I had a horrid cold the other day, chiefly sand & dust irritation I think, & I felt rotten for a day or two, but the excitement of battle proved a splendid cure. A tip for the future!

I heard from D.B. last mail . . . his time of command is up on Nov 22nd so I don't think we shall see him again. I hear Lyell is due to come out with the next draft, and as he is senior to me, it would mean his taking command from me. But I can't complain can I! I've had the regiment 6 months, I've commanded it in action; the men & officers were splendid & did awfully well, so what more can I expect? It's only fair that the senior ones should get the good jobs. So don't be surprised if I get regulated to Major as 2nd in command, or even down to my real rank as Captain, if Henderson & other senior officers come out. But it's rotten if it happens, 'cos people who don't know will wonder why.

The trip to Baghdad was even more horrendous than the visit to the dentist:

26 October 1917

. . . The journey takes 4 days, 2 days each way, over most appalling roads with 2ft ruts and clouds & clouds of dust, really quite indescribable. You have to get down as best as you can, as there are no regular means of course, I mean no railway or anything like that. But there are motor lorries going backwards & forwards with rations etc & you have to pick up lifts here & there in those. It's a very rough & jolty journey & very tiring as you may imagine. We are about 70 miles out, & you do about ½ the journey each day, an experience I can tell you! Yesterday I started at 6.30 & got in here at 11, driving through bitter cold N. wind all the way.

During his three days in Baghdad he 'didn't have much time to do anything except see the dentist & do some shopping – of course we are clean out of all luxuries etc up here so I had heaps of commissions to do for lots of people, & that took up a good deal of time . . .'

As for the dentist:

. . . A very good one – found a wisdom tooth badly gone & so he killed nerves & things & sort of ½ finished it, but I have to go & see him in about a week's time. However, he is coming to ½ way house, so I shan't have to go so far thank goodness. . . .

I see Genl Brooking, our General, has been given a K.C.M.G. as a reward for his services in the capture of Ramadi, so they are evidently well pleased with him and all he did. It's good to have been in such a successful show.

As things settled down after the campaign more letters came through with news from home, although still in rather an erratic way.

29 October 1917

Very many thanks for a letter dated 22nd August which I got yesterday. I have had letters from you dated later than that, so I suppose this is one of those mails that comes by Colombo. In it you talk of Dick's coming home on leave & in one I got a few days ago you describe his doings on leave! So things are a bit topsy turvey. It had a gorgeous little bag of lavender in it; thanks ever so much. . . .

So glad to hear Ben is so well again. She wrote me such a cheery letter which I got yesterday & says she knows she is so much better herself.

It's an awful day today, nothing but dust & sand, one of the worst dust storms we've had. We have got some more kit up now & I now have a tent & a bed & a clean shirt, so am quite a swell. Also a pair of pyjamas which I got from the Red X in Baghdad the other day. So nice after sleeping in one's clothes for six weeks.

Not much excitement here just at present, we are still busy digging & don't get much time for anything else. . . .

Sorry to hear Capon is still unwell – I'm afraid he's come to the end of his really active capabilities and after the war we shall have to look out for another factotum . . . Capon will be a great loss & the family will have to devise a pension scheme for him.

7 November 1917

I haven't much news for you . . . Yesterday we went out on a reconnaissance about 5 miles beyond the outposts but saw nothing. In today's communiqué I see we have got Tekrit, north of Baghdad. I wonder what our next move will be. I am sending along a card which they give us out here, a ghastly production but I'm afraid it's the best I can do. We just got Ramadi in time to appear in the card as you can see – all the other names are former scraps out here.

Yes, I see London has been raided a good deal lately, but Ben writes to say how wonderfully calmly people take it all. So glad to hear the specialist's opinion on Capon is so hopeful but it must be awkward having him on the sick list. . . . Thanks most awfully for writing to the matron & sending her a parcel, I know she will appreciate it. Certainly the things you put in sound most alluring & I think you couldn't have chosen better. Lucky getting that bit of sandalwood soap! . . . I had a line from Jim a day or two ago, & he tells me he expects to be sent out here soon, but has to go to India first. I wonder if we shall meet! Specs still exempted! Disgraceful I call it. Surely he can hold a gun straight in a trench, or do *something* to finish the war. . . .

I wrote & told Nell she could put our engagement in the paper if she liked. Several people have seen Paul's & asked if it was my brother.

11 November 1917

. . . I wrote to you 2 or 3 days ago so haven't much further news. We got the home papers today with the wire about our Ramadi show in them, but I see they are very non-committal & told you nothing beyond that the action was a success. . . . Nell's birthday today, she is 20, so is getting quite grown up! I hope Jane finished her present in time & I hope Mrs Fielding won't be shocked! Nell writes very cheerily & of course is wild at the prospect of my coming home next year. I hope the dear child realises that is only an outside chance & may not be possible, but I'm going to have a jolly good try.

My chief bit of news this mail is that Col. D.B. is definitely giving up command & Jack Hogg has been appointed to succeed him. He is the son of Col. Hogg you know at Camberley & is at present commanding our 3rd Bn in India. He is an awful nice man & we are lucky to get him. The official letter says he will proceed to Mesopotamia 'in due course' which may mean anything. So when he arrives *and* Lyell, I shall drop to humble Captain again!

I went out shooting this morning, it's the first holiday the men have had since we left Baghdad last September. We have been so busy marching & digging that we haven't had time for any 'days off'. It's rather a krewst here, as you have to have an escort to go out any distance from camp, rather novel conditions to shoot under! However, nothing exciting happened & we brought back 6 partridges & 2 grouse so had quite a nice little outing.

Yes, Ben told me all about the air raids; terrible they sound and it's good to get some inside news as the papers tell us so little. They must do a lot of damage of course; you can't *miss* anything, bound to hit something flying over London.

Thanks most awfully for your contribution towards the Mess – Fortnum & Mason parcel. It's most awfully good of you & we shall all appreciate it awfully *when* it arrives. I was particularly anxious to do something – however small – in return for all the good work fellows who have served under me while I've been in command have done for me. I could not have been better served & I am frightfully glad to feel that you too are helping – I do hope the things turn up in time for Christmas, but things take years to arrive to this 'outpost of empire' nowadays. . . .

You say in your letter of Aug 21st that you sometimes feel a bit anxious about me, but please don't my dear mother. I really & truly am awful fit now & am feeling so well & all in this cold weather one ought to keep as well as anything.

18 November 1917

I got a lovely surprise today in the shape of a really gorgeous pipe from you. You had to post ridiculously early apparently to catch the Christmas mail for these parts, and your parcel turned up today! But that's no matter, the point is the rippingness of the present. Thanks ever and ever so much for it Mother; it's a regular 'just what I wanted' and such a gorgeous pipe too; I'm awful proud of it and it's the envy of the Brigade. . . .

23 November 1917

I haven't heard from you again since I last wrote, but I have to write tonight as we are going out on a reconnaisance for the next 3 or 4 days & we shan't be back until after mail day . . . I am taking out a column of cavalry & infantry & guns tomorrow, and am commanding the show. It's awful good fun getting these mixed columns to command, as it's good practice in handling troops & very good experience. The amusing part is of course that most of the senior officers in the column are really senior to me, being real Majors etc, but I am senior to them *pro tem* by virtue of being an acting Lieut Col! So it's a bit of luck for me, isn't it. However when Hogg & Lyell join & I have to revert, I shall only take part in these affairs as a humble captain again, rather a drop from commanding a force to commanding a company! The fortune of war –

Good news from Palestine isn't it, & just as well perhaps considering the rather depressing series of events in Russia & Italy. Really the Russians are rather trying, but I fancy we have cleared them out of our calculations altogether now. The Italian news is uncertain, but they seem to be preparing us for worse. Poor old England & France! We are bearing the whole weight of the war between us. I rather fancy America's entry will make all the difference, especially her air fleet.

Awfully sad about Genl. Maude wasn't it, so awfully sudden too. They say it was Cholera, but no one seems to know for certain. He was undoubtedly a very good man, with an extraordinary amount of energy & attention to detail – and he is a great loss.

I must have my bath now, & use some of the bath salts you sent. I used one cube the other day & it was gorgeous.

1 December 1917

. . . Today a plum pudding arrived from you, so we are all right for Christmas in that direction anyhow. Our trouble is a Turkey (one is tempted to pun here, but I will refrain!) or a goose, but there are apparently none to be had. Thanks awfully for the pudding, you'll be glad to hear of its safe arrival I know.

Life is strenuous for us – at least for the men – these days. Dig, dig, dig all day, but last week we were lucky & went out on a 4 days reconnaisance about 15 miles up the river. 'Berryman's column' it was called, and . . . we had quite a nice 4 days out; ooo, it was cold, no tents & this old wind blowing the whole time. We came across some Turks one day & they fired a few shots at us, but did no harm. But it was good training for us all, as we were in hostile country & never knew what mightn't turn up. And it was a very pleasant change too from our life of late, cooped up inside barbed wire & all here –

Lyell hasn't joined yet. Yesterday I got a wire asking me to inform him of his wife's death in Lansdowne. Did you ever hear of anything so tragic? She had just had a son, but from all accounts was going on well. Poor Lyell had to leave Lansdowne a week before the child was born, so perhaps the worry of it all killed her, poor woman. I don't know *what* Dolly Lyell will do now; I believe he was devoted to her, & it will be such an awful shock to him, poor man. I have wired the sad news to him to try & catch him at Baghdad before he arrives here, I think it's better he should know as soon as possible rather than wait till he gets here.

Later Just got a wire from Lyell to say he is applying for leave.

Mrs 'Dolly' Lyell and Mrs Bobby Reed were both as much casualties of the war as men killed in battle. With all the best

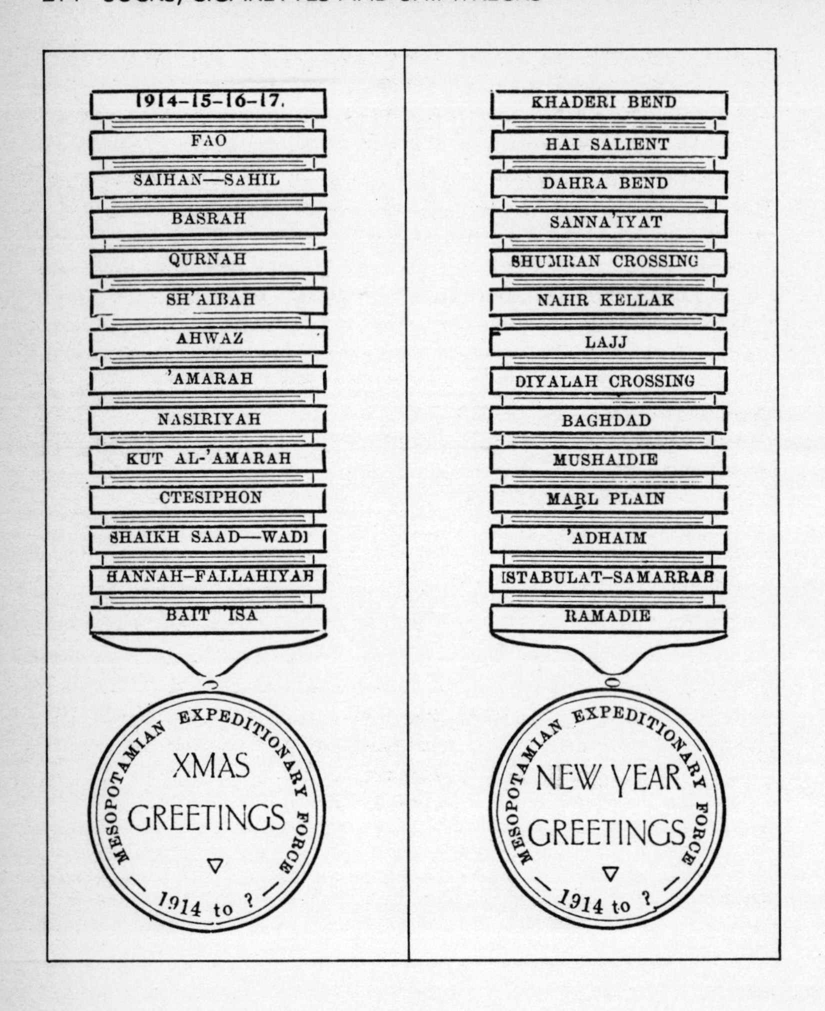

Christmas card from 'Mespot', 1917

doctors on active service the medical facilities of a remote hill station left much to be desired.

. . . Really Babs Davids being married seems very hard to believe, they both are so absurdly young. As you say, it must be hard to feed a sudden inrush of people for a weekend, & even your truly marvellous capacity for meeting these somewhat alarming situations must be taxed these days, but I have no doubt you still succeed in making a little go a long way & I'm sure no one leaves Delaford either hungry or sad. Whiskey at 8*s* 6*d* a bottle! My word, we pay 33*s* a dozen here, but I suppose we are spoilt children.

Yes, mother, I have had my wish of leading my men into action, & indeed they did not fail me. . . .

You say Specs you think will be roped in at last – well, it's about time, & his work can hardly be put down as of national importance! I got a lovely box of cigars from old Fielding today, very sporting of the old man. He wrote such a nice letter in reply to my 'ultimatum' about getting married next year. I wish you could manage to put in a few days there, but I know it's difficult, but the rest of the family are all very anxious to meet you, I'm sure you would like them all most awfully.

He wrote of the Christmas festivities, such as they were, but the weather and the conditions in camp were the dominant theme of his letters in December.

17 December 1917

Since I last wrote we have had a good hard frost each night . . . & the water in our basins frozen solid. . . . We haven't got any thick khaki yet, only the drill stuff . . . One hears such a lot about the hot weather out here, but not a soul ever told me of this really bitter winter. Consequently we all made preparations for the summer & none for the winter. After all you can do with very few clothes in the summer, but you want a whole heap & lots of blankets too in the winter. . . . We all find the cold keeps us awake at night, in tents you see, & the only possible time to have a bath is midday, when there is a tiny bit of heat in the sun.

Day before yesterday we had to go out on a 15 miles reconnaissance, stay out one night, & we came back yesterday. Two Turkish deserters gave themselves up to us, they were rather miserable specimens, & seemed absolutely fed up, & complained of ill treatment, scanty food & clothes, & no pay, so let's hope this represents the general condition of their army out here. We had to bivouac the one night we spent out, so you can imagine how cold it was, & there were 7 degrees of frost that night too!

Christmas Eve, 1917

. . . This past week has shown us what Mesopotamia can do in the way of rain & mud. We had 24 hours rain last Wednesday and the whole camp was turned into a quagmire; but it dried up in the wind of the next few days, though the weather remained raw & very cold. . . . All our men have got warm clothing and they need it badly, but officers are still without it, except one or two lucky ones who happened to have some. Today my one & only pair of riding breeches has gone to the wash – fancy washing clothes in the icy Euphrates this weather! I'm glad I'm not a dhobi – so I am shivering in shorts and a greatcoat. We are getting some thicker khaki from government stores, but it hasn't turned up yet.

Their Christmas was quiet. Gertrude's pudding had been eaten about a week before – 'we are getting so many for Christmas & as yours had arrived I thought we had better get through it now. It was voted excellent, & so it was, & I didn't get the sixpence though I had a good try!' The Fortnum & Mason parcel had still not arrived, although he got 'a lovely tin of nuts from Rosamond . . . a very welcome gift indeed'. However, they had plum puddings and crackers and some luxuries especially ordered from India and made merry in the evening, although some of the sports had to be cancelled because of the weather.

He is still concerned about the air raids – 'I hear from all sides of the bomb in Piccadilly and how Swann & Edgars were strafed: a good shot wasn't it, though I don't suppose they do much actual aiming' – and Capon:

Please let me know if I can do anything for him; I think we boys ought to buy him an annuity or something as he has served us faithfully & well all these years. If you are writing to the others you might suggest it to them, & meantime make inquiries as to what's the best thing we can do for him. There are many calls on our pockets nowadays, but I think this is a special case.

His other news was that Colonel Hogg had arrived at last – 'so I am no longer in command but am an acting Major & 2nd in command now. Lyell has gone back to India on a month's leave.' But, as he said in an earlier letter, reporting Colonel Hogg's appointment: 'I can't complain, can I; I've had my innings & a jolly good one too.'

DICK'S & TOPHER'S 'KREWST'

While Jim was censoring cables in Singapore and Ted campaigning in Mespot, Paul had managed to spend enough time in England to get engaged to Nancy Swann, and Dick and Topher were apparently enjoying what Ted referred to as their 'krewst' in France.

Dick's letters were scrappy compared with Ted's, and Topher's have not survived, assuming that he wrote any, but, with comments from Ted it is possible to get some idea of what was happening. Ted was still a bit confused about the situation. Answering a letter of Gertrude's which was probably written at the end of January 1917 he says, 'So glad Dick & Topher have joined up, but I cannot quite grasp what Topher's position is in a native cavalry regiment. I suppose you say you have three sons in the Indian Army now!'

Meanwhile Dick was writing from France.

22 January 1917

Many thanks for sending the boots. I think you said you had sent my blue suit to Lesley Roberts [tailors] & my greatcoat. If not please send it to them & get it pressed. Also ask Dreda to send to that shop where you get O.F.[elsted] ties & get one for me. Can you give her the money. I dunno when I shall get home but I want to wangle it same time as Paul. I've got no respectable uniform at all, & I shall have to wear mufti.

Topher is quite happy with me I think. He's awful fed up as he gets no letters nowadays!

I will write to Lesley & Roberts & tell them to get my mufti ready.

And, in a postscript over the page:

Quite forgot I *must* have some dress shirts & collars got ready. Please have *all* those dress shirts of mine done up, some are Paul's I know but get them done as well, then there'll be no mistake. There are some that came home in my kit [he drew a sketch] like this with *14* not 14½ inside. You needn't get the 14½ washed also my white waistcoats. *Don't* send them to the wash, but to a shirt dresser; they do these things so much better &

one doesn't economise on leave. It wouldn't be a bad idea to send my dress clothes to Lesley & R. with the dinner jacket & tell them to press them.

I daresay *my* dress shirts are in the black tin box I left behind.

All this most important.

Any dress ties get 'em washed.

1 February 1917

. . . You might buy some leather buttons 4 big 6 small like you took off that coat & get Capon to clean them with *dark* polish every day till they look old. I want some more & hate 'em new.

I hope to get home about 10th.

Love from Topher & me

He got a cake from you today.

Ted wrote on 10 March, answering one of Gertrude's letters dated 7 February: 'Poor Dick, I expect he feels the cold a bit, but he's jolly lucky being able to get hold of Topher to help him along. I wonder if Dick got his leave or not.'

Dick did not get his leave.

13 February 1917

Many thanks for the 2 parcels you sent us the other day. I would have written before only of course I imagined I was coming on leave, so I thought I'd be able to get away any day, one never knows. I believe the cold weather is over at last. Anyhow it didn't freeze so much last night. I am glad you recovered my blue coat. What luck eh?

Many thanks for the *Daily Sketch*, and please thank Dreda for *The Stage*. Topher seems keen on getting a commission, dunno' quite how he is going to wangle it, we must see what we can do.

I sent you a wire yesterday saying leave was stopped for a bit. I do hope Paul is not home yet. Dreda wrote Topher on the 5th that Paul hoped to be home in 14 days so that makes the 19th & I might get home about then. I see Ben has a munition job.

I hear news of Jane & Chubbie from a friend who called there.

Was there something about Dick's friend, Evelyn, in the copy of *The Stage* that Dreda had sent him?

We gather from Ted's letter of 24 April, answering two letters of Gertrude's written at the end of February and the beginning of March, that Dick had some leave after all:

Yes, it was lucky, Dick & Paul just managing to meet wasn't it. I wrote

Dick a long letter from Karachi telling him all about June, but of course I haven't had time to hear from him yet. I had a very long & interesting letter from Paul last week; he is awfully pleased with life isn't he, & he told me all about his romance & his Nance, *most* interesting.

Dick's being on leave would, of course, account for the gap in his letters, not that he was the most regular of correspondents.

24 March 1917

Just a line. Many thanks for yours. I am so glad Jim is safe. Topher & I are quite alright.

Send some chocolate *plain* Fortnum & Mason or Cadbury Vanila (not milk) little plain chunks too, lots & often.

Love to all,
Dick.

The news of the sinking of the *Tyndareus* at the end of February had only just got through.

Sunday, 1 April 1917

So sorry I haven't written for such ages, but it's been imposs. We've been fairly on the move every day a different place, sometimes sleeping in the open other times lucky to get a stable. Cold as blazes too. Always sort of under the impression we'd been in action in 24 hrs, but nothing ever happened and for the present things seem quiet.

Topher & I are both very fit in spite of it all.

You might send me one or two pairs of loofa socks. Size 7. If you have sent chocolate you needn't send any more as I can get it now. Many thanks for the porridge it's awfully good & we now have time to eat it.

I wonder if you got my will! See I've at last been Gazetted. I'll write again soon.

5 April 1917

Many thanks for your letter and the *Daily Mirror*. The porridge & chocolate have not arrived yet, but I expect they will soon. We still have some of the last lot of porridge. Jim's regiment do seem to have been heroes. I am so anxious to read what the papers say. Isn't this weather beastly. Snow & rain & cold & mud, however at present we are fairly comfortable & can make fires in old tins.

We are both very fit; someone I met tother day said I was getting fatter. Can you send me a little Lux. I am sending a watch home to be mended.

Get it done as soon as you can & have a protector thing for it. Topher uses it & always smashes it, & it's a good watch.

Easter Day, 8 April 1917

Many thanks for the handkerchief. I am using it today. It arrived just right. The porridge & chocolate & cake all arrived safe. The chocolate just what I like & in the small pieces too. Much easier to carry one or two in your pocket.

Send me some porridge once a week. I will send you the money as I charge the mess. Happy Easter to you all.

Topher must have written to his mother in greater detail, as Ted, answering a letter of hers written on 11 April, comments: 'Dick & Topher seem to have had a hardish time lately, & I'm glad they are back in rest for a bit.' Meanwhile Dick continues his staccato requests – one can hardly call them letters.

15 April 1917

Many thanks for your letter & the DM [*Daily Mirror*]. I expect the porridge will arrive soon.

I wonder if you could find out about a small lightweight tent. The advt was often in the field [sic] & I meant to have seen about it when I came home but forgot. The stores may have it. It costs £7 & weighs 4 or vice versa, can't remember.

Wet & beastly today. Must catch post.

This seems to have been almost too much, even from Dick who could do no wrong. The note on the envelope is a terse 'tent' heavily underlined.

18 April 1917

Could you make me some white bands to tie round the arm. About as wide as this [he sketched them] & measure twice round the arm for length. They are for my stretcher bearers.

So many thanks for cake, porridge & Lux. Most welcome nowadays.

Love from both,
Dick

'BANDS' wrote Gertrude on the envelope.

30 April 1917

Many thanks indeed for parcel cake porridge etc. The créme-de-menthé sweets are awfully good. The armlets too are quite alright, the rest you say will roll up alright. Did I tell you I wanted 16. If you could sew a biggish red S.B. on them it would be nice, cut the SB out of a bit of stuff, no desperate hurry.

Lovely now, so warm & I wish I was at home. I had a long letter from Ben. Tell her when you see her. I wonder if you have seen about the tent.

Post going, more later.

6 May 1917

Many thanks for the parcel porridge cake etc. Most welcome. Put in some Lux next time. The tent has arrived & is lovely, keeps the rain out too, Topher & I put it up. The watch too has come, thanks so much for all. I want a pair of *Jaeger* putties, would you send me some please. Thin sort if possible, dont know if they make two weights.

I saw Nell's brother [Jack Fielding] the other day. Fancy meeting him just on the road.

Oh I know what I want, a pair of grey riding breeches in the big black tin box in the lumber room. They are in with that red coat & things I didn't take to India. They are the same stuff as that suit of mine.

I am sending you £5 to pay postage etc for all these things. I see the cake & porridge always cost 1*s* 4*d* to send.

Send us some penny packets of seed, mustard & cress, radishes, carrots, sweet peas & taters, lettuce, vegetable marrow, eh? Scarlet runners. Send me *John Bull* every week will you?

10 May 1917

In one of those boxes upstairs you will find a fairly large, nicely bound, red book written in Hindustani. I forget if there is a name in, anyhow it belonged to somebody in the I.C.S. Would you send it to me please, as I am going to give it to some padre man.

We get another glimpse of Dick and Topher from Ted's letter of 28 June, in answer to Gertrude's of 16 May: 'So glad to hear Dick & Topher are flourishing. The latter must be rather tired of roughing it, & he must feel the poor old 16th being cut up very much, he must have lost so many pals.'

Meanwhile Dick, incorrigibly light-hearted and lovable in spite of everything, wrote again, this time not even dating his letter:

Many thanks for those S.B. bands. If some day you see in the paper I have the D.S.O. you'll know it's for the smart appearance of the stretcher bearers, & I'll give you a bit of it.

Please send me another pair of shorts. I'll probably be sending some thick clothes home for you to keep safely!

Tell Ben I dined with that nice looking Stephen last night. 'Dined' sounds grand but I wish you could see the conditions. The radishes are coming up.

And in a postscript: 'Topher is clearing away breakfast and sends his love. You needn't send any more porridge.'

1 June 1917

Many thanks for the *Sketch* & *Spectator* & *Pictorial.*

What an awful raid I saw that was. I do hope they don't get to Guildford. Hot as blazes nowadays. I love it.

Topher is always saying I never have any work to do! When you write to him say you hear 'Richard says he is working very hard nowadays & says he gets so tired, so mind you look after him well.' It will make him laugh.

2 June 1917

Topher thanks you for his letter today.

Would you pay the enclosed for me please, send bills with money then they'll understand.

Would you send us a packet of enclosed instead of porridge. Good it sounds, goodness knows what it tastes like.

The plants are growing A.1. Topher says the beans are nearly ready to eat, & we are to have a veg marrow for dinner tomorrow. Quick an' all.

With apologies for Topher's bill, we must excuse the Tommies.

Topher says he caught some fish the other day. I've not caught one yet. 'Sawful.

I am looking forward to the boots & leathers.

PS. Topher says if you can find an old fishing reel he'd like it.

There were some things even Dick could not ask his mother to send. The following request was addressed to Dreda.

19 February 1917

Please send me one or two of those awful common khaki made up bow ties with a thing on the back to fix it to your collar stud, you know the sort, and it must have the allies flag or something on the bow parts, something bright & big. I'm sure they make them.

Lemonade powder will be awfully welcome.

Best love to all & I hope you've seen Cicely.

Yr loving Dick

Dear Mother,

So sorry I never wrote to you at Totland Bay & by this time you are back & I hope all the better for your holiday. You never do want to go. Eggo etc arrived today and we hope to have buttered eggs tomorrow morning for breakfast. Your face is fat in that photograph isn't it, but p'raps you *are* fatter nowadays.

Wd you send some more eggo. That cake was awfully good.

I must send some more thick clothes home. Such a clutter as Topher is always saying.

We have a dear little kitten in our mess, our mascot we call it, black and white.

9 June 1917

Many thanks for the parcel. Clothes, cake, sweets etc. Eggo isn't as good as cook's eggs is it? Sorry you haven't any spare money to invest. Why not sell out the £600 in the War Loan. It won't be unpatriotic, and put it in the enclosed. It's a good thing I know . . . only I suppose old Hill and all will be against it. The stars are quite right. The ones I wanted.

Your bedroom must look nice after it's been painted. My bedroom at present is a greenhouse up against a wall. No glass, but there's some corrugated iron, and only a little rain comes in. The vine inside is growing . . . but of course it's all over the place as there's no one to tie it up.

21 June 1917

Dear Mother,

Many thanks for your letter from Totland Bay. I hope the clothes'll come soon. We've managed to get a Gramophone after all & the records are awfully good. Fancy getting a leaf out of the Garden of Eden, and fancy having a son in command of a regt. I expect it's a relief to Ted to have D.B. out of his way for a bit. . . . Those raids were alarming. I hope they don't try Guildford again. More clothes lumbering home me dear! Huge parcel but undo it & get out that German hospital placard, rather interesting.

I do hope Ted sticks to the Command, but I doubt it, his being only a Capt, yet quite capable.

Dreda tells me she is going on the land after all, how will she like it in the winter.

We've tried the Eggo. Jolly good & Topher has also made some cherry jam, most awfully good . . . Topher is a great fisherman. . . .

Send some more books during the next week or two. I'll want them, also some lemonade powder.

3 July 1917

Many thanks for the parcel that arrived last night. The wretched gramophone needles were all over the place, however I collected most. They were very welcome as we had just run out.

I enclose papers about some of my shares. Keep 'em safe. I hope you'll be able to buy Graysons & sell out the war loan. But I suppose old Hill will say no, but why shouldn't you invest where you like. Your income should be a great deal more than it is, our grandparents idea of safe consols at 3% was rotten & if only your money was properly invested you'd be quite rich.

I sent you a watch, a pair of sox & some bits of shell. You might send me some elastic so that I can make a wrist band to go through the watch. That spring is rotten, at odd moments the watch shoots off as if from a catapult! Hence the damage.

Lovely weather & I wish I was at home.

P.S. Did anyone ever find my blue serge coat?

The reference to the King in the next letter is a little obscure. Perhaps His Majesty had been visiting his son, Prince Albert, on Paul's ship, the *Malaya*. And Gertrude had evidently taken over the search for the 'awful common khaki made up bow ties' after all:

6 July 1917

Many thanks for your letter. Sorry to have given you so much trouble about the ties. Never mind if you cannot get them. I thought you'd easily get them at a poky little drapers. Topher's present has arrived, it's lovely and he's awfully pleased.

I hope Dreda will have a good time at Bognor. Will she live at the farm.

I was wondering if Paul would have an F.F. with the King.

Here's the address of a good stockbroker. I'd wish you'd write to him and tell him how your capital is invested & ask him how it could be improved upon. He's absolutely sound & you need not do anything even if you are allowed to. Tell him your son is a friend of Major Dykes. . . . You'll realise how badly off you are considering the capital you've always had. He may want paying for his information, I will do that.

We all hope the war will end in August!

11 July 1917

Glad you got the watch safe. I haven't sent off that big parcel yet, it's all ready, but it has never been directed.

I do hope Capon will get better, but I suppose he has the same thing as Mabel Jones's mother, & must be a cripple for the rest of his life. Whatever will you do without him. You watch the stocks in the papers . . . and do write to Williams it would be interesting. Our seeds back here HAVE grown. Veg marrows climbing all over the place, & of course the lettuces are lovely, & all the messes in the rgt come & get them, Topher & I are so popular. Topher says he hopes to be home soon.

Awful these raids. I'm glad to be away from the shells.

1 August 1917

I am so glad Ted is all right again & has rejoined. I dunno' if you ever got my letter telling you dysentery was not so dreadful as people at home think.

I hope to be home next month sometime, & shall spend it quietly at Guildford.

The postscript to this letter makes one wonder what he meant by 'quietly'.

With a view to my being home in Sept? *perhaps*, please have my evening dress shirts sent to the cleaners *not the wash*. Do you remember that number we worried so much about last time? Paul had one on the ship I know. Those are the ones I want to go & I enclose a cheque to pay for the dressing of them. *Don't* please send them to the wash, they do spoil them so. There are the ones I bought in London but I've no idea which they were unless they are all in the suitcase together. They might go too if you know them. Have you found my blue coat?

19 August 1917

I hope perhaps to be home on 25th. I wonder if you have found the blue coat. I am telling Lesley Roberts to send my clothes to Guildford, and another small parcel will arrive with some collars. I shall come home on Sat.

Best love to all,
yr loving son,
Richard

One senses the relief with which Gertrude wrote on the envelope: 'Richard saying he is coming home'.

With Dick in England and no letters of Topher's extant we have to rely on Ted's answers to Gertrude's for news of the 'Krewst'. It had obviously been a happy one, with Topher putting his gardening skills to good use and Dick enjoying his role of protective elder brother, but it seems it was inevitably due to come to an end.

Dick had raised the question of Topher's future in a letter to Ted at the end of June. Writing to Gertrude on 14 August Ted says, 'Really I don't know what's best for Topher. I sympathize with him immensely, he must be so heartily sick of being a Tommy, & besides I expect he'd like to earn a little more pay. Surely a commission in the A.S.C. would not be impossible, a stammer wouldn't matter there, & he's seen enough scrapping to warrant his going into the A.S.C.'

Dick had enjoyed his leave and Topher was also expected home – though we've heard *that* one before! – but Ted was still more concerned with his youngest brother's long term prospects. 'I'm very anxious to hear what job Topher has managed to get,' he wrote on 7 November, 'whether he got gunners or tanks. Really awfully good of Genl Robertson to take such an interest in him.' However he was glad to hear that Topher had turned up on leave at last. 'I hope he enjoyed it – wish I'd known I should like to have sent him the price of a sherry & bitters at least.'

Dick was back in France at the beginning of December.

Sunday 9 December 1917

Thank you and the girls most awfully for that lovely box. It arrived most opportunely too. Thoroughly wet, tired & bored, & with no prospect of anything for dinner but bully, & lo & behold that box of delicacies. We've been living like dukes. Too good of you to send it & it was like a conjuring trick, things never seemed to end coming out. We've eaten all the almonds, & that butter is lovely, & the mince pies too.

Did you have all that frost? We were sleeping in the fields then. Awfully cold but really not as terrible as it sounds. I have hopes of being home soon. Perhaps for Christmas . . .

By 'we' Dick was referring to himself and his fellow officers, not himself and his youngest brother who had been with him for nearly a year. The 'Krewst' which they had clearly both enjoyed and which was, in time, to become one of the family legends, was now over, but it would be logical, through the medium of Ted's letters, to follow Topher's fortunes for a while.

In his letter of 30 December, answering Gertrude's of two months before, Ted writes:

Poor Dick, yes he would hate the mud & cold I know, and now he's losing Topher he won't be any better off. As regards Topher's commission, I expect the poor boy has had more than enough in the ranks, though as you say he was well enough off as Dick's groom: all the same if he wants the commission it seems hard on him not to let him get it and he'll be home some time training now. His stammer would certainly be a difficulty & I hope he manages to do something for it.

Apparently some sort of speech therapy was fixed up for Topher, either before or coinciding with his training for a commission.

You all give me hopeful news about Topher & the curing of his stammering. I do hope you'll be able to tell me of considerable improvement, if not a complete cure, in some future letters. The boy has done splendidly I think & I'm sure we are all jolly proud of him, and I think he deserves a jolly long rest; even if it involves strenuous training he will at least be well housed and fed and will be away from the strain & stress of the front.

A month later he wrote again about Topher, this time slightly less happily, 'I'm glad to hear that Topher's stammering is so much better. He doesn't seem to have struck a very bright spot at first, but I expect by now he has joined his cadet school & things will probably be better there.' It seems they weren't as Ted, writing on 16 July, 'I *do* wish they'd give Topher a commission. Couldn't Dick go over & see the C.O. & rout round a bit. It's a shame as you say to expect the poor boy to go back to the ranks after all he's done.'

He is still worried in his letter of 23 July: 'I do hope Topher finds a suitable job: he ought to be able to get into the A.S.C. easy enough; . . . by now I expect he is fixed up; I sincerely hope so. But I don't think they are doing him very well considering his service. I wish I were home, then I'm sure I could buzz round & go and see his colonel etc & get things moving. . . .'

Seeing that, at the age of twenty one, Topher threw up a good job abroad to come home and enlist as soon as war broke out and had served in the trenches 1916–17, Ted probably had a point. The stammer had been a stumbling block but apparently this had now been virtually cured. However by August things were better: 'I am so glad Topher has started on his way to a commission, & I think the A.S.C. should do him well.' Ted had asked Cox to send Topher some money but we don't know whether he ever got it.

In October, answering letters written at the end of August, Ted was able to write, 'I'm most awfully glad Topher has passed out & done so well, & I hope he'll get a good job somewhere now. He seemed to be on the verge of going to Egypt in your letter.'

Meanwhile, what was happening to Dick?

In his long letter of 1 February, after his comments about

Topher, Ted writes: 'Poor Dick! I know how he must hate all that slush & cold. You say he has been away from his regiment. What's he been doing I wonder?' Apparently, like his brothers, he had been 'loosing all his kit, & not being able to take his shirt off for a month! Quite like old times, I know so well what he feels like. After a bit you begin to feel you never want to take off anything, & then that awful "scratching" period begins, & you simply *have* to take it off! Aren't I horrid! I suppose he was all through the Cambrai business, as I see the Indian Cavalry were engaged.'

As Dick did not always date his letters or give a full address from which he was writing it is not easy to follow his movements. After a long silence, partly explained by references to 'a lovely leave', there was a little bunch of such letters, written on scraps of paper, all stuffed into one envelope on which Gertrude had written 'Richard, dated March 7, 10 & 11th Marseilles'. However, what seems to be the first letter in the series was from the 'South Western Hotel, Southampton', and was obviously written at Whitsun, which was sometime in May that year. Dick was once more going overseas, trying to take a dog with him:

I got Jane on board all right & imagining I had scored & was safe, left her in charge of the steward. When I went back the Master of the Ship had arrived & said I could not possibly take her. I argued etc & told him I had escaped the A.M.L.O. & Embarkation officer & he had no right to stop me. All to no purpose, and as she cannot travel during Whitsun she leaves here, on Wednesday & will be delivered at Delaford. A doggy porter has her in charge at present.

I have just had some tea here as I am not going yet.

He appears to have gone to Egypt but, typically, was trying to arrange a transfer.

On Active Service
WITH THE BRITISH EXPEDITIONARY FORCE. Y.M.C.A. Tuesday.

Arrived over here this morning, the place I said I thought we should go to. Awaiting orders now to go by train. Specs that means 5 or 6 days in the blooming thing. Hot, dusty, dirty, but I believe the scenery in some parts is luvvly. Very hot here this morning. Just had a shave & hair cut, so sleepy I went to sleep while I was getting my hair cut.

What about the dog eh? If she does not arrive Wed write to the porter in charge, parcels office, Sthpton.

c/o Cox & Co. Alexandria,
to be called for

There appears to have been a delay for some reason about half way to Alexandria:

Friday 25th

Here I am waiting at the place I expected to wait, and I am going to try & wangle a job here if possible, though I doubt if it will come off. Don't write to where I said till I tell you for certain. It's gorgeous weather here but an awful lot of dust blowing about. We had a 3 days train journey, but it was not so bad as many I have experienced.

That was a lovely leave.

E.F.C.
OFFICERS' REST HOUSE & MESS
Sunday 26 May 1918

I wrote yesterday & gave you an address as I may get a letter before I have to leave. Anyhow I am trying to wangle an exchange & stay with a hospital there if possible. I don't know if they will sanction it, if they do I think I shall apply for some leave from here! Still lovely weather here not too hot yet. I've met several men I know & I am leaving a letter for Ted at Cox's in case he comes through, he might have time to arrange a meeting if our visits clash. [Ted, still in Mespot, was hoping for some home leave.] The biscuits & milk & kettle were awfully useful in the train, although troop train journeys are done very much more comfortably than in the early days. We had several quite long stops at odd stations at odd times & we could get a good wash & decent meals, four in a first class carriage for 2 nights wasn't too much of a crush either.

I wonder if you found that envelope with my statement of leave granted. There are two lots of two each. One lot was in with that yellow ticket. Hope you are using my meat card & butter etc. The 13s.

E.F.C.
OFFICERS' REST HOUSE AND MESS
Monday

Still here yer see but so far I've heard nothing of my application for an exchange. Early yet . . . It's so fine here that I imagine it's lovely at home & everybody on the river every day & tennis & so on. I have not seen or heard anything of Ted yet. I wonder if you have. I hope you'll be able to write soon & will not have written too many to Alex before you get my last letter. We eat white bread now & there's lots of jam & stuff, but I wish I was home all the same. Did Jane got to the dance on Tuesday. Give my love to Eleanor.

By 1st June he was back in Marseilles.

I called at Cox yesterday but no letters had arrived. So I hope you get the letter asking you to write here. I have not been able to go down today as I am attached to a hospital for temporary duty & have been orderly officer today & could not get out. Like a prisoner in a cage. I must try & go down tomorrow. I shall be here for a bit, I expect, as they are keeping me to await the result of my application for a transfer.

Would you send those brown shoes that are in the old boudoir, that's where I saw them last.

Any news of Ted?

57th General Hospital
B.E.F. France
5 June 1918

Many thanks for your letter. I was glad to find it yesterday when I called. I knew all the letters you wrote would go whirling off to Egypt but I could not stop them. I have heard nothing yet, however they are keeping me back very kindly, till news arrives. Wonder if Ted has arrived. . . . I am sorry I missed Paul's letter, I hope he sends one to me here. So the dog arrived back safe, how good of that old porter to write you a letter. . . . Send me those 3 blue paper books of French Hugos there are about in the spare room or else upstairs in the room over the lumber room.

Monday 10 June 1918

Two letters arrived at the hospital today. I see they take four days. So you have at last heard from Ted, his leave certainly does seem uncertain . . . I got some things from Cox today that have been there since I arrived in France Oct/16. My camp bed, a chair & 500 cigars. I am glad to say that although so old the cigars are in quite good condition & I am having an awful f.f. with the C.O. over them as he likes them & I have given him some. . . . Some afternoons we go down & bathe but the water is very dirty – bits of cabbage & decaying vegetable matter of all kinds floating about.

A raquet came up from Cox, a good one, press, case & all, I had forgotten I had it, all the strings are bust though. I may send it home as it would be worth re-stringing . . . might do one for the girls.

I have got about 80 patients under my care! I've not absolutely given up all hope of having to go on, but I have definitely heard they will not sanction an exchange, if I don't have to go yet something might be worked, but I doubt it.

I have had one game of tennis but . . . the court is hopeless . . . big sort of undulations going lengthways & if you stand on top of the undulating surface on the service line, it's like serving the ball from the top of a hill, and you can get a tremendous slash in. . . .

I wish I hadn't stopped you writing here, I don't expect I shall go yet. You never know though.

15 June 1918

I am still here & if only I'd thought of it I'd have asked you to go on writing till I wire. Goodness knows how long a wire will take but if I do go I will wire thus: SEND MY WATCH. Then you'll know I am off & not write any more here.

The shoes are taking ages to come. I have just written to Ben.

I got Dreda's letter.

15 June 1918

My dear Dreda,

Thanks awfully for your letter, I shall look forward to getting the other one later on as I shall probably have to go worse luck. You'll hardly believe it, but I am quite interested in my work here. Lots of malaria cases which I know how to treat & none of these other M.O.s seem to know anything about. Dysentery too. Don't know how long my enthusiasm will *last* but I shall be sorry to go.

I'm so glad Jane arrived back safely. How exciting Freddy flying over and doing all those wonderful stunts. What fun if he comes to where I go, I am afraid I shall be sent away soon.

I am glad Topher has got to the A.S.C. at Aldershot I hope he makes a success of it, he's sure to.

The brown shoes haven't arrived yet, they should be here soon but parcels seem to take much longer than letters.

Gorgeous weather and the bathing is lovely, but it's a different life altogether from the last months with you all. I did enjoy that & I'd love to get home again, but must save up some money first.

Best love to all. I am going to wire mother 'send my watch' when I leave. Then she'll know.

21 June 1918

Dear Mother,

I am sending you a telegram this morning 'send my watch'– It's a nuisance, but I could not wangle the exchange, but I might possibly get back if I still want to from the other end.

After leaving France both Dick and Topher, by different routes and at different times, found themselves in Egypt. They were later to meet again in Palestine.

'MESPOT' 1918

The first half of 1918 was to bring changes for other members of the family and once again we rely mainly on Ted's letters for their stories. He was still very much 'at the front' and mails were taking a long time to get through. As well as being held up by the weather – 'wet and cold & the motors simply can't get along the none too good roads here' – they had, of course, to give place to essential supplies of food and ammunition. 'No sign of the good things from Fortnum & Mason,' he wrote on 7 January, '& I have had no Christmas parcels from Nell & the girls though they all said they sent them.'

Although they were up at the front, things were quiet, their only excitement for many weeks being 'one of the very rare visits of a Turkish aeroplane':

> He was very high up, barely distinguishable, and I should think he must have been on his way somewhere else. Anyhow he wasn't stopping here, and our 'Archies' shelled him – unsuccessfully – to speed him on his way and he disappeared into the distance. One of our planes which fly round here pretty well every day has not returned and they can get no news of it. A rotten country to get lost or stranded in, this, I should think, as it is very sparsely inhabited, and then mostly by unfriendly Arabs.

He later reports that the missing airmen had had to come down owing to engine trouble and had been captured by Turks, 'though they got back to within 14 miles of here. Bad luck wasn't it.'

Letters were still uncertain. 'We don't expect them nowadays much under a fortnight or 3 weeks' interval', he wrote on 21 January, but he had had a wire, just one word: 'Congratulations.' The General had earlier sent him a wire saying that he had been awarded a Brevet Majority for his part in the Battle of Ramadi. 'So I suppose you have seen it in some list. I do hope they give some of the other officers and men something . . . as they did all the dirty work and deserve a reward.' As well as the immediate awards on the field (see Chapter 14), Lieutenant Maclear was awarded the M.C., and two native officers were given the Indian Order of Merit, and one the Order of British India.

News from home was at least two months out of date. Writing at the end of January in answer to a letter of Gertrude's dated 21 November he says, 'You were writing of Paul's wedding which I suppose is a *fait accompli* now. I had a long letter from him last mail and he seemed very excited about it all,' and in a rather homesick letter to Jinny, 'So I suppose old Paul is married now. *Lucky devil* I say. I hear you were bridesmaid so I ought to be getting long descriptions in a few weeks.' He apologized for not answering a letter he had received 'about Christmas time':

. . . I've been that busy I haven't had much time for writing, except to old Nell, ha, ha – I'm still very ill, with Nellitis I mean: and I see no chance of ever getting any better – a hopeless case I'm afraid – and to think I haven't seen the dear child for over 2 years. I do loathe this war.

We have been in the front line for nearly 5 months & we are getting rather tired of it, for though not in actual touch with the enemy, yet we have to keep our eyes skinned the whole time. . . .

I say, I told you didn't I, how *fearfully* bucked Nell was with the undies you made her; thanks awfully for making such ripping ones. I got some *very* old letters of hers last week, dated last July! In those she said Mrs F. had said she thought she ought to be getting her trousseau, & they went off and bought some Japanese silk for undies on the strength of it! Mind you help like hell in getting Nell's things for the wedding, trousseau an' all: the child is to be clothed *perfectly* right down to her nethermost garments: she's such a dear that nothing but the best is good enough for her – (So you see I'm still pretty bad!)

He is still looking for news of Paul's wedding, which seems to have been subject to the same sort of confusion as Jim's. On 1 February he writes: 'I suppose Paul is married now, but I was not aware of the date, which was being perpetually changed I gather, so I could not cable. In any case the cable between Bombay & London is unable to be used for private wires now . . . and cables are being sent by post if you please!' He had also begun to make wistful plans for his own wedding:

Now I hear of the shortage of sugar & currants etc at home I can appreciate your plum pudding (already eaten) much more. *We* still get rich Christmas cake with thick sugar and almond icing from India . . . if I come home this year it seems I'll have to bring my wedding cake with me! I think it could easily be managed . . . the difficulty lies in getting it home to England. They seem to have sunk fewer ships in the last 3 weeks, but America says they have withdrawn a lot of submarines.

12 February 1918

Ink again you will notice, for we have come back some 30 miles or so and . . . Baghdad is within 4 hours by cattle truck, so we are indeed in the haunts of semi-civilization once more. I have got heaps of ink tablets and have rigged up an ink pot and am using my fountain pen as a dipper, as it has long since ceased to carry out its fountain duties.

We had a comfortable journey down; 3 days marching and 2 halting not by any means strenuous. The roads and weather were perfect for marching. They have done a lot to improve the roads, mending them etc, and they use a lovely pink sort of stone, which they get from the sand dunes close by, to do the metalling with. A most gorgeous colour, it must have absorbed the sunsets of a thousand years to get like that.

Our new camp is out in a bare dusty place, the edge of the desert. All right now, but it will be a warm spot in the hot weather I'm afraid. Not a tree or shade of any kind: two miles from the river and a dusty road running straight in front. And there is a railway line running within 20 yards of our tents, a novelty now, not having seen a train for 6 months (we all stare at the train as it goes by daily!) but I expect we shall get sufficiently bored with it before we see the last of it. Still it's a blessing to be on the rail again. One isn't quite so cut off . . . and you feel nearer home somehow.

Lyell joined us yesterday. Poor man, he is very hard hit, but it must be a blessing to him to be employed. So I am no longer 2nd in command now, & though my brevet saves me from dropping to captain's rank it doesn't save me from dropping to captain's pay. . . .

I hear the leave rules are out, but I have not seen them yet. I am told they are on the liberal side. I wonder if I shall be able to get home this year. It seems absurdly near now, & if I *do* manage it I ought to be home in about 3 months time . . .

He enjoys being by the railway. 'There are a lot of L.S.W.R. engines in use on the line,' he writes in his letter of 20 February, 'So familiar they look and sound as they go puffing by, and of course the Queens all swear they can recognise old friends in them; and I have no doubt they have all buzzed through Guildford station one time or another.' There is still no news of the Fortnum & Mason Christmas box, but Dreda has sent him a photograph of the 1914 star:

. . . and right proud I am to have qualified for it. I'm afraid it will lead to many discussions, as of course there has been equally heavy fighting and a good deal heavier in many cases since those early days. But it's nice to think that the old army (though, heaven knows, no one respects & admires the new army more than I do) will be practically the only ones to get it, including many territorials . . . who did magnificent work. Anyhow it has been given, up to a certain date, & there the matter begins & ends – if you get it, you get it; if you don't, you don't.

I have written to Nell, making some sort of preliminary arrangements for the wedding. I *hope* to arrive home about the middle of May, & be married round about 1st June, though of course it's impossible to say definitely. In any case I will be wiring to her when I start, and I hope she will wire on to you. I hear leave is on the liberal side this year: I sincerely hope so.

By the way, we are moving up a bit tomorrow; afraid I can't say where or why, nothing very exciting, but I may not be able to catch the next mail, as we are going off into the blue on 20lbs kit. This is just to warn you in case you don't hear next mail, but with this fortnightly business I may be able to scribble a short line.

He did not have as much to say about this expedition as he had about the campaign of the previous Autumn. Admittedly, although successful, it was not as exciting and he was more preoccupied with news from home and the chance of leave.

4 March 1918

. . . I have been wondering if I was surprised when I got James's wire containing the really splendid news of his & Ben's forthcoming wedding. Looking back & remembering various things in Ben's letters of late perhaps I ought not to have been. Be that as it may, the fact remains I am more glad than I can say and it's one of the best bits of news I've heard for a long time. It's a real comfort to know dear old Ben has found happiness again and she deserves some indeed. She will make James a splendid old wife and he indeed is lucky, as also is she. For we all know James, and taking it all round it is, as Shakespeare has it, a consummation devoutly to be wished. At least that's *my* opinion, & I feel sure it is shared by all.

James Tucker was a friend from Camberley days – it had been his feet that had wrought such havoc with a tea table as he swept down the razzle-dazzle on the Vicarage lawn – and he had become a barrister, although now employed on some sort of civilian war work in London.

I have applied for leave home, but if I get it and when lies on the knees of the Gods. . . . I hope Paul managed to fit in his wedding all right. In your letters (24th Dec, 2nd & 9th Jan, just received) you say his leave was doubtful, at least the exact date was. As you say Lincolnshire [Nancy's home county] is a long way off. What will you say to Gloucester I wonder! . . . I have perforce to leave all arrangements entirely in the Fieldings' hands as I can only suggest a few things – as I have already done – & it's otherwise impossible to communicate except by uncertain &

expensive cables. So I have asked Ben to act as 'agent' for me & have asked Nell to refer all questions on which there is any doubt to her. And now Ben is going to get married & I'm sorry I asked simply because she will have lots of affairs of her own to think about. Perhaps you could help if required?

If you want to communicate with me you can write to Cox, 16, Charing Cross Road & leave any messages there . . . Be very careful about my rank, initials, & Regt as both Dick & Jim bank there I believe, & Cox has already muddled us up once or twice. . . .

I have to write to Ben & Nell today. I had letters from Dreda & Jinny too yesterday, please thank them & I will write when I find time . . . I had a long letter from old Ben & there are one or two rather important things I want to say to her.

He wrote briefly on 8 March:

Tomorrow we march 18 miles after a few days stay here, and after that I dunno what happens. I suppose we shall march clean away from our tents – as usual! – though we have stayed here long enough to let them catch us up. All well here. Our 'planes have been bombing the wretched Turk today, their usual daily amusement! We have had no Hun over lately – tap wood! – but I don't think he's very well off for 'planes or very enterprising either. . . .

P.S. Fortnum & Mason's things haven't turned up yet. It is *so* disappointing.

His next letter does say something about this Spring Campaign.

17 March 1918

. . . I see in Reuters wires that mention is made of the occupation of Hit, but of course there has been no fighting as the Turks discreetly retire as soon as we show any signs of concentrating or advancing. I have seen a good many prisoners & deserters coming through & they all look pretty miserable, ill clad and hungry and thoroughly fed up with everything. . . .

I'm longing to get the next mail, we haven't had one for just a fortnight now. It ought to tell me if Paul's wedding came off all right as it had been arranged for 17th Jan when I last heard. I ought to be getting a line from him too as I haven't heard for a long time. I wonder if old Nell has found time to go to Delaford for a bit. I do hope so. Then there's old Ben's wedding I'm longing to hear all about that, and there's all sorts of news I want to hear. . . .

Writing on 22 March he has more to say about the weather and local conditions than the campaign itself:

. . . It's still very cold here, especially when that N.W. wind blows . . . And we have had a fair amount of rain, I got wet through and dry again 3 times the other day! Road scraping & mending is still the general order of the day, though I trust our march tomorrow will give us a bit of a rest from this dull job. . . . Leave opens on 7th April, but no further news about English leave yet.

By 25 March Ted has received two letters from home with all the news of Paul's wedding. In an earlier letter he had commented on the rationing at home: 'How amusing about the "bring your own sugar" to the wedding! I wonder if I can bring a bag home with me but I believe it is not allowed. . . .' Now he writes: 'Meat appears hard to get at home, but I am sure it is a good thing to have compulsory rationing . . . if I come home I shall have to have sugar & meat cards & I'm sure I shan't know how to use them, & I hope I shan't be put in prison for eating too much!'

And yet another recurring theme: 'So Specs is still exempt! Ah well, I expect he will be roped in before long. How can he – well, never mind, I suppose he knows best – I do believe it is going to rain in a few minutes, a huge black cloud has turned up so I may have to stop while it goes on. . . .' They were once again without their tents and he was writing in the open, using boxes captured from the Turks as a desk and chair.

By his next letter, however, his mind is full of the campaign.

30 March 1918

Just a scribble to say I'm all right. I suppose in the midst of all the terrfic fighting in France they have found room in the papers for a brief reference to our little show out here – the regiment have been in it: we weren't in the actual fighting, but took part in the pursuit which was a great show. We followed the retreating Turks for miles at a tremendous pace & roped in hundreds of prisoners and got any amount of booty in the shape of ammunition and kit and guns of every kind. . . . The sight on the road which the Turks retreated along was a wonderful one, strewn with kit & equipment & wounded & prisoners all the way along, and it has been a really wonderful experience to follow a beaten army in retreat . . . I am quite all right and very fit and well . . . I'm very busy just now and have only time for a short scribble. Awful luck the regiment getting in for 2 such successful shows as Ramadi & this one have been.

3 April 1918

I've no letter of yours to answer as we've had no mail for 10 days . . .

but we are right in front of everyone now and they have a difficult enough job in getting rations up to us. I scribbled you a line on Saturday just to tell you all was well & the fighting safely over . . . we are staying up here for a bit and shall eventually march back to our hot weather quarters . . . when we've finished all there is to do here & when someone comes to take our place. Ever since Sunday night we have had wretched weather. A real hurricane sprang up & rain fell in torrents. We had managed to put up 3 Turkish bell tents we had captured but the one I was sleeping in blew down in the night & we couldn't possibly put it up again in that gale so we just lay there & got wet. . . .

I had a wire from Jim on Sunday saying he was coming out here early this month. I wonder if I shall see him, but there are so many places he might be sent to off the beaten track that as likely as not we shall miss each other.

I went on a reconnaissance across the river yesterday. We visited a perfectly charming little village, all surrounded by palm trees & growing wheat. We were received by the Sheikh under the village mulberry tree, where he placed rugs & cushions for us to sit on – and then he gave us coffee, very nice indeed & made from fresh baked & ground coffee beans. He said he was delighted we had driven the Turk out, as they hate the Turk and his cruel ways and he seems to treat the Arab very badly. Eventually we left him and he gave us eggs & fowls & dates and a nice big fat sheep as parting presents – most welcome as rations are short up here . . .

It's a long way from here to home, & I should think it would take *at least* 6 weeks from the time I started. But at present I have no news about leave. It begins for the men next week, but I'm afraid ours won't be able to go yet, as we are up here and probably can't be spared for the present.

I'm sorry for such a scrawl but it's jolly hard to find anywhere to write . . . But it's all great fun really, especially as it has all been so successful.

He wrote a long letter on 24 April, which he began by thanking her for letters dated 30 January and 5 February:

. . . I believe there are mails of a much later date in the country somewhere and they may turn up at any minute.

A good deal has happened to me since I last scrawled a few lines during & after the Khan Baghdad fighting. I haven't told you much about it I'm afraid. Truth to tell there isn't very much to say about it. Besides when one reads of all this terrible fighting in France our rotten little side shows seem so absurd as to be hardly worth mentioning. Of course the whole topic of our thoughts & conversations for the whole 4 or 5 weeks has been the Western Front.

We can imagine Gertrude's impatience as he continues on this topic for at least another page before he says:

I simply can't write much about all this, but please don't think I'm dismissing the subject lightly. We are all of us deeply concerned and I'm afraid a little worried at times. It comes I fancy from a feeling of absolute impotence, of 'not being there' sort of feeling; not from any pessimism or lack of confidence in those wonderful troops who are going through it all. One feels so powerless to help out here. We all know & realise that it must fall to someone's lot to serve in these parts . . . but it is very hard to get rid of the feeling that the Western Front is where men are wanted, & the Western Front is where we all would be if we had our wish. . . .

I have been given a job for the hot weather: instructor at an officers' school, sort of teaching young officers & getting them in touch with the latest idea. I did not apply for it but they just ordered me to come and take up the appointment. It is only temporary, of course . . . We are in Baghdad . . . in a house with electric light & fans, so we ought to be fairly comfy for the summer anyhow. . . .

My leave has been refused, as so very few are being given home leave this year, except on very urgent affairs. Mere marriage apparently does not come under this head, so poor old Nell & I must possess ourselves in patience for a little longer. Poor child, I feel so frightfully sorry for her, & somehow it seems to be my fault for coming out to this rotten country & getting stuck here. As it is I don't think I shall bother about taking leave to India this year, even if I could get it, which seems doubtful now I have got this job.

I hope to meet Jim in a day or two. He is on his way up river from the base, & should be here shortly . . . I shall be jolly glad to see a member of the family again, as Jim has seen you all much later than I have, even though he must have been away more than a year.

The remainder of his letter consists of comments on family news:

Of course the chief item in your letter is dear old Ben's engagement. I can't think why she thought it would be a shock to me, I was surprised, of course, as not being on the spot so to speak I wasn't in touch with the latest developments. But 'pleased' is hardly the word to express my feelings. . . . However all this is ancient history now of course & they are married & settled down & all. . . .

Your letters too are full of Paul's wedding which seems to have gone off with a bang eventually, after having been put off many times. I haven't had a word from either him or Nance, though I sent them something, or they chose something. Anyhow I have paid the bill! & Ben said my present was a very nice one, though I haven't the vaguest idea what it was! But nowadays letters so often go astray that I'm not worrying about it. For heaven's sake don't tell them this, by the way. I'm sure to hear sooner or later if it's not been sunk or lost. . . .

By the way, on my way down here from the regiment to railhead I stopped at the latter place one night with a pal who was in charge of all our stores, tents, etc which we couldn't get during the active operations. He was busy sending up as much as he could every day to the regiment up the line as soon as we had come back, and of course a good many things had accumulated there. I asked him at once if there was a Fortnum & Mason box for the mess there, & he said 'Oh yes, I sent it up today!' So I must have actually passed it on the road the very day I left the regiment! So it's taken all this time to reach us! Doubtless you will get a scrawl from the mess president about it, but I'm afraid I've missed all the good things by coming here. However, as long as it's turned up safely, that's the main thing.

Please apologise to the others for my not writing but really the excuse 'no time' is genuine . . . I can't remember if I've written since I heard of Jinny's engagement. Anyhow I'm jolly glad to hear it & I'm longing to hear who he is & all about him, as at present he is a mere name to me. Anyhow it's splendid news, & my advice to them is to get married *at once*! I've tried waiting & it's not a success!

30 April 1918

Very many thanks for several letters from you. Our long lost mails have at last turned up & I have letters dated 30th Jan, 13th Feb, 20th Feb, 26th Feb. I'm afraid I'm most awfully busy nowadays and I have only just time for a bare scribble to you. My chief news of course is that I have met Jim. He turned up one day & rang me up & came & stayed with me that night & is here again tonight. He is most awfully fit & we have had great talks on things & people. He doesn't seem to have changed a bit since I last saw him. I've been so busy that I really can't remember when I last wrote, but anyhow I have got this job as Instructor . . . but starting off the school of course involves a whole heap of work, and I literally haven't had a minute to spare & what I have had I've spent with Jim.

Of course we are all fearfully anxious for news from the Western Front; none too good it seems just at present but . . . we must & will stick it out. It's so *worth* it, to win now, and it's just a question of endurance & surely surely we can hold out as long as anybody. It's hard to say cheer up I expect but I do say it all the same mother I'm so sleepy & haven't written to Nell for a week & she must have a line . . .

He was more optimistic about the war in his letter of 8 May and was inspired to write at length about the ability of the ordinary

'Britisher' to stick it out, but he has plenty to say about the family as well. He had had letters from home in which 'the prevailing topic was old Ben's wedding' and, as Gertrude had merely mentioned 'it had gone off all right', he was 'longing to get next mails letters with fuller descriptions'.

. . . Your letter too is the only one that mentions Nell, you say she is 'very pretty' – I'm sure of that, the dear child – but thin – well, as far as I can make out everyone at home is thin nowadays & Nell says she is very fit & well. All the same I am longing for letters . . . as they all promised to write & tell me all about old Nell, and of course I'm wildly excited to hear. I had a wee note from her at Delaford, very hurriedly written, but she seemed very full of life.

He writes again of his meetings with Jim:

. . . He was living in camp the other side of the river, and as there is only one bridge, supplemented by a spasmodic ferry, it was rather hard for him to get across. . . . I was awfully busy too, however we saw a good deal of each other, and had great talks over old times, & he told me a good deal of stop press news, tho' I was able to put him wise on a good many points as he had been without a mail for a long time. He is most awfully fit & well, & it was ripping seeing him again. He has gone off now to join his regiment. We had several dinners together at the club here and he may try and wangle it to be sent on this course later on, in which case I should have to lecture him!

He refers lightly to his latest campaign, 'You sent me one or two cuttings about Hit & the fighting up there. Yes we were in that, but there wasn't much doing, except our pursuit of the Turk, which was most exciting. But I wrote & told you we had been up there didn't I.' But he had not told her that during the pursuit, after the Khan Baghdad fighting, he had received the surrender of Nazim Bey, the commander of the 50th Turkish Division and his staff. He must have been very satisfied when he sent this scribbled message to his commanding officer.

12th INF BDE
H D 3 27/4

Herewith Turkish commander NASIM BEY and staff. There are now 11 officers and 468 Turkish prisoners in camp here

Received *EF Maude* Major
EM 12 Bde

P. C. Hadithal
E. R. P. Berryman

Ted's letter continues:

What exciting adventures my last lot of letters seem to have had! both Ben & Nell say they were stamped 'damaged by sea water' so I expect they could a tale unfold. It is a comfort to think they do roll up eventually. I think the mails are *marvellous;* irregular of course, but at least they arrive nearly always; I have the greatest admiration for the mail service.

I had a long letter from Paul describing the wedding an' all. He seems deliriously happy, & his letter was most enthusiastic. I *am* being left behind aren't I! Three members of the family engaged *and* married since I set the fashion in engagement anyhow [he remembers Wiggy] – 'tho' Ben was engaged then of course – and I expect & hope Jinny will not wait too long. Poor old Nell, I am so sorry for her, & she's awfully plucky & patient about it all. But what can one do?

I *am* so glad my cable to Ben hit off the exact day. I must confess it wasn't meant to [he must mean it was sheer chance that it did] but it was rather hard to send off private wires just then, as we were right up at the front – during the Hit business it was – however I managed to persuade the field telegraph to take it, & I'm extra pleased if Ben was so anxious to hear from me. . . .

So glad to hear Capon is so much better & can do a little work now. You seem to have discovered a wonderful doctor in London for him. . . .

Gertrude was evidently considering moving:

I suppose with all the family getting married you would be more comfortable in a smaller house, but when the family comes to stay it will be rather a problem.

Well, the old home is beginning to break up – sad but inevitable I suppose – but we have no complaints – we have been together a tremendous lot despite our scattered professions. And we couldn't have had a finer training ground than we have had, or a finer example than you, mother, and we all owe you a very deep debt of gratitude for all you have done, and I only hope our own homes will be as happy and comfortable and well managed as the one we have known so long has always been. . . .

My news is little enough I'm afraid. I have been in bed these last 3 days. It appears that I had a 'sharp attack' of sandfly fever . . . then about a week ago I began to get something really saucy in the headache line & on Sat & Sun it felt as if someone was making a tank inside my head & I thought it was going to burst. Jim was here, and was *awfully* good to me, & got doctors & medicine etc; I'm afraid he was rather worried but of course I'm perfectly all right really. Sandfly fever always leaves you with heads like that, & they are getting less every day & will probably be quite gone tomorrow.

He was not able to do so much for Jim when he had an attack of it about a week later. Jim had been in hospital for two days before Ted heard of it. 'I went & saw him once or twice' he says in a letter dated 14 May, '& he seemed very fit each time & had got over the worst of it, but I was too busy to go oftener.' However he had been able to give Jim one of the pieces of soap from a parcel he had just received, containing soap, bath salts, and chocolate.

He did not write again for a fortnight:

This old infantry school has kept me very busy. . . . We work from 5–8 every morning outdoors, lectures 10.30 to 1 & private work for students and correcting papers etc for us in the afternoon. And as the weather is warming up it takes it out of you a bit. . . . This morning I met the Russian General Baratoff, who used to command the Russian troops who were working with us out here. But of course all that's bust up now & he has come in to us. He suddenly rolled up here this morning, with all his staff and several generals etc. He was dressed just like a Cossack out of a book, double breasted coat an' all & medals & swords & a very hot-looking sheepskin hat, most unsuitable for the weather I should think. . . . It was interesting to meet him, though of course our conversation was limited!

I didn't see Jim again after that Sunday I saw him in hospital. He . . . went off pretty soon to join his regiment & I have heard from him once since then.

By his next letter he had at last heard more about Ben's wedding and Nell's visit to Guildford for it.

2 June 1918

Many thanks for your letter of 25th and 2 really excellent snap shots of Ben & James & Dreda & the best man, I'm most awfully glad to have them, & incidentally I'm jolly proud of my sisters. (I wonder if Specs took one of Nell, by the way? I know she was only a guest at the show & not a performer but I should love to have a real good snap of her.) I heard from Nell too, of course, all about the wedding & her visit. She did enjoy it so, & I'm sure it did her all the good in the world to get away for a bit. I'm so awfully glad the dear child was looking so pretty & well, but I haven't heard *half* enough about her yet. You see I seldom if ever get a description of her & just this glimpse I have got from you & Ben has made me wild to hear more. However another mail is on its way upstream I believe, so perhaps I'll be satisfied in a day or two . . . You refer to 'rather a friend of Jane's' in your letter, by name Garden, who is I gather the 'Murray Gordon' of her wire; am I right? I wonder, as, beyond the wire & the slight reference to him in your letter, I am completely in the dark regarding the whole affair.

He was right: Murray Garden was a Canadian barrister, who was currently serving with the Canadian forces in Europe. Jane had met him in London – probably at her famous shop.

22 June 1918

I can't remember if I've written to you lately, I know I've been most frightfully busy with this old school and haven't had much time. The course ends next week & then we have a week off & the next one begins.

I hear from Jim very often. He wants me to get him a lot of things like hair oil & writing paper. There is an officer from his rgt on the course so I'll get him to take a box up to Jim for me, though I may be able to manage a visit myself in the 'holidays'. . . . He seems very fit and enthusiastic.

I had a line from Nell dated 22 April & she had some letters from me . . . I'm afraid I was rather optimistic & hopeful about leave then. But if there was a chance at all I simply had to sort of warn Nell, didn't I, and I'm afraid I raised the poor child's hopes too much. I feel rather angry with myself for having done so, & there still seems practically no chance of my coming home this year.

The following poem, which Ted dedicated and sent to Nell, was published in a magazine – probably *Blackwood's*.

DAWN IN BIVOUAC

A flicker of dawn in the reddening East:
  A cluster of clouds in the melting grey:
A quickening stir amongst man and beast,
  Drowsily conscious of coming day.

A sentry's challenge – a stray dog's bark –
  Cut the silence – From where we lie
The guns stand out in the lessening dark
  In grim silhouette against the sky.

A whistle shrills through the cool, sweet dawn;
  The camp is astir as the thin note dies:
An oath, a jest, and a laggard's yawn
  From his rough, warm blankets unwilling to rise.

A shouted order, a snatch of song
  Smoke from the camp-fires hanging low;
In a jingling column, ghostly, strong,
  Down to water the gun-teams go.

Two hours later the camp is bare,
  High overhead a bullet sings:
(There's a sniper up in those hills somewhere)
  Into the desert the rear-guard swings.

It was signed 'Cotswold'

* * *

By the beginning of July Ted's stint at the officers' training school was nearly over. 'They are changing all of us instructors gradually, as we had all got a bit stale and jaded working at this pressure in this climate. So I am only staying one more course . . . I shan't be sorry to leave though I must say I have learnt a lot & have met very many good fellows.' He managed to fit in his visit to Jim.

10 July 1918
[his birthday]

. . . I drove up in a car, a 3 hour journey from here . . . I found Jim very fit & happy in his new regiment & he seems to have got among a remarkably nice lot of officers. I had quite a good time while I was there, didn't do much except a good deal of talking. . . . The hot spell is over for the present & we are having really quite respectable weather, round about 105°–110° or so with a breeze, which has risen to a wind today, with lots of dust.

Meanwhile Dick was still writing from Egypt.

11 July 1918

Haven't had a letter from you for ages. I expect you have written to Alex but I haven't managed to get hold of them yet. I am now with 39 Indian General Hospital E.E.F. but I expect by the time you get this I shall be moved on, they seem to have a knack of shifting one about in this country. I am quite happy here on the sea shore, & lovely bathing but nothing much else to do. . . . We were nearly torpedoed on the way out.

The torpedo got within a few feet of the ship, but we were swinging round & just swung in time. Most exciting, & we finished up by the torpedo & the ship going along side by side.

I wonder if Ted is home & married.

Ted was still regretting raising their hopes.

16 July 1918

As you know by now I was all too foolishly optimistic about my leave, and it was refused . . . Of course I still have a chance, but not for some time yet I'm afraid & in any case I'm not going to be so foolish as to even hint at an off chance next time & I shan't say a word till I'm really on the way!

I wonder if Dick will go to India or Egypt. If I was he I would choose Egypt but I know how much he likes India. . . .

I should think lobbing – or is it bobbing? – the hair would suit Rosamond admirably, just the type of face for it (this will make her hoot, I know! my love to her; & I must write).

Artie Woolridge a Major! I don't want to sneer at the new army & there are hundreds & thousands of thundering good fellows in it I know but still – they do get on quickly don't they. Here I am with 14 years service next month, & only a captain still! Brevets aren't much good I'm afraid. Oh well, I can't grouse, I'm still alive & whole, which is better than fifty million promotions isn't it. There's only one souvenir I want after this war & that's

your loving son
Ted

By his next letter Dick had had news of Ted.

22 July 1918

Many thanks for your letter written June 24th, which Cox sent on to me here. The silly fools haven't sent the original letters yet, they must be wandering about somewhere & will turn up in the end I suppose . . . So Ted never got home after all. How disappointing for Nell. He seems a great swell in Baghdad & must be nice for Jim & he to be together.

Nell, 1918

We are in tents on the sea shore . . . nothing to do, outside work. I am registrar, don't know quite what it means, but I seem to sign my name to a lot of odd letters & papers every day & so far everything has gone satisfactorily. We've got a tennis court of sorts made in the sand, but it's very difficult to get anything hard here. All the paths are made of wire netting put on top of the sand, & the old original wire netting road by which all the troops marched up to Gaza runs through our camp. Imagine the miles & miles of wire netting there is down.

Did you ever find those papers of mine. I want:

1. That yellow return ticket
2. (a) One paper giving me 6 weeks leave
   (b) another paper granting me 4 weeks leave.

a & b were in duplicate so will you send them in separate envelopes by different mails in case they get sunk.

By 28 July Ted had received '4 lovely long letters' from Gertrude.

I'm afraid all my home letters now are rather pathetic as they are mostly in answer to my letters written saying I was coming home & you were sort of expecting wires and cables and things. The mails are most erratic just at present, & some letters written much later than others seem to arrive first. But after all it doesn't matter much as long as they do turn up eventually, & that I think is the most wonderful part, how really regular they are & how few get lost, practically none nowadays – tap wood!

Nell had evidently been staying with Ben and James and they had all gone to Delaford for the weekend.

I'm so glad Nell was looking so well and nice . . . I long to see the dear child again, & I feel I'm treating her very badly by being so long away & keeping her waiting so. But I'm afraid it can't be helped. . . . In your April 23rd letter you had had letters from me of Feb 12 & 20th, saying I might be coming home. Yes, it's 2½ years now since I left; hope it won't be 2½ years more before I'm home again! The news from France is really most encouraging isn't it . . . I wonder if things are really taking a turn for the better, permanently at last. Please God they are.

Although Dick's address was 39 Indian General Hospital, Egyptian Expeditionary Force, he seems by now to be in Palestine.

29 July 1918

. . . People seem to have their letters numbered out here. This one of mine is no 1, & I have noted it. So number yours & we can tell which is sunk!

You seem to have had a big house party the Sunday you wrote. How nice having Evelyn down, I expect you'll like her the more you see of her.

The eyeglasses haven't arrived, suppose they came by parcel post & got sunk. . . . I wonder if you will ever find those papers of mine . . .

Still boiling hot here. I must go & look at the sights I think soon. Not far & it's a pity to be in the Holy Land & not see them all. I will take my camera & send you some pictures.

Ted has been buying winter clothes. 'I'm determined not to be caught like I was last time,' he writes on 6 August, '& have to spend the winter in khaki drill. . . . I had to put on woolly waistcoats etc to try on these coats, can you imagine it in this heat!'

. . . You speak of Nell again . . . staying with Ben . . . Poor child, I'm afraid all the frocks & frills she bought are not much good as regards the reason why they were bought: & I feel so miserable about it all. I have wistful letters from her saying how she is not counting on my coming home too much, but she was sure I would manage it somehow. But what can one do? I'm longing to get home, but if they won't let you go – well there it is. I certainly think I stand a good chance next spring, meanwhile, with the cold weather coming on out here, and the fighting season with it, I feel it is my duty to stay on & see it through . . . I have *no* compunction in trying to dodge the hot weather! so I shall begin to worry them again after Christmas. How awfully good Ben was to Nell, I can never thank her enough, & Nell was most enthusiastic about her visit an' all. You have all been most awfully god to the dear child, & I know she is being well looked after. . . .

After commenting on Topher's progress towards his commission he wonders 'if Dick ever managed to wangle that exchange, but I fancy it's difficult for anyone in the Indian establishment to stay in France nowadays.'

As it seemed to be Dick's custom to try to negotiate a change as soon as he was posted to a new job, usually without success, it is not clear whether his next letter refers to the same negotiations or some other effort.

7 August 1918

Cannot wangle this exchange so I shall be going on some old time I expect. Not yet awhile. Don't write here any more anyhow. I shall be able to pick up the other letters later on. Getting hotter here every day. I must go & call for some more letters, I expect there are some.

Ted's next news warranted a wire as well as a letter.

11 August 1918

Just a line to confirm my wire which I hope you got & understood to say I have been given a staff job, Brigade Major 34th Bde. I'm delighted with the appointment, as a Brigade Majorship is undoubtedly a good job, & I am lucky to get one first go . . . I applied for staff employ 3 or 4 months ago on the advice of Genl Brooking & others, and after all, after dropping from C.O. to a company commander where I had the same work & responsibility as officers of 2 & 3 years service, I thought it better all round to try & improve my prospects. You see I've got somebody else to think of now! It's a splendid job . . . I must explain what it is. A Brigade (Infantry) is as you know commanded by a brigadier general, who has two staff officers under him, a Bde Major & a staff captain. The B.M. does all the operations training & fighting, & the S.C. all the administrative & disciplinary work of the Brigade, so obviously B.M. is more interesting & it is the senior job of the two. My general is one Wauchope, a charming man & a very good soldier & a glutton for work. So I am indeed lucky to serve under him. I knew him in Amara last year, so I'm not quite in such a funk as I might be. Of course it's only a job & I'm not leaving the regiment for good; normally a staff billet lasts 4 years, but one can't tell nowadays. In any case rest assured I am mighty pleased with the appointment. I am sorry to leave the regt in many ways, having been so long with them & all through the war so far with them, but there are wider views to take & broader issues to consider. . . . My address will be, Major ERPB, BRIGADE MAJOR, 34th INFANTRY BDE. M.E.F. So cease sending c/o Cox & *don't* put the regiment now; just as I have written above is correct. . . .

This is only a scribble to let you know my movements. My new Brigade is on the same 'front' as Jim's regiment, but not in the same division: but we shan't be very far off each other & I expect we shall meet.

He managed to snatch three days' sightseeing before taking up his new appointment, and wrote a long letter to Gertrude describing the Biblical and Classical sites he had visited – Nejef, Jonah's Mosque at Kufah, the ruins of Babylon, Ezekiel's tomb – she must have been very impressed

On 16 August Dick writes: 'That crop and glasses turned up the other day, but some of those letters have been lost I am sure. I never got Paul's, for instance, you remember he said he had sent me an important letter, & you forwarded it to Cox, Alexandria. My eye glasses must have been sunk I think.'

He has, for the time being at any rate, given up his attempt to get back to Marseilles – 'doubt if I can manage it' – and seems to be prepared for a fairly long stay where he is – 'I've written for some bulbs & flowers to grow in the sand here! . . . The figs are just getting ripe. I eat them all day, you know how fond I am of them don't you? [One of his letters still extant from Cordwalles, his prep school, asks in large childish writing for 'some figs', so maybe she did know.] . . . I wish I was at home in this lovely weather. I shall never take leave again unless it's summer time.' And in a P.S. – 'Can you pay King's bill?'

In his next letter dated 20 August, after commenting on the news in hers he goes on:

We've just had a convoy in & being registrar I have to receive them an' all.

Did Ruth ever go to Marseilles? I wrote & told her where to write to.

I've written to Evelyn this mail, I wonder if she has been to see you again.

Nancy's brother is near here I hear. I must go over & see him tomorrow. I only heard yesterday he was in the offing & I've been wondering how we are related, & I have decided that we are no relation at all until Paul gets a baby, then we shall both be uncles to the same child, so must be related somehow.

Found my grey suit?

Meanwhile Ted was settling into his new job.

26 August 1918

. . . I arrived just over a week ago after a rackety train journey & then 4 hours in a car, thanks to engine trouble & burst tyres. I didn't get here till after 9 at night & the Brigade had quite given me up! Anyhow I arrived safely with all my goods & chattels. . . . I have settled down more or less & am getting over the initial strangeness of things, though of course I find office work quite familiar after having done so many years of it in the regiment as quartermaster & adjutant. . . .

The Brigade is the end of all things on the front. Beyond us is the desert and – presumably! – the Turk, but where heaven knows, except that it's a very long way off – so life is fairly peaceful, though it promises to be strenuous when the colder weather sets in & training & possibly active operations begin.

The river here is a lovely clear sea-blue, beautifully clean & running over a sandy shingly bed. There is lots of grass & greenery round here, dried & burnt now after the summer, but I believe it is lovely in the late winter & early spring after rain . . . lots of wild flowers, poppies & clover. But the river is the thing that delights me so; to see the lovely crystal-clear stream, blue as the Mediterranean, is a perfect joy after being on the banks of the same river lower down where it runs thick & dirty thanks to its muddy & silted-up bed.

Isn't the news from France good & reassuring nowadays? I *am* so glad for all your sakes at home, after all the anxious times you had in March, April & May. Has the turning point in our favour been reached I wonder? It seems almost safe to say so.

He reports rumours that the mails of the latter half of June have been lost and goes on:

. . . I shall be awful disappointed, as they wd contain Ben's letters telling me of Nell's stay with her about which I have heard nothing yet. . . .

Haven't seen or heard from Jim lately. He is on this line somewhere but some way back.

5 September 1918

No mail yet, the last letter I got from you was just a month ago but it seems longer somehow . . . Tremendous rumours about mail having been sunk . . . they say it was torpedoed but they managed to beach the ship at Malta & save the mails. . . .

What really splendid news comes almost hourly from France . . . what must you think of all us out here doing absolutely nothing while all that fighting is going on at home, I can't think. There seems to be practically no enemy to fight here, & whenever we make a move he retires. I wish we could feel we were really doing something to help, but it's very hard to imagine one is.

9 September 1918

Quite unexpectedly a mail turned up yesterday, at least I never thought I should get any letters, but I did, including one from you of July 2nd, for which many thanks. I had a line from Ben too & one or two letters from Nell. . . . It's still very hot all day, with nice cool nights & fresh mornings. But the day heat is very trying, damp south winds and still sticky days with intermittent dust storms of some violence, very unpleasant as you may imagine. This damp season is called, as I think I must have told you, the date-ripener, and is doubtless excellent for finishing off the dates, but I don't know that I can find much to say in its favour. . . .

Ben seems very happy & comfy in her little suburban house, I got a cheery line from her condoling with my refused leave – especially after she had taken such a lot of trouble to help Nell an' all. . . .

I am very busy just at present, & get up early to go all over the place with the General but his other staff officer is sick this morning & in bed, so the General has gone off by himself & left me behind to see to things if necessary. However as nothing is happening I thought I'd write to you.

Dick was on the move again.

15 September 1918

Very many thanks for your letter & that lavender. The first letters direct here, & today I am off on some other stunt! Go on addressing here though, they will roll up some old time. It's a nuisance being pushed off, as I am quite happy here, but 'c'est la guerre' . . .

What a pity they are turning Ruth's hospital into a malaria place. Nothing else to do but give quinine. No dressings or anything. Didn't she ever write about a transfer to Marseilles. I wrote to her when I was there, but she never said anything & cannot have got my letter. . . .

It's a pity I have to leave the garden I started. Some seeds are coming up, but they seem to find some difficulty in the sand.

I have an amusing chameleon who is a great friend, & is great at catching flies. Huge long tongues they have, that flip out in an extraordinary way & nab the fly. It's no good giving you any other address, I don't think.

Dick's stunt appears to have been the defeat of the Turks in Palestine.

21 September 1918

Many thanks for your letters . . . Of course all our success in the last few days will be stale news by the time you get this, what will happen will have happened, however we seem to have got Johnny Turk on the run. I of course am moved off, and am with a Field Amb.

What a nuisance you cannot find those papers. I have asked for some more.

Ted is doing well then isn't he. A Brigade Major now. How pleased Nell must be . . .

I am seriously thinking of going back to Assam if I can get away in November. Things must be nearly over here & if I stay on I'll only be mucking about in India, nothing to do with the war, & I shall get stuck for another year for certain. After all, I've done 4 years now . . . I will cable you where to write. This is what I will say so don't lose this & I will keep a copy.

QUITE WELL = c/o Messrs Cox & Co, Calcutta.

So if you get a cable saying 'quite well' you will know where to write, put 'to be called for' on top. And will you write to Cox & Co (Ind dep) at the same time asking them to send £50 to my account with their Calcutta agents. I am writing Cox London to that effect.

I don't suppose I shall have time to write again for a bit. I've just seized this opportunity.

However four days later he managed to scribble another mysterious note.

25 September 1918

I've just got a letter from XX D[eccan] H[orse], also Ben's. Yours had a lot of lavender in it. Cox sent me a letter for Ted, too, awaiting his arrival. Pathetic eh. I've sent it on. If I cable my quite well stunt would you please post the enclosed. I am communicating with Assam & hear there are plenty of jobs. . . . I shall be sorry if I go & miss Topher. . . .

P.S. If I cable please send this letter. If no cable *don't* send it, tear it up.

Ted writes of the news from Palestine.

29 September 1918

Not much news here. September – always a bad month East of Suez – has been particularly rotten, *very* hot. . . . This time last year we were scrapping at Ramadi & I'm sure it wasn't as hot as this.

The news is good isn't it. What a sweeping success from Palestine, it simply *must* affect the situation here sooner or later, as the entire Turkish army seems to have been utterly routed and rounded up for the chief part & they must be completely disorganized & have lost all their guns. Salonika too sends out refreshingly good communiqués almost daily. If I had stayed with the regt I should be on my way to S. now. So they ought to be well in it as there's lots to do there yet. . . .

What an extraordinary epidemic of flu there has been at home – of course we all say it's good old sandfly fever same as everyone gets out here; it sounds just the same – it seems most likely, doesn't it, that that is what stopped the Boche offensive in the end, either that or some other epidemic. . . .

Gertrude had had a holiday in the Isle of Wight with friends and Ted comments:

So glad you were able to get away to Totland Bay for a bit of a rest and change: the Morses seem so remote these days though of course I remember 'Dumps' as well as anything, and 'young Morse' as Paul called him one day years ago at Camberley – enormously tall isn't he, so I don't see how he could help being wounded sooner or later. I hope he's all right.

I got a lovely bit of seaweed in your last letter, it smells gorgeously of the sea . . . I'd just love to sit on a beach again & throw stones into the sea and eat buns covered with sand!

Leave, for some reason, was suddenly generous and, if it had not been for his new job as Brigade Major, Ted would have stood a good chance. However his general had promised to help him the following year and in the meantime he was going to apply in order to get on the list with the rider that he could not be spared just yet:

. . . Besides I don't think one ought to go away just now when there is a chance of things happening . . . I know there's Nell waiting at the other end, bravely as ever poor child, and some people may think I ought to get home just as soon as ever I can. I *know* there is that point of view and I'm dreadfully sorry about the whole thing, but she & I have exchanged long correspondence about it all, & if we are both worth the other's waiting for – in our own opinion I mean! (and we've come to the conclusion we are, you'll be glad to hear!) well we must just wait till the Empire can spare us, that's all – And it certainly looks more hopeful all round now.

Dick's application to go to India came through sooner than he expected.

3 October 1918

I hear today I shall be off to India in time to get there by Nov 23rd, and I hope by then the war will be nearly over. Anyhow it's done with here I think. I shall send you the cable later on, if I send it now I doubt if you'd understand what it means. I must give you time to get my letter. . . .

I had a line from Topher. I am glad he has got his commission at last. I don't suppose he will come out here, as I doubt if they'll keep even the people they have got. . . .

I hope Paul has been home & enjoyed his leave.

I've got no mufti if I do go to India!

8 October 1918

I must soon be sending a cable. Quite well. No good sending it now as I don't think you will know what it means as you won't have got my letter explaining.

Many thanks for your no 1 letter. I've forgotten to put the numbers on mine, but anyhow I can always tell if I get yours.

I enclose a cheque for £10 to pay all those bills. It's a pity you can't find those papers. I can't think where they have got to. Please look in a leather pocket book of mine & send me the address of that firm of coffee growers in the Nilgiri Hills.

Ted was still feeling the frustration of being away from the main front.

7 October 1918

. . . We are of course all sharing the good news from France & Palestine. . . . one feels somehow there is a lot going on that one ought to be giving a hand in . . .

. . . I had to take a letter for the Turkish C-in-C yesterday under a flag of truce – Awful squeamish marching boldly out beyond our outposts waving a towel on the end of a light tent pole & hoping no one would have a shot at you! However all passed off well & a Turkish officer came out & I gave him the letter & then came home safely.

I've lost my British Warm, my Burberry, a pr boots & about 10 or 12 tins of baccy, & a waterproof cape – that's a good bit isn't it! They were all in a kit bag & somehow or other got mislaid on the way up here; sickening – I hope I'll be getting a trench coat out soonish, I asked Ben to see about one, but it does take such ages to get things out from home.

10 October 1918

Very many thanks for an unexpected letter that came from you yesterday dated July 23, it seems to have come a long way round somehow . . . So glad your rest & change at Totland were so pleasing & good for you, I know they would be and you wanted and deserved a few days off. Coo – as Nell says – what wouldn't I give for even one day's real loaf on the sands. However that'll all come some day & meanwhile I suppose we must all get down to it & finish off this little matter we've got in hand. . . .

He is a little anxious about what he calls a 'peace offensive' from the Germans.

. . . It sounds attractive in its way, but somehow I feel sure the Allies will have nothing to do with it. Wilson is the big man now . . . & I don't think he will listen to any peace proposals till the Allies are in a position to dictate terms. My contention is Don't let's listen to any of these specious proposals for peace conferences etc – let's go on till we can say what *we* want & with the power & victory behind us we can enforce our wishes. After all we've made tremendous sacrifices to get thus far, and we have got on so magnificently lately and really turned the corner at last, that it would be *wrong*, I feel sure, to stop now. It means more sorrow, more sadness I know to go on, but as I say I think it's our duty to go on and finish the thing off properly. Otherwise it only means a repetition of it all someday, and a thousand times more sorrow and sadness and sacrifice than a completion of the job will involve.

What a dissertation! But I do feel so strongly on these points . . . I say, you got at Teddy Darwen all right, & quite right too I think – unless he can produce good sound reasons I don't see why he shouldn't shoulder a gun & go to the wars – and fancy not *wanting* to do something for old England, instead of making cardboard or something. However p'raps he's gone now. Anyway you are indeed in a position to criticize – talk about your sons, my dear Mother, you are doing splendid war work yourself, and anything we do we owe to you & you only, just because you are our Mother.

17 October 1918

Some more papers have just come in from Cox, about mid-August, but no more letters yet – I wonder what's happened to them, & I've got none from Nell at all, either today or with yours 2 days ago! I suppose she's come a fearful toss over the address, & put the regiment, Cox, *and* 34th Bde on the envelope, so no wonder the post office is a wee bit confused.

I had rather a krewst 2 nights ago. I suddenly got a wire from Jim to say he was dining with Col Lumb of the 1st Bn! & would I go down & stay the night. Of course I hadn't the vaguest idea where anyone lived or was in camp, as they are nothing to do with us, but after much telephoning & enquiry I found out where they were & wangled a car, stuck a bed & some bedding & kit into it & dashed off. I found them eventually after wading through seas and fogs of dust and we had a very cheery evening. I stayed the night with Lumb as he had more room in his tent than Jim had, Jim's being a tiny little thing as wide as Dick's motorbike garage & about half as high! I saw Jim for a few minutes next morning, but he was rather busy & I had to get back to camp, so we didn't have much time. He was looking very fit & well & seemed very happy. He said I was looking ever so much fitter than when he last saw me, & I certainly feel much fitter in myself.

Gertrude had evidently met someone who had been in the campaign with Ted the previous Autumn:

I know Nepean quite well, an awful nice fellow & got a D.S.O. on the field for gallantry at Ramadi, badly wounded & stuck to his job like a man. But I think he's laying it on a bit thick about me, & I *don't* think you ought to have told me all that! However, no harm done, as most of it or all of it if you like is quite untrue – at any rate it's nice to know people say they appreciate you. . . .

I'm most awfully glad Topher has passed out & done so well.

I'm sure I paid Hacker's bill, I distinctly remember asking Cox to send him £3. 3*s*, you might ask. I am sending along £1.7*s* 6*d* for Savage; so sorry you have been worried with these bills – Hacker's is for a pair of riding breeches I lost with all my kit at sea, so I don't score much there!

Dick again:

20 October 1918

. . . Fancy finding those papers at last, but there are 2 more like them somewhere. Anyhow I can claim some part of the money with these . . . I sent you a cable today saying 'Quite well' & I hope you've got my letter telling you what it means, otherwise you will be wondering. . . . I wonder if Topher has arrived in the country yet. I expect he was stopped when all our successes were known & there won't be much doing out here now. . . .

Wish I could have been there that weekend when everyone was at home. I am so glad Evelyn came over. . . .

I wangled a day's leave the other day & went down to Jerusalem. No good being out here without going there is it? Most interesting, but it seems such a pity to build over all those sacred spots like Calvary & the Manger. I quite long to go to church again some Christmas time at home and sing 'Hark the herald angels' and 'There's a green hill' & 'While shepherds watch'.The hill isn't green, & there are a lot of houses built in the field where the shepherds were, but I'll be able to think to myself I've seen them.

How did Gertrude react to the idea that Mrs Alexander's Good Friday hymn, 'There is a green hill far away' could be sung at Christmas! Well, it was Dick who said it and he had obviously gone to a lot of trouble over the Holy Places especially for her. By the time she finished reading the letter she had almost certainly forgiven him.

There's the place where Solomon's Temple was originally built, & the only thing remaining there is a huge rock with a hole in it where the sacrifices were offered, & the blood & ashes all used to run through this hole into a tank beneath & so out. There's a lovely view from the Mount of Olives. I went there about 7 this morning, so as to get out to Bethlehem & back in time. It's curious too, that the Holy Sepulchre and the place where the Cross was are only about 20 yards apart. Both quite close in the same church. I always imagined the sepulchre was a long way away. I have sent you a little mother-of-pearl cross & a Star of Bethlehem and a book marker from Bethlehem. Goodness knows when they will arrive. It is difficult to get anything useful. Anyhow you can wear the cross sometimes & use the book marker & look at the star. The mother-of-pearl comes from the Red

Sea & the people in Bethlehem make all these things. I wish you could see it all. . . .

I am sending some little napkin rings made out of olive wood from Jerusalem, also some beads made out of Mecca fruit, they call it, & olive wood. You have a bead necklace for a muff chain which you'll promptly break on your bicycle handle! & the girls can have the others. I'll try & say who is to have them when I write again.

I hope I shall meet old Topher. I can borrow some money perhaps.

25 October 1918

Topher & I are at present quite near each other. He is in a camp expecting to go off any moment, and I expect any moment to be sent to India. Wish they'd hurry up & let me know. We had some rain here the first time for ages, & huge sand storms blowing. All the news is good isn't it, the war is over here. I must send you a cable if I can afford it!

Best love to all,
yr loving son,
Richard

1 November 1918

. . . I sent a letter saying Topher & I are quite near each other. I discovered him by chance. All private cables are stopped or I would have sent one to say we had met, but the one saying quite well went just before the order came out. I haven't gone yet and am rather sick about it as I do not see how I can get to Assam now by the 23rd. Anyhow I expect to be sent any day. Funny sending a cable quite well, 'cos just after I for some reason or other got a bad throat & for the first time for many years was made to stay in bed. Couldn't swallow or smoke & generally felt rotten. However I made a rapid recovery & did not reckon on being fit, even by today, but thank goodness I am. Topher is seedy now. Rotten country eh? He's got diarrhoea, but I went and fetched him this evening & have put him in a tent next to me & got him a couple of days ex-duty, so he will soon be all right. . . .

I am waiting for No 5 letter now. Wonder if I can run across Jim or Ted in India!

9 November 1918

I have got two letters of yours Oct 4 and 8 in which you say you have not heard from me. I hope by this time you have, & got my letter directing you what to do when the cable arrives. I am back again with 39 Hospital, hoping I am on my way to India. But there is a hitch somewhere & goodness knows when I shall get away. 'Snice to be back here. . . . I was sorry to leave Topher behind. He came to see me off, & he will always be able to go over to our camp & see a change of face. Goodness knows when I shall see him again. He is quite fit & happy, only like everyone wonders what's going to happen to him. Many thanks for all those papers & the photographs of Evelyn. . . . I haven't heard from Evelyn for ages, but I must write as it's my turn. Topher seems to have cut me out there altogether.

I imagine I am going to India for 3 years. Save save save & then come home for good & do a small practice there. But the quicker I go, the sooner I'll be back.

21 November 1918

Just a line to tell you I am leaving Egypt today for Bombay. I have a nice ship & know the O.C. well & it ought to be a nice voyage. Luckily I have only been kept in Suez a day & much to the disgust of one or two others I am getting away first.

I haven't heard from Topher once since I left Ludd.

I hope I shall find some letters in Calcutta.

Here, apart from references to him in other letters, we say goodbye to Dick.

THE LAST BATTLE AND AFTERWARDS

Although the war was over in Palestine Ted and Jim still had some unexpected fighting ahead of them. On 30 October Ted wrote to Nell:

Darling Child,

Just a scribble as near 'the day' as I can get it – honestly old lady I simply haven't had a minute since 21st of the month to write to you in – for 9 days we have been marching hard & long, & the last 5 have had fighting in addition – heavy fighting too, but the Brigade did splendid work, tho' I say it as shouldn't, and we had some hard fights with the Turk and some stern chases after him – into bivuoac after dark at 7 or so, then on again at midnight, fighting early next morning, perhaps all day, that's been our programme – but it has all ended very happily – you will have seen by now how many prisoners were captured, I haven't the vaguest idea, but I saw several thousands this morning – it has been hard work & we are all pretty well done, but the final success is worth anything. My Brigade was on the right bank of the river & we had as much fighting as we wanted, & it was all most awfully interesting for me of course in my new job – and very frightening at times too! However no harm done, except some splinters of shell in my arm & hand, as one burst rather unpleasantly close one day, but beyond being rather painful for a day or two it was nothing.

Anyhow old lady here's to yesterday – the great 29th October, the greatest day of my life in lots of ways – 29th Oct 1914 I first went into the trenches in France; 29–10–15 I spects you remember rather well don't you dear! – & then 29th Oct 1918 I finish (I hope!) with the war, for there was no fighting today, just huge mobs of surrendering Turks. . . .

By the way, the Divisional General explained the whole battle by a rough picture in the sand this morning – he showed where our Brigade was with reference to the other Brigades engaged, & said 'and these are the people who won the battle & accepted the first surrenders'; very nice of him wasn't it – we got about 10,000 prisoners & 40 guns;

Two days later he managed a letter to Gertrude.

2 November 1918

I haven't written for ever such a long time, nearly a fortnight now, but you will understand why. We have had a very busy time indeed, as you will probably have seen by the accounts in the papers, but it all ended up successfully with the surrender of the whole Turkish army opposed to us, followed next day by the announcement that an armistice had been declared with Turkey – so we only got our show finished with one day to spare! . . .

Our casualties were not very heavy but the time was one of the most strenuous I ever spent – I *am* so glad I took part in it all & saw the best of the fighting, as now I feel I have done something at last to help things on. My brigade had its full share of the fighting, & it was all so interesting to me in my new job as Bde Major as of course I had tons of work to do & I *was* so tired & sleepy at times. Jim's regiment was across the river but I have heard nothing of him . . . We have been busy clearing up the mess on the battlefield since then, & collecting all the booty & guns & prisoners – it's the first action my brigade has been in & they did awfully well & the general is most fearfully pleased of course. . . .

Well, I must end up – sorry I've given such a vague description of things, but it's all been such a rush & hurry itself for the last 10 days that really I'm not quite clear when or where or how we marched & fought, except that it was long & hard & often & we were absolutely dog tired at times & wondered how on earth we should ever crawl another yard – it's been a great show & we are all fearfully pleased with ourselves.

He managed later to write an account of the action.

3 November 1918

I am sending along a very rough and ready description of our doings of the last few days which may be of interest to you. It's all rather a confused memory as we were so hurried & pushed & there were times of such utter weariness that I can't quite remember exactly what happened. It is however a fairly coherent account I think, & I hope you will like it.

It's loverly weather here now, very fortunately for us, as of course we have no kit to speak of – We have bagged a Turkish tent for meals, but otherwise are leading a very primitive existence.

We are still clearing up all the mess & booty left by the Turk on the battlefield. There's an awful lot of rubbish but a lot of valuable stuff like guns & machine guns which all has to be laboriously gathered together. . . . As usual friend Turk has left us a large legacy of flies which are very trying. I ate a whole tin of malted milk tablets one hungry day during the show, a tin you sent years ago, & they came in awful handy. I have no news of Jim or his regt, they are across the river somewhere . . . *Nov 6* later: just heard news of Austria being out of it – splendid isn't it.

> Operations on TIGRIS 21st–30th Oct 1918 ending in Surrender of Turkish Army under HAQQI BEY at 7 a.m. on 30th Oct

On 21st we marched as soon as it was dark and reached camp before dawn on 22nd, stayed in camp till nightfall and marched on again that night, reaching our next camp early morning on 23rd. This was about 6 miles from the first Turkish position, a formidable line of hills running roughly at right angles to the Tigris & guarding both banks, with many trenches and gun positions, and althogether a nasty looking place to tackle. There was a certain amount of patrol work & artillery fire this day (23rd), but no fighting. Our bde hadn't much to do, as 2 other bdes were in front of us. Orders were out to attack the positions next day 24th, but on the morning of the 24th our patrols found the Turkish position empty. He had retired during the night, & so we pushed on hard behind him at once. We camped that night in the gorge formed by the river breaking through the hills, and another brigade went on ahead of us. At 5 a.m. next morning (25th) we pushed on, along a most extraordinary road. It ran along the sides of the hills, just above the river, and the hills here are split up into innumerable raveines. Consequently the road wound in and out of these ravines and wandered up and down, in and out, the whole way. We could only take pack animals along it, so steep was it and tortuous, not a hundred yards straight in ten miles of it. Yet in some marvellous way the guns came along it later in the day, tho' heaven knows how they managed it. But then gunners are always doing wonderful things. I just mention the road as an example of the difficulties of the advance. The country we have been operating in is very much broken up with small hills and big dry 'wadis', broad stony river beds which rapidly become torrents in the rainy season. Consequently the Turk had a choice of innumerable positions where he could (and did!) hold us up and stop our advance.

Well, we reached camp that evening 25th, & were off again next morning at 5 a.m. & had our first fight that day 26th Oct. The bde in front of us met the Turk in a very strong position and had not been able to turn him out. The Turk held all the cards; all aproaches to the position were under close shell fire, and the ground in front of the position was an open plain. We pushed in some of our troops, but did not attempt anything serious till we were able to work round his flank towards evening. All that day (26th) the 2 brigades hung on under shell fire, & all that night too, & next morning (27th) patrols found the Turk had once more slipped away in the night. So off we went at 7 a.m. on 27th in hot pursuit, marched all day without finding him, & camped that night for food & rest at 6 p.m. By this time men & animals were pretty done, after hard & continuous marching over bad roads, & a day & night fighting. However we had to hurry on and catch up the Turk, who we knew must be tired too by now.

While all this had been going on, a cavalry brigade, after a wide detour of nearly 50 miles, had crossed the Tigris *behind* the Turk, i.e. between him and Mosul, & so cut him off from his base. Of course Haqqi Bey, the Turkish commander, went for the cavalry & tried to knock him out, but they put up a splendid fight & held on & the Turk could find no escape there. Turkish reinforcements – 1000 of them – were sent down from Mosul to destroy the cavalry, but instead were captured by them! Meantime however the cavalry were hard pressed, and it was imperative that we should push on up the river & join hands with them. So off we went again at 3 a.m. on 28th, marched till 12 noon & found the enemy in position. The Bde then attacked & by 2 o'clock had driven him from his position, & captured 200 prisoners & 10 machine guns. We got into camp by 6, with orders to pursue hard as soon as the men had rested. More troops however came up – in the shape of already tired & battered brigades – & they took on the pursuit as well as they could, as we were absolutely done.

But we were off at 5.30 a.m. again on the 29th, & found our advanced troops again in action by 9 a.m. We had a bit of a rest and at 1.30 p.m were again on the move, this time to attack once more. The men went forward splendidly under heavy shell fire and tremendous machine gun fire, but the position was too strong for our small force, & was held determinedly by the Turk, who knew he had our cavalry just behind him, so he had to fight or surrender, & he certainly fought alright. Night fell on the usual confusion of the battlefield, units and brigades mixed up, tired, and thristy and the enemy still in his position. We had no troops near to throw into the fight, & we wondered what was going to happen next day. Another division was operating on the other bank of the river, & they had managed to send over a few troops to help the cavalry, but they couldn't do much to help us, as there was no bridge across. They helped with the long range guns a lot, but it was infantry we wanted. It was an anxious night, the 29th Oct, & the early hours of the 30th, as we thought the Turk would counter attack our thin & exhausted line. But we were to reap the reward of the preseverance and gallantry of our troops sooner than we expected, and at 7 a.m. on 30th the Turk surrendered everywhere. He seemed to come from all corners of the field, & we were indeed glad he had decided not to try and drive us out! Great long columns of them were collected & marched off to the prisoners' camps, & we were left in possession of the battlefield and the way to Mosul was open. That was at 7 a.m. on 30th Oct, and next day we got orders through that hostilities were to cease as an armistice had been signed between the Allies and Turkey on the evening of the 30th. So we only just made our bag in time –

a few hours later and they would not have been prisoners of war. We had marched hard and long and fought hard to catch them and it was a most satisfactory ending to the operations.

The prisoners number nine or ten thousand; over 40 guns have been captured & well over 100 machine guns besides much miscellaneous booty. This does not sound much compared with the colossal captures in Palestine & elsewhere, but it is at any rate, all there is to capture, & one can't do more than that!

The men have been absolutely marvellous. They have been asked to do a very difficult job, hard marching when they were dog tired, hard fighting on little water & short rations and to overcome all sorts of difficulties incidental to campaigning in this country. But they have done all that was asked of them & have never failed, and it is splendid to know their efforts have been so tremendously successful.

13 November 1918

I'm afraid I've got very much behindhand with my correspondence lately, but we've been very busy all the last 4 weeks. I hope you got a line or two from me giving an account of our doings lately. . . . The old and battered Mesopotamia E.F. got in one good blow before the finish, and I *am* so glad & proud I was there, & in such a fine brigade too, which did splendid work, & we were 'well in at the death', our regiments being in the front line & receiving the first surrenders. Genl. Wauchope is of course fearfully pleased, & he & I agree that we couldn't have wished for a better ending to our personal share in this great war . . .

Well, of course, THE only thing now is the wonderful news from Europe. So it's all over at last. It's all too stupendous . . . to grasp at first, & it must take time for each and all of us to realise what it all means. The great point is without any doubt that the anxiety of all you dear people at home is relieved now, after more than 4 years of terrible waiting & wonderful patience, courage & sacrifice. . . . It's all, as I say, too big a subject to write on, but it is enough to know that it is all over now. And isn't it gorgeous to be on the winning side! Not that one ever doubted for one minute that it would ever be otherwise in the end – but there have been anxious moments. Well, we've got heaps & heaps to be thankful for . . . and that's enough for the present.

Meanwhile we are sitting on some mud flats by the river, in wet & rainy weather, making the best of things. Our recent advance up the Tigris landed us many many miles away from tents and railways & we were on short rations & no tents for nearly a month . . . I am glad to say we have come back a bit, about 50 miles from our final battlefield, & right glad I am too, as there is no longer any 'front' to be at – thank heavens! it is best to be back near railways & comparative comfort.

We arrived 2 days ago & a mail arrived at the same time. I got a line from you, very many thanks. It was dated Sept 2nd. Thanks awfully for sending the woollie, but it hasn't arrived yet, tho' doubtless it will in a day or so. The winter is on us now so it will come in very handy.

You ask about several men in the Queens. Of course I am not with them now, as I'm miles away from my old brigade and the regiment an' all. In any case the regiment, I mean *my* rgt – left the country some weeks ago for Salonica I think . . . I envied them awfully when I heard they were off as we thought they would be sure to have some fun, & at the time it looked as if we should get little or none, but as it happens it has turned out just the reverse. . . .

Nell was 21 on the 11th, a great day all round wasn't it. Easy enough for me to remember now isn't it with 2 events, Nell's birthday & peace. Isn't the child growing up fast! She was only 18 when I left & I shall be in an awful funk meeting her again! But you all say such gorgeous things about her that I expect it will be all right.

Hooray here's the sun, the first time for four days & we may be able to dry some of our very damp kit. Lunchtime too, I get infernally hungry these days. I do hope the food position and the coal one too improve rapidly now. But I fear things will take months to become normal again. But it's worth it isn't it. But I do want to come home so much.

16 November 1918

A lovely parcel arrived from you today, containing a gorgeous new shetland woollie and some soap & scent & a wee sponge & some bath salts & cocoa & 2 lavender bags – *most* acceptable my dear mother, each and all of them, and very many thanks indeed . . . it's very cold o' nights nowadays & sleeping in a tent one wants a woollie & really that grey one you sent me before is rather worn out nowadays. . . .

The general & I have been riding about all the morning & looking at people building railways. I met many officers of Jim's regiment who were at work on the line. He is up the river a bit, making a road they tell me, & is quite fit & well. His regiment came under a good deal of shell fire in this last show it seems. . . .

Ted discovered that he had officially been reported wounded, so he cabled Nell on November 1st 'to put her mind at ease' in case alarming wires arrive home.' He also tried to send one to Gertrude: 'I wired to you the day after the surrender of old Haqqi & his merry men,' he writes in his letter of the 13th, 'but we got news that no cables were being sent ex-Mesopotamia unless paid for at a post office . . . so my cable never went. And as we were miles from any post office I couldn't send a wire till yesterday when we got to one – I sent one off to old Nell, & then found I hadn't enough to send

Hakki and his merry men.
(Sketch by Lieut. Balburnie of the Royal West Kents)

one to you! & no one else had any money (just a fluke I had a few rupees) so I added "tell mother" to Nell's wire which I thought was the best way, otherwise I would have wired you too – I hope it arrived all right.'

23 November 1918

. . . I see the King & the Army Council & India Office have all sent us nice messages about these last operations. We are awfully pleased they are so appreciative & we like to think our little battles out here don't go quite unnoticed in the welter of fighting on the Western Front. It was good honest fighting & hard marching: just the old bullet & bayonet (& the man behind them) no gas or tanks or other modern horrors!

You had got my letters of June 10th & 16th, what years ago! Yes, I had a great time with Jim then. I haven't seen him since our battlefighting – so you had sons advancing up both banks of the Tigris in that show. I had a line from him a day or two ago telling me his experiences. I'm so glad he got into a fight as he always wanted to 'strike a blow for freedom' as he put it. . . .

Delaford seems to have witnessed some cheery weekends of late, & Paul at the top of his form – I suppose he's busily engaged now in taking over Hun ships, and perhaps the 'Great Silent' is a wee bit more talkative now that naval censorship has been removed. . . .

From all accounts the wildest scenes took place in London on several successive nights after Peace night & Reuter gives us glimpses of revels & streets rendered impassable owing to dancers, 'many of whom were in fancy dress'. For ourselves, I was wakened on a wet miserable night – Nov 11 – by a signaller with a message just saying the Armistice had been signed and hostilities had ceased that morning. I donned a British warm & slippers & went & woke the General up & told him; he grunted & next morning I apologized for having woken him but excused myself on the grounds that the news *was* rather epoch-making: & his only reply was 'Did you wake me up? I don't remember it!'

My cold reception there made me wonder if anyone else would like to hear the news – I decided they would, so slopped off in the mud & rain to the West Kent regiment next door, & after much difficulty woke their C.O. & 2nd in cmd, who took rather more interest than the General had; they got up & came out of their tents & we watched the next brigade to us – some 2 miles off – entirely losing their heads and sending off Very lights & S.O.S. rockets & various other coloured signals. Meantime the rain came down harder & I decided the rest of the Brigade must await the news till next morning. I waded back to my tent – wet & muddy & cold but happy, anyhow! – & wrote out messages for the others & turned in. Next morning at 6 I sent the messages & a few rounds of cheering told me they had arrived at any rate. We had a bonfire or two that week, & used up all our signal rockets & S.O.S signals, & since then have been solemnly digesting the wonderful fact of Peace.

The war was over but there was no immediate prospect of going home. 'No news as to our movements or chances of leave or anything,' he writes on 8 December, 'Even Rumour is silent once more, after being particularly active *and* unreliable a few days ago.' Jim was off to Salonica but they managed to meet again before he left.

2 December 1918

. . . I had Jim to stay a day & a night last week. After many wires (he got most of mine after he met me!) we eventually met at the railhead in fact we arrived there from two different directions at precisely the same time. . . . He arrived about 10 one day & went about 10 the next. I was most awful pleased to see him looking frightfully fit & well, & full of his experiences in the last show up the Tigris. We had some good old talks & hoots about everything & generally swapped lies about things in general. I was glad one of the family has had a chance to meet my present mess mates. I wish he could have stayed longer, but he had a party of men with him so I don't quite know how he managed to wangle even a day off!

Christmas had passed off quietly, with a parcel of goodies from Gertrude and some delicious nuts from Rosamond, which they had had to 'bang with spoons & knives and things' as they had no nut crackers. He describes the Christmas 'Babylonian Race meeting: awfully well run, nice railed-off paddocks & rails, a grandstand made of sandbags (no fear of *that* collapsing anyhow!) and all the paraphernalia of a real racecourse. I love all the crowd & noise & excitement & ripping horses all nicely groomed & prancing about & the jockeys in their bright colours – shocking isn't it! . . . Anyhow I've promised to take Nell to the 1919 Derby. . . .'

Early in December they were 'busy polishing up & practising for a ceremonial parade in a day or two when the Corps commander is presenting some awards given for this last fighting we've had' but this had to be postponed because of rain. It eventually took place: 'Our big parade went off very well and the aeroplanes "flew past" General Cobbe, a most novel performance. Afterwards they gave a display of dives & loops and wonderful things, really most thrilling to watch. It was a colossal parade, miles & miles of troops it seemed, horse, foot, & guns, & big tractor caterpillar engines drawing the guns. We had no tanks, as there aren't any out here, but it was a good show of modern arms taking it all round.'

Ted was always one to look to the future. He had enjoyed the fly past, and as early as 23 November he was writing, with reference to letters that had taken just 2 months to arrive: 'I hope they'll get a bit quicker now & possibly a bit more regular – I see they are starting aerial mails in many places, but I imagine our mails are far too big to expect anything like that from home to here.' By 18 December he had this to say: 'What about these aeroplanes cruising about the world now? I didn't see the one that flew from Cairo to Damascus & then on to Baghdad – a wonderful flight wasn't it – And they say London to Calcutta in 4 days, for the mails, & it can't be a very far cry from that to passenger carrying. The war has certainly advanced flying beyond all knowledge.' Gertrude sent him a cutting about flying which evoked the comment 'Truly there are undreamt of possibilities . . . we must expect rapid developments as soon as the world settles down & big commercial firms can give their attention to flying. I wish I could fly home. Stewart [a friend] tells me he is going to!' and early in 1919 he noted that a letter from Topher was 'marked "E.E.F. Aerial post" so I suppose it came by aeroplane.'

There was still no prospect of going home. The brigade was detailed as part of the 'post bellum' garrison of Mesopotamia which meant they would be there for another year at least. Ted was not sure whether he would remain as Brigade Major as there would be a lot of officers senior to him who would be wanting staff jobs. He didn't really mind what happened as long as he was given some home leave soon.

'Jane's lucky getting Murray home for a spell,' he writes on 16 January, 'I can see Nell and me coming in a good last in the marriage stakes! I've just read your letter . . . & I see you rag me about getting the wind up about Nell & my wedding & the long wait. It's not exactly that, I know she's young & all that, & there's lots of time – but still I should like to get married all the same.' Nell of course was 'tremendously pleased about the peace' but was 'keeping her head splendidly' and did not expect him to 'come clattering home at once.' She had spent her momentous 21st birthday nursing the rest of her family who were down with the flu that was then sweeping the world. Gertrude had succumbed too. 'So unlike you to "go sick!"' wrote Ted, 'and I'm much relieved to hear you got over it all right. Really it is most alarming isn't it. . . . I told you I think we had it out here, & whole regiments of 800 or 900 men were reduced to 200 and under . . . there were not many deaths but for the time being those who got it were absolutely useless.' He thought he might have had a touch of it during the last few days fighting – 'I felt rotten for 2 or 3 days with fever at night' and then at the end of January he went down with a curious recurring fever, succumbing at 10.30 on Monday morning for three weeks running, with a high temperature that lasted for two days. After the fourth successive go he was sent to hospital for tests and observation, feeling a perfect fraud, but admitting that he did not feel like doing anything much.

It was during one of these bouts of fever that he received a cable from Gertrude just saying 'congratulations'. His mysterious reply was worthy of Dick. 'If it is for what I suppose it is, I can't think why I haven't heard from old Nell as I presume she has similar information to you.' The explanation comes in a long letter from hospital written on 16 February: 'Jim told me he was writing to you about the D.S.O. (Was that what your cable of congratulations was about?). Surely you didn't expect me to write & tell you; hardly my job I think! However, I'm so awfully glad for your sake & Nell's sake, you seem so frightfully pleased all of you, so that bucks me up a lot, but I feel I don't deserve it in the least, & my general must have lied very hard indeed when sending my name in! Genl Cobbe pinned a bit of ribbon on to me at that big parade I told you about.' He had received an immediate award of the D.S.O. for staying in action although wounded.

With nothing much else to do, he wrote at great length at this time answering letters that were now less than a month old. He had a big batch in February, including a Christmas card from Paul & Nance. 'What splendid news about the expected infant', he writes to Gertrude. 'I'm most awfully pleased, & I'm sure it's quite time you were a grandmother.'

'So you've kept all our war letters,' he writes later. 'I suppose they will be interesting some day, in fact I'd very much like to see some of mine written in the early days of France, for I can't remember a single thing, except that it was rather unpleasant at times, & that the Boche seemed to have about 100 guns to each one of ours.'

Ted's fever continued to baffle the doctors who finally decided that he was unfit to serve another hot weather in that climate and was run down having been too long without leave. On 12 March he wrote:

> They won't send me home from here, as I am Indian Army, & I have to go to India – isn't it sickening, as I don't know what will happen now & my chance of leave home seems to be dwindling away once more. . . . Rather curious in your letter of Feb 5 you say you are glad I'm so fit, 'and mind you keep so' you add. Very sorry, but I'm afraid I failed to carry out your instructions. . . . How I hate all this uncertainty – I mean about being able to get home this year. It's no good denying it, & I've simply got to face facts, it *is* uncertain whether I'll be able to manage now. Poor old Nell, I'm frightfully anxious about it all, & she's such a dear & so splendidly patient. However it's good to be alive & well, there's always that to put in the balance on the other side, & someday things will straighten out I suppose. . . .

On the eve of his departure for India he wrote, 'Being invalided out of the country means, I suppose, that I lose my job. I'm sorry in a way, but it is made easier by the fact that the whole brigade is new . . . and on the whole I want to get back to the regiment. I think I've been long enough away. I should like to get home for a bit this summer, & then bring Nell out to Lansdowne to a nice peaceful existence after the strenuous life of the last few years. But "man proposes, etc" & I'm too old a plaything of Fate to make anything in the way of elaborate plans as far ahead as that.' But he cheers up in a brief postscript: 'Goodbye Mesopotamia!'

Dick, of course, was already in India but this was where he wanted to be. He was still very much the Dick who wangled exchanges and tried to take his dogs on active service. '*How* I laughed at Dick's collection of beasts he took to Assam with him!' commented Ted just before he sailed for India himself. 'No one but he would dream of doing such a thing & how he explained to everyone on the train I can't imagine! How he dare! as we used to say.' Unfortunately no complete record of Dick's menagerie survives, but it included a mynah bird, probably the chameleon, almost certainly at least one dog and possibly even a monkey.

Meanwhile there was news of Jim and Topher. 'So you've got on to Jim at last,' writes Ted in this same letter. 'And you say you think he might have been home in a fortnight after writing your letter. Perhaps by this time he has come & gone again. It seems I'll be the last to get home, if Topher gets home in April – Dick & I came out more or less the same time in '15 didn't we, but he's been back since of course, so I think it's really time I came back for a bit.'

In April, however, Topher was still very much on active service in Palestine. 'Very little news this week,' he wrote on the 9th, 'the unrest has quietened down since the return of General Allenby. One has to walk about armed with a revolver these days. No chance of any leave yet as it is all stopped, also demobilization. . . . Paul again on leave, same as he was before the war, always on leave. . . .'

Easter Day 1919

We are now at Ismailia, a very pretty little place on the Canal, also a very big lake . . . We are supposed to be here until the breaking up of the Army of Occupation. Leave is still closed, but demobilization has started again. No doubt you saw in the paper that a Major Cecil Jarvis of the 20th Deccan Horse had been murdered by the Egyptians down south. I knew him & he was a friend of Dick's. I was only speaking to him a few weeks before he was murdered. We all have to walk about armed these days, which is a bit of a nuisance. . . . Sorry such a dull letter, but there is absolutely no news. I have been to church today, in a Y.M.C.A. hut which is just near our camp.

He also had his adventures on water, though on a smaller scale than his brothers.

13 May 1919

Since writing quite exciting things have happened. I have saved a man from drowning during some aquatic sports which we held the other day. I was one of the judges in the novices' race and was out in a boat at the time. The race started all right, but one fellow got into difficulties about 30 yards from my boat, and, being the only swimmer in the boat, I had to dive in with all my clothes on, I just caught the fellow as he was going down the second time. This is the 3rd time in about a month that I have gone into the sea with all my clothes on, the 2 previous times accidents of course.

While sailing the other day we had to pull up the centre board because we were in shallow water, but of course forgot to put it down & over we went, luckily quite near land, and really it was funny, I swallowed practically the whole lake through laughing. What's much more annoying is that I have spoilt 2 watches, I must send them home to you to get mended.

Would you please send me that pair of binoculars belonging to Dick, I think, which were when I last saw them in Rosamond's room, also his prismatic compass, which *was* on the sideboard of the new boudoir. I must have them, and I'm not going to buy them when things are so near the end, also very expensive. Send them by registered post. They will be taken great care of, in fact I shall hardly ever use them, but have to be fully equipped in case of emergency. No news of leave, but it has really started, 3 officers have already gone.

Topher had jokingly said he was thinking of putting in for urgent leave on the grounds that both Jane & Ted were going to be married and Ted to receive the D.S.O. For Ted had written on 13 April to say that he was going home. He had cabled Nell, of course. He had been granted four months sick leave on the grounds of general debility and expected to be home about the middle of May. Ted's last communication of the war was a telegram from Southampton, dated 12 May, addressed to his future in-laws:

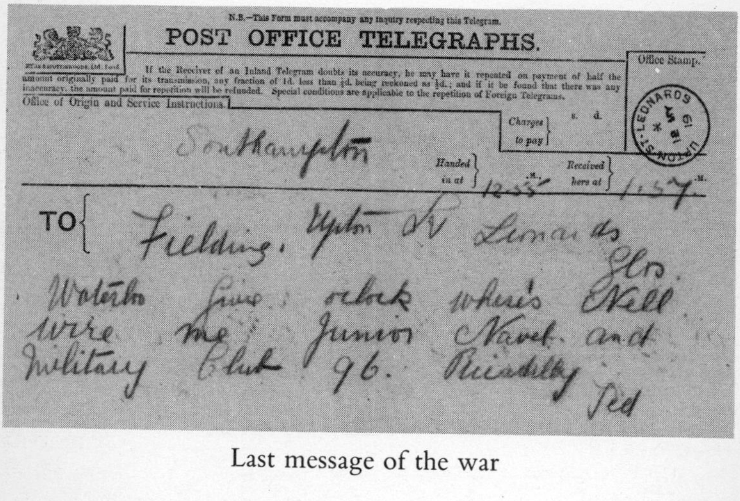
POST OFFICE TELEGRAPHS.

Southampton

TO Fielding. Upton St Leonards Glos.

Waterloo five o'clock where's Nell wire me Junior Naval and Military Club 96. Piccadilly Ted

Last message of the war

Fielding Upton St Leonards, Glos.

Waterloo five o'clock. Where's Nell Wire me Junior Naval and Military Club 96 Piccadilly. Ted.

A month later he was married on the day that his Mention in Despatches was published in the papers.

Ted and Nell

EPILOGUE: HAPPY FAMILIES

It seems a little ironic that a war should bring about so many unexpected reunions while in the peace that followed the members of the family were once more scattered across the world: Dick and Ted to their different parts of India; Jim back to Portugal; Topher farming in Kenya; and Paul serving on the China station. Jane had sailed to Canada and the other girls settled down in various parts of England with their husbands. Of course they did meet from time to time but it was to be nearly forty years before they were all in England again – all except Dick, who died in 1936, a year before his mother. For the rest of them, their wives and husbands (they all married eventually) and such members of succeeding generations who could come, there was a grand family gathering at Ben's house in Bookham in the summer of 1954.

They must have known that this would be the last time they would all be together – for some the last time that they would meet any of the others at all – but they did not allow this to cloud the joy of reunion or the recollections of former days. They had brought photographs, books and old games to augment the exclamations of 'Do you remember – ?' and 'Wasn't it fun when – !' and, after dinner, they sat down together to play 'Happy Families' with the old, pink-backed pack of their childhood. It was fascinating to watch the years fall away as they became the children they had once been. Those who used to cheat were still cheating unashamedly, those who argued found their old sparring partners ready with the ripostes of their youth, while those who had kept the peace automatically asserted their former authority. At any moment you felt that the Mater would walk in to see what they were all doing. Yes, it was indeed a Happy Family.